CARABANCHEL

This book is dedicated to my loyal wife

CARABANCHEL

The Last Brit in Europe's Hellhole Prison

Christopher Chance

MAINSTREAM
PUBLISHING
EDINBURGH AND LONDON

First published in Great Britain in 2005 by
MAINSTREAM PUBLISHING COMPANY
(EDINBURGH) LTD
7 Albany Street
Edinburgh EH1 3UG

ISBN 1 84018 967 3

A catalogue record for this book is available
from the British Library

Typeset in Apollo and Gill Sans Condensed

Printed in Great Britain by
Clays Ltd, St Ives plc

CONTENTS

ONE

THE MOUTH OF THE BEAST

The noise of rattling chains and the stench of acrid tobacco smoke accompanied me on my journey to hell. My fellow passengers jabbered in Spanish – their native tongue – as they tried to hide their fear with meaningless banter. We were all chained together with handcuffs fitted so tight that my hands were swollen and throbbing. They had changed colour and become a bluish grey with mottled redness around the knuckles. The swelling increased with each kilometre of the drive from the law courts in central Madrid across the city to the infamous Carabanchel prison.

My brain felt just like my hands – throbbing and stuffed with cotton wool – as I thought about how stupid I had been to drive half a tonne of Morocco's finest herb, hashish, from the Costa del Sol to Burgos and get caught by the secret police as I approached Madrid. It was May 1998 and I was a *preventivo* (remand prisoner) awaiting my trial. I had lived in Spain since 1993, developing my martial-arts business before I became involved with hashish smugglers on the Costa del Crime, and now I was being given an intimate introduction to its penal system.

The Spanish chatter and the pulsing pain signals from my hands and head blended with the engine noise of the stinking Spanish police van to form an insistent drone that I fought to stave off with prayer. The sadness in my heart made my chest feel as though a large stone had been placed inside my ribcage as I asked my God for

9

forgiveness and the strength to survive the impending trials and misery of the Carabanchel: the Devil's shithouse.

I also prayed for my loved ones, especially my wife, who would have to survive alone in our *finca*, a farmhouse in the hills above the Costa del Sol in southern Spain. I was so focused on my Act of Contrition, I didn't realise I had entered the Devil's waiting room. I was so intent on prayer, I wasn't yet quite aware of the silence. It then dawned on me that the van had stopped, the engine and my fellow passengers were silent and the thick, swirling tobacco smoke was escaping out of the driver's open door.

I came back to reality with the crashing open of the van's metal doors and the sudden commotion of screaming *funcionarios*: Spanish prison officers. Pain raced through me as I was yanked out of my stiff, crouched position by the man next to me. We had to move as one because our wrists were shackled together. The prison officers screamed obscenities at us as their hostile eyes scanned each of us in turn. They prodded us menacingly into line with their long truncheons, making us face a high, grey concrete wall.

I was being roughly frisked by a screw in a dark-blue uniform as two green-uniformed *Guardia Civil* officers approached me. The screw finished patting me down as the fatter of the two officers unholstered his pistol and placed the barrel on my temple while his colleague unlocked the handcuffs. First, he unlocked the handcuff attaching me to my fellow prisoner, then he unlocked the bracelets that bound my wrists together. The blood flowed achingly into my swollen hands as I rubbed them together, and the *Guardia Civil* officers moved along the line with pistol and key.

The Spaniard standing next to me was trembling with fright, his bottom lip was quivering out of control as tears trickled down his cheeks. He whimpered and wept as his handcuffs were released. The fat copper grunted like the pig that he was then punched him hard in the guts. The prisoner fell to his knees holding his stomach and wept unashamedly as one of the screws strode across the yard and yanked him to his feet by grabbing his hair whilst screaming and spitting into his face.

It occurred to me that this man's fear had been gnawing at him all day because of the folklore he'd heard about the Carabanchel. I imagined that the Carabanchel was the bogeyman used by the mothers of Madrid to keep their children on the straight and narrow: he was weeping before he was assaulted. I knew very little about this prison but I could feel the malevolence here. I knew in my heart that I had entered a different world, a dangerous, evil world where officials rule with violence and impunity. I had just witnessed an assault on one of their own, so what chance did I have as a *giri* (an offensive word for a foreigner, as disagreeable as the term 'nigger')? Not much, I feared, but did I have the weapons and shields to survive the netherworld of the Carabanchel? I am an ex-professional soldier and a professional martial-artist, so I hoped I had the moral fibre and nous to keep out of trouble while I was locked up in here.

I would later read about eight prisoners who were killed under suspicious circumstances in Spanish jails during 1997, which was only the previous year. I would also read a United Nations General Assembly Report of the Committee Against Torture stating that many cases of ill-treatment appeared to constitute manifestations of racial discrimination. Fuck me! No wonder these gypsy spicks and Moroccans were shitting themselves.

The wild-eyed screw who seemed to be in charge was screaming instructions for us all to strip naked. My fellow prisoners obediently shed their clothing in an instant, but I struggled to take off my bloodstained clothes. As I exposed myself, the screws gathered round for a closer look at the massive bruising around my torso, seemingly enjoying the spectacle. My arms and thighs were blue and yellow with bruises that overlapped each other. My lips were swollen, hiding shattered teeth, as were my fingers and thumbs, which had both thumbnails and several fingernails missing from them. My testicles became the butt of more entertainment because they had been kicked black and blue and were massively swollen.

The screws were quite amused with my battered body, but the pièce de résistance for them came when I squatted over a mirror so they could check my rectum for contraband. My arsehole had been so badly kicked by the Spanish secret police that my little freckle was now a three-inch-long gash of weeping pus and blood. This was met with great hilarity. The laughter increased as the screws discovered the stitched wounds around my head – the results of a pistol-whipping: the handiwork of the secret police.

A burly screw picked up my clothes with the end of his truncheon then indicated that I should enter a small room, which I did as he flicked my clothes in behind me. I started to dress. My fellow prisoners trooped in, obviously relieved because I had taken the edge off the screws' malevolence with my injuries.

Paco, an educated Spaniard, said, 'If it wasn't for you showing your broken body, I think we all would have been roughed up.'

'Maybe you're right,' I replied, as the tiny room quickly filled with tobacco smoke and unwashed spicks.

An ugly screw with one giant eyebrow stretching right across his face from one eye to the other prodded me with his truncheon to get me out of the tiny room. He then violently pushed me into a brightly lit, large room with white tiles and metal tables. The bully with the giant eyebrow yelled at me to go to the nearest table, manned by two very big prison officers. As I neared the table, one of the screws grabbed my wrist and pulled me to the table where his large, fat colleague waited with an ink roller. My fingerprints were to be put on the sheet of white paper that bore my name, with the word '*Peligroso*' stamped in red next to it. My command of the Spanish language wasn't so good then, but I knew this word meant 'Dangerous'. I then realised that I was going to have an especially rough ride in this place.

My fingers and thumbs were still hurting from the stomping I'd received from the secret police, so I intended not to press down too hard on the ink stone. These two screws were not concerned about my discomfort, though. They just wanted to stamp my fingerprints on all the right parts of the sheet of paper then get rid of me. It was futile to resist so I allowed my fingers and thumbs to be painfully inked and forcefully pressed down. The big, ugly screw was behaving as though I was being difficult, but I wasn't; I was trying to be helpful.

I realised he wanted me to struggle away from him so he could justify beating me about the head with his truncheon. But I didn't give him the satisfaction because I handle pain well and could read him like a book.

The final digit was my thumb. This was his last chance to extract a cry of pain or to get some retaliation from me. He roughly put his own thumb on the raw flesh where my thumbnail used to be and pressed hard, smearing blood on his own fingers as he rolled my thumb first on the ink stone and then onto the white paper. It was excruciatingly painful and difficult for me to find my words, but well worth it to see his face as I lied to him, '*Yo tengo Sida* [I have Aids], *Señor Funcionario.*'

His face transformed into a slab of Cheddar cheese as he quickly went to the lavatory to scrub my blood from his hands. On his return to the room he dug furiously into a cardboard box full of surgical gloves, regretting his thoughtlessness. The oafish spick had thumbed off the scabs where my nails used to be before the stamping boots of my arresting officers, the secret police, had torn them off. Red blood and black ink don't look nice when mixed, but there were no hand-washing facilities in this room and now they wanted to take my photograph.

I was shoved in the direction of another table, where two screws were waiting to take my photo against a white wall with a metric ruler on it to indicate my height. The screws grabbed me, forcing me violently against the wall, disturbing one of the stitched wounds on the back of my head and smearing blood on the white-painted bricks.

The wild-eyed screw, who was obviously the boss, threw a toilet roll at me, so I took some paper off to wipe the blood and ink from my hands. He charged at me, screaming into my face, and vehemently slammed me against the wall then pointed at the bloodstain there. The bog roll was intended to clean the wall, not my hands. I pulled some more paper off it and started wiping off the blood. I had just about finished when the next internee came crashing against the wall to have his mug shot taken. I was pushed to the next metal table where two screws were sitting surrounded by filing cabinets and swirling tobacco smoke.

'*Nombre?*' snarled the fat, greasy one.

'Chance,' I replied. 'Christopher Chance.'

'*Fecha de nacimiento?*'

'*No comprendo. No hablo mucho Español,*' I stammered through my broken teeth.

'What is the date of your birth, Englishman?' said the hard-looking screw sitting next to Fatso.

'Oh, yes, er . . . 27 November, 1940,' I said.

'*Ciudad?*' said Fatso.

'Where is your home town, Englishman?' said the hardcase.

'Widnes in England.'

'You will wish you had never left there. Now go to that officer over there. He has some nice things for you,' he said, pointing across the room to a screw standing behind a counter waiting to issue washing-and-shaving kit and other sundry items.

For the first time I went to the next screw unassisted by a shove. This one handed me a plastic bag as he studied me over the rim of his spectacles. He then slowly handed me each item and slid a sheet of paper across the counter for me to sign. I checked it to see that it wasn't anything other than a stores list, then I signed it, puzzled, because amongst the issued items were three condoms.

Looking over the rims of his spectacles again, he jerked his thumb in the direction of a corridor where another screw was impatiently beckoning me to get into a shower cubicle. The cold water was already cascading from a pipe in the ceiling. My new escort shoved me into the shower before I undressed, so my clothing got drenched. I painfully pulled off my clothes and stepped under the freezing spray. I used my new bar of soap, which was rose-scented and most enjoyable, but the screw realised I was enjoying the experience so he glared at me and screamed for me to get out. Apart from the word '*giri*' I couldn't understand anything he said, but I gathered he wanted me to get out of the shower.

I noticed that, as he'd screamed at me, he'd been ogling my genitals, so I turned my back to dry myself. I feared that I would meet many perverts in this evil place. He watched me dry and dress myself, his eyes darting around my torso trying to get a glimpse of my dick. His interest in me died as I pulled on my trousers. Now he wanted to see the dick of the next prisoner.

I had just put the towel in my plastic bag when another screw beckoned me to follow him. He was tall and skinny and looked as though he should have been an undertaker rather than a prison officer. I followed him along the corridor a few paces, then he stopped and poked me with his truncheon to make me walk in front of him. He said nothing as our footsteps echoed along the dismal corridors and staircases. The muffled echoes of manly voices drifted around me, adding to the shock and bewilderment of finding myself in the grey, metal-and-concrete maw of this Spanish judicial beast.

I turned my head to ask my escort where he was taking me, but the words would not come out as I looked into his dark, oily face as he twirled his forefinger, indicating that I look to my front. In that lonely corridor with that eerie face, I knew I was in the worst place I could possibly be. I had to condition myself to survive this dreadful satellite of human bondage.

Apprehension and adrenalin coursed through my veins as I moved through this evil, architectural beast called the Carabanchel. In amongst our footfalls my imagination picked up the whimpering of souls past and I sensed the pervading corruption hiding in the concrete. My thoughts were racing as we followed our echoing, haunting footsteps along this eerie corridor with its daunting ceiling high above us. Whose ghosts were trapped up there? God only knew.

The corridor opened out into what can best be described as an amphitheatre, with one single tier running around the perimeter wall, which rose from the black-and-white, shiny, tiled floor to a domed roof high above me. A glass window high up in the wall just beneath the giant dome filtered the last of the daylight down onto the control tower in the centre of the atrium. The tower looked like a giant Dalek out of *Dr Who*.

Through the glass surround of the Dalek I could see several prison officers going about their business. One of them disappeared downwards, so there must have been more floors below ground. The Dalek had a flat top with a handrail running around its circumference and I could see a screw patrolling it. He was possibly 20 ft above the ground, looking down on me. Our eyes met and, even from this distance, I could see the hostility in his gaze.

Architecture often delights me, but this building exuded evil. The message here was quite clear: intimidation by design. I felt the architect had wanted to put gargoyles in here but they'd been deemed an unnecessary expense: gargoyles might have softened the impact. The hub of the prison was designed to strike fear into all who entered and I felt intimidated right then, standing under what was possibly the largest dome in Spain. Several prison wings branched off of this hub like the spokes of a wheel. My escort prodded me with his truncheon, indicating that I should walk clockwise around the Dalek.

A prison officer called from the tower: *'Galería cinco, Rafael.'*

'Sí. Venga,' my escort replied, his voice reverberating around the atrium. Touching me with his truncheon, he pointed at a massive iron gate, with a big, black number five above it.

As we approached the gate, I detected movement in the darkness beyond: somebody was opening it. The gate crashed open and my escort pushed me with his truncheon into the dark entrance, wherein lurked my new keeper, whose menacing eyes bored into me as the tall, skinny one disappeared wordlessly, his receding footsteps echoing around the atrium.

TWO

THE TEETH OF THE BEAST

If the eyes are the windows to the soul, then this prison officer didn't have one. It was like looking at a face with two glass eyes. He was either drunk or deranged. I could smell whisky so I guessed he was drunk, but another look into his eyes told me he was both drunk and mad.

'*Venga, giri*,' he slurred, pointing his truncheon behind him along the dark corridor. All of my survival instincts were creating a third eye in the back of my head as I walked in front of this troglodyte swinging his club behind me.

I've been in some dark alleys in my time, but this was the gut-wrenching alley to end all others; this was hormone gridlock: the heavy breathing, the primeval shuffle of the club-wielding anthropoid sneaking up behind me. The adrenalin coursing through me was my weapon, my Excalibur, the controlled aggression that would trash anyone who tried to seriously hurt me. My ridiculous imagination cranked down and the apprehension diminished slightly as the light from a television flickered on the tiled wall up ahead. I could see a gate ahead of me and then an office from which the light of the television was shining.

A snarl from behind stopped me in front of an office door. A truncheon pushed me against the cold wall opposite it, and a threatening gesture with the truncheon informed me that I had to stand just where I was and not move, or else! Again, I understood just one word: '*giri*'.

I stood here looking around me, trying to take it all in, trying to keep control of my thoughts, trying to hold on to my senses, the apprehension that pounded in my head making me feel giddy and nervous. Cockroaches appeared on the walls. I wondered if they were real, because if so, they were the biggest cockroaches I had ever seen. The first rat appeared and it was so big that I half-expected it to produce a top hat and perform a trick or two. I wondered if I was dreaming and getting mixed up with *Alice in Wonderland*; maybe I would awake in a moment to find myself at home. No such luck: loud laughter brought me back to reality as the screws saw something funny on the television.

I studied the screws in their smoke-filled office, but I could only see their silhouettes. In the light from the television screen I could see they each had a can of beer. I could just about see the familiar San Miguel logo on the cans. They were smoking and peering through the haze at transvestites and transsexuals prancing on the screen – Spaniards with thick facial hair dressed in skirts and blouses, wearing thick, bright-red lipstick, lifting their skirts to show the nation their frilly knickers. Both the television audience and the screws were laughing heartily at this sad insult to manhood, but scenes like this are a daily occurrence on Spanish television. Bulls and transvestites are big in Spanish culture; seemingly, so is cruelty.

I observed my keeper throwing his cigarette to the floor. He stepped on it as he came lurching out of the office waving his truncheon at me to stand still while he opened a big iron gate, then beckoned me in to the poorly lit staircase of the *galería*. I walked up a few more steps to be confronted by another iron gate, which my escort noisily opened. We stepped onto a terrazzo-type floor that housed two rows of cells situated along each side of the gallery, the far end of which I couldn't quite see because of the poor lighting. Above me were another three floors of cells running down each side of the gallery with a safety net stretching across the first floor. I could hear the muffled noises of locked up prisoners and the cooing of pigeons. Rats scurried here and there fearlessly, while cockroaches, alarmed by human footfalls, darted away.

Another iron gate was being noisily unlocked by the drunken

screw, his patience being tested by the usual drunkard's inability to find the keyhole in bad light. Curses flowed as his big nightstick clattered to the floor and rolled to my feet, where it lay resting against my shoe. At last he turned the key in the lock and smashed the door against the wall with a deafening clang of metal.

I stood motionless, mortified, with the truncheon against my foot as he jerkily looked around trying to find it. He stiffened as he located the truncheon resting against my shoe; an eerie coldness emanated from him as his eyes glittered with spine-chilling madness. The hostile silence seemed to cast deafness upon me, as though the whole prison was in the frozen silence of suspended animation.

The spell was broken by the pounding of my heart, and with my dry mouth I softly said, '*Señor, está aquí*,' pointing my finger down to my foot. My mad keeper warily stooped to pick up his truncheon as I silently prayed, 'Please, God, don't let him stumble into me.'

He stood erect now and pointed the truncheon at my face: '*Muy bien, giri*.' Then he prodded me through the gate and onto the stairway to reach the upper floors, where more gates awaited us. At last, we reached the top floor, where he pushed me through the gate to walk the length of the gallery to a cell somewhere near the end: a cavity in the rotten tooth of this mouldy Spanish beast.

He hit the handrail with his big stick as we walked, heralding his approach. I visualised inmates wondering nervously which cell would be visited by this mad creep who everybody knew was on duty this night. I got a whiff of the pungent, familiar stink of hashish, as did my mad escort. He signalled me to be silent with a pouting kiss on his forefinger accompanied by a hiss. I stood still to watch him sniff around a cell door then he quickly slid back a metal shutter to expose a peephole. He peered through the hole in the door and muttered angrily to himself as he noisily slammed back the shutter.

'*Venga, giri*,' he said, waving his big stick to indicate that I should walk in front of him. I was nearing the end of the gallery when he stopped me at cell no. 98, where he inserted a key, slammed back the massive bolt and pulled the heavy iron door open, allowing the light to spill out onto the gallery.

My escort stepped back nodding his head, indicating for me to enter the cell. As I entered, two Arab occupants stood to attention next to their beds, having flung back their bed-sheets untidily in their efforts to get up quickly to greet the screw. He came in behind me sniffing noisily, like a bloodhound sniffing for cannabis, which we all knew was not in the air here. The cell smelt pleasantly of pine disinfectant, while the two Arabs exuded exotic aftershave or body lotion; totally alien to this foul-smelling rat-hole and this stinking turd dressed in gravy-stained blue serge.

'*Otro giri*,' he snarled, stepping backwards to exit the cell.

'*Sí, señor, muy bien, señor*,' said the two Arabs in unison as the turd made threatening gestures with his truncheon then noisily slammed shut the heavy iron door and crashed home the big sliding bolt.

Through the echo of the crashing door I could hear the tinkle of the turning key: the final act of the Spanish beast, masticating and swallowing me down into its evil gullet to begin the violent journey through its foul intestines to be eventually shat out of its decaying arsehole sometime in the future. I began my first night of madness in the Carabanchel.

We three stood motionless, listening as the screw's footfalls faded into silence, then the Arabs grabbed my hands to vigorously pump a welcoming handshake, painfully squeezing my tender fingers. This genuine, heartfelt welcome from two complete strangers washed away all sense of trepidation as they jabbered at me in Arabic, French, Spanish and finally German, my second language. My new friends' names were Hassan and Tribak. They were both Algerians and were over 6-ft tall with hard, lean, athletic bodies.

They quickly made up the third bed in the cell, which was really cramped with three beds and three blokes moving about. The cell had a toilet and a washbasin with a cold tap, both made of concrete. Because colliding and squeezing past each other was unavoidable in such a small space, we soon developed a habit for our morning rituals. Tribak would be up first to wash and shave while Hassan and I stayed in bed and chatted. Tribak would then make his bed neat and tidy and sit on it talking to me while Hassan washed and shaved. By the time Hassan was finished, the duty screw would have opened the cell door and my Arab friends would leave the cell so I could shit and shave in private.

The Arabs always used the heaving communal shithouse in the prison yard because they had a thing about shitting in the cell, whereas I had a thing about shitting in the unbelievable filth of the communal lavatories. Neither Tribak nor Hassan shat in our cell during my time with them.

We scrubbed our cell clean and bleached it daily to keep out the cockroaches. Everything was neatly stowed away and our shoes were kept in a cardboard box under the sink. At the doorway to the cell we removed our shoes and put on flip-flops or slippers so that gunge from the yard and gallery was not walked into the cell. There was an ever-present carpet of snot and phlegm on the gallery floors, staircases and yard, put there by the constant hawking and gobbing of the Spanish prisoners. The sound of discharging nostrils and splattering head-gunge is constant in all Spanish prisons.

Back on this first day my cellmates looked on in shock as I removed my shirt, revealing my injuries. The pain I was suffering from the simple act of undressing was plain to see. They sat on the edge of their beds, open-mouthed as I removed my trousers, revealing the monstrous bruises on my legs.

'*Polizei?*' Hassan asked.

'*Ja,*' I replied.

Hatred shone in both Hassan's and Tribak's eyes as they swore amongst themselves in disgust. Hassan passed me one of his clean T-shirts telling me it was to be used for sleeping in or lounging in the cell – I wasn't to take it out of the cell. He then gave me a pair of flip-flops, again to be used only in the cell. Tribak handed me a lumberjack-style shirt to wear as I liked, the genuine smile on his face telling me this was a gift he knew I would truly appreciate.

We chatted for a while, the two of them telling me about their wives living in Düsseldorf in the beautiful homes they had bought. They showed me photos of their wives when they were *fräuleins*, not so long ago. They were beautiful girls. Now I knew why these blokes spoke such good kraut.

I settled down to sleep as Tribak switched off the light. '*Gute Nacht. Schlaf gut,*' we each said in stage whispers as I pulled the sheet over me. Thoughts came rushing into my brain, driving home the realisation that I was in the most abysmal situation. I thought about my wife Susan and the anguish and distress she must have been suffering at that very moment as I was lying there thinking about her.

The scar across my heart was being cut right then and would grow bigger with every day I spent in this dreadful place. Realising the misery and suffering I had caused to Susan created the first incision of the cold, steel claw of guilt, which began its gouging journey across my heart, sending my spirits plunging to unknown depths.

Despair clouded my mind and I gave up the notion of sleep as guilt and frustration broke down the barriers to my soul, invading the innermost segments of my mind and causing silent tears to overflow and trickle uncontrollably down my face into the pillow. Carabanchel was not causing this: no, it was the vision of Susan, the heartache, the numbing sadness, the stark failure of providing security and happiness for her, my fragmented peace of mind exploded by my stupidity.

My mind raced. I had to beware of self-pity. I had to root out all negative thoughts about myself: my body would mend quickly; my mind was well trained in adversity; Susan was tough, clever and not short of moral fibre. This was my first night in hell, so I had to get the barriers up, control my thoughts, promote a mindset of courage and invincibility, rely on my military and martial-arts experiences: in short, get a grip!

Self-discipline was the key to survival in this netherworld, so the next day I would start composing my own rules. I reflected on my years of martial-arts training and the notion came to me to adopt the byword of the samurai: Bushido – the rigid discipline of the ancient corps d'élite who withstood the hordes of Kublai Khan's Mongols, the Chinese and the Russians. I promised myself that I would never surrender to anyone or anything that could possibly shame me.

Waves of tiredness swept over me and I felt that sleep was coming after all. I lay awaiting the embrace of sleep but the numbing silence created a roar in my ears and a kaleidoscope of lights began to appear behind my closed eyelids. I suddenly felt the urge to pray, so

THE TEETH OF THE BEAST

I gathered my thoughts and tried to remember the words to the prayers I used to say as a child. My mind was pulling back the layers of time when suddenly my vacuum of silence was pierced by a spine-chilling scream from the depths of the gallery.

Tribak leapt from his bed and crept to the door. With the point of a pencil he moved the shutter on the spyhole. He then gave a running commentary to Hassan in Arabic, who then relayed the information to me in German. Four screws were savagely beating into unconsciousness a crazed Spanish prisoner who shared a cell with a transsexual whom he had just stabbed and started to rape. The rapist was notorious and Hassan reckoned the screws had probably taken bets on the hour in which he'd strike, because he'd been put in that cell that afternoon and the screws had responded to the scream too quickly. They must have been waiting for it to happen.

Tribak reported that the spick was now unconscious, but Don Ignasius was now breaking the rapist's ankle by frenziedly striking it with his truncheon. Don Ignasius was the screw that had brought me to my cell earlier. Tribak beckoned me to have a look at the scene below, so in the darkness I got out of bed and went to look through the peephole, through which I witnessed Don Ignasius grinning and prodding the limp, badly injured ankle of the unconscious rapist. I watched him raise his truncheon above his head and crash it down sickeningly into the rapist's knee, the crack echoing around the gallery followed by the sound of his weird laughter.

The poor light on the gallery contrasted with the bright light shining out of the cell, making the whole scene seem surreal. It was as though I was watching an old black-and-white horror film, with long, sinister shadows being cast across the landing. I half expected to hear a panic-stricken piano from the days of silent movies, but the only sound was feigned laughter from the lunatic screws. I made a mental note of this sicko screw, because this type of pitiless brutality and cruelty suggests a total absence of inner feelings, and it was quite obviously unusual for screws to be brought to book for any ill-treatment they dished out. The uniformed brute was no better than the rapist, and I had to assume that this kind of activity was normal around here. I went back to my bed and immediately fell into a fitful sleep.

A wailing siren awoke me on my first morning in the Carabanchel; it was *recuento*, the first body count of the day. The shouts of the abusive screws and the noise of crashing bolts echoed loudly around the prison. Hassan and Tribak were early risers and their beds were neatly made up, the two of them ready to leave the cell. I made my bed and was about to wash and shave when the bolt crashed back and the door swung open, revealing a little man wearing baggy serge trousers and a light-blue shirt with a metal badge pinned to the right breast pocket.

This little man in a big uniform, a little brain with a big mouth, was glaring at me now, so I looked deep into his eyes, peering into the glittering madness that belied his composed expression. There was a blend of icy cruelty and tongue-tied shyness – manifestations of a deep sense of inadequacy – hiding behind his uniform, his armour. This vicious, unintelligent tyrant was nothing outside these walls, but in here he was Mister Big. He turned away from me to flash his hostile eyes at the Algerians, then, with a contemptuous snort, was gone.

Hassan had warned me about this tyrant. His name was Don Juan, but the inmates knew him as Hitler. He had grasses on every landing, so I had to be careful and courteous with this creature. If you gave him cause to be angry, he would write your name in his pocket diary and the next time he was on night shift he would visit your cell with four of his big pals with big sticks.

Hassan informed me that I was the only Englishman on this gallery, so when I'd washed, I should slide the bolt on the cell door and join them down below on the ground floor. Everybody left the landings to go down and walk around the bottom of the gallery before the breakfast gate was opened. I finished my ablutions and gave my bed-sheets a final tweak, then quickly mopped the doorway with bleach. I hurriedly laced up my shoes and set off along the gallery to the stairs at the far end of the landing.

I felt I had forgotten something. I dashed back to shoot the massive bolt on cell no. 98. I gave myself a bollocking for being so stupid: 'Think, think, you silly bastard,' I said to myself as I headed for the stairs.

My senses were heightened and my apprehension increased as I realised all eyes were on me, the new boy. There seemed to be a thousand faces looking up at me as I moved along the landing, some of them blatantly staring at me while others just glanced furtively. The noise drifting up from the mouths below was deafening. It seemed as though everybody was shouting, and behind that noise was the sound of shuffling feet, hundreds of them.

When I reached the end of the landing to go down the stairs, I noticed the white-tiled walls were soiled with snot and phlegm. This was truly a bad place to be, an enormous health hazard occupied by consumptive junkies who gobbed their innards all over the show. I jostled into the throng on the ground floor to look for the Algerians. It didn't take long before I clocked Tribak waving to me from about 30 metres away. I was relieved to see a friendly face in an environment where everybody appeared grim and intimidating. Maybe I was paranoid but I felt oppressed and threatened just then.

Hassan appeared just as a big, iron gate opened and the throng moved through it to the *comedor* (dining hall), where breakfast awaited us. A queue formed and filled the corridor leading from the gallery to the dining hall, which I couldn't yet see because there was a corner to get around first. While we were all slowly shuffling forward, several greasy types barged through to get to the front of the queue.

'*Gitanos*,' said Hassan.

'*Zigeuner hunde*,' said Tribak.

'Gypsy scumbags,' said a man standing behind me. I turned to see a friendly face smiling at me.

'Hi. I'm from Holland,' he said. 'You can call me Dutch, if you like. That's what most people here call me and my countrymen.'

'Chancer,' I said, shaking his hand.

He looked into my eyes and said, 'I'll speak to you later on the *pateo* [prison yard]. Enjoy your breakfast, my friend, it's normally the best meal of the day.'

My turn soon came to pick up a *bandeja* (metal tray), which I loaded with bread, jam, margarine and a plastic cup of milky coffee. Hassan pointed to a table where one man sat eating alone. He told me that this was the English table, and that everyone was expected to sit in their own national groups at mealtimes. I joined my 'countryman', who happened to be an American sitting at the wrong table. The Yank turned out to be quite mad so I was pleased when he left the table muttering something about a game of chess.

Because I was so hungry I enjoyed my bread and jam. I hadn't eaten for 20 hours. The last food I'd had was at midday the day before and I couldn't eat much as the shit had played havoc with my broken teeth. A mouthful of bread and jam with a swig of hot coffee to soften it was a real treat. I enjoyed it so much I went for second helpings. I soon learned that breakfast was the best meal of the day because the Spanish kitchen staff couldn't really fuck up jam and bread.

I sat alone at the English table trying to take everything in. No matter which way I looked I was confronted with eyes staring back at me. Everyone I clocked looked away instantly, except the occupants of the clog table, who smiled and waved. Dutch was obviously gobbing off about me as I could see his head nodding in my direction.

About 20 ft to my right was a table full of Negroes who averted their gaze as one, as though I had shouted the command, 'Eyes front!' I later found out this table was known as the nignog table, just as all the other international tables were named after their ethnic groupings. This may seem politically incorrect to people who have never ventured out of their street, but it served as a useful point of reference in this big, noisy dining hall.

The *comedor* was spacious and high, the roof held up by steel trusses that were painted green and coated with pigeon shit. The pigeons were waiting patiently for me to finish so they could swoop down for my crumbs and shit all over the table, which was bolted to the concrete floor, as were the rows and rows of long wooden benches.

Each table seated about ten men and had a green, gingham plastic covering that made the pigeon shit really stand out. Between the benches and tables I could see rat shit, so I correctly assumed that armies of cockroaches and germ-ridden rats visited these tables when the prisoners and pigeons had vacated them.

THE TEETH OF THE BEAST

The tables were international territories, jealously guarded to keep foreigners out. The table to my left was kraut; to my right were two wop (Italian) tables; beyond them were the rusks (Russian) tables; to my front were the clogs (Dutch) and behind me were the frogs (French). Several wog (Arab) tables were behind the frogs and several rows of spick (Spanish and South American) tables took up much of the space between the clogs and the food service area. Right at the rear of the dining hall were the Basque tables, and as far away from them as they could possibly be put were the spick gypo (Spanish gypsy) tables. Spanish gypsies were looked upon by their fellow countrymen as being the lowest form of life on the planet, and every other nationality in here agreed with them. According to a 1998 report by the Commission on Human Rights over 80 per cent of adult Spanish gypsies were functionally illiterate. In all of my years in Spain I have met many gypsies, none of whom could read or write.

I finished my breakfast and was sitting, lost in thought, when the *comedor* screw ordered me out. I was the last bloke to leave the tables. They would close the gallery after breakfast so everybody got locked outside in the prison yard. Most of the prisoners were already walking clockwise around the *pateo*. Some blokes were jogging, while others were running hard. I joined the walking throng and settled into a brisk walk, trying to ignore the pain in my weeping arse and getting accustomed to the oppressive height of everything. Bricks and concrete seemed to be growing all around me, towering over me no matter where I looked.

The noise of discharging nostrils and hawking spicks is not conducive to serious thought or exercise; it is quite disturbing and interrupts concentration. Walking over phlegm-spattered concrete takes a bit of getting used to and to avoid stepping in spick head-shite you would need to be the world hopscotch champion. I could feel the eyes staring at me: the screws – perverts, queers, psychos; and then the prisoners – transsexuals, paedophiles, rapists, killers and international villains from all over.

I stood up tall, head held high, an Englishman whose imagination was running away with him, feeling a bit like the lone rabbi at Yasser Arafat's birthday parade. Time would tell though that this wasn't my imagination: I was in a cauldron of evil, which bubbled all around me.

I jumped when a greasy hand touched my elbow; an oily, unwashed gypsy was rabbiting on about coffee and pointing to what I was later to learn was the *economato*, the prison shop. I twigged what he wanted but, not knowing enough Spanish to explain that I was skint, I simply said 'no'. His sly, oily face changed from simpering begging to total hatred. Suddenly, out of the strolling groups of prisoners, I clocked five greasy spicks closing in on me. To my right I saw Tribak and Hassan moving quickly towards me, shouting a warning because the begging spick had a weapon in his hand: a *pinchou*, which is a spike of steel about 9-in. long.

With a long, lunging thrust he tried to stab me in the solar plexus. The oily turd was clearly inexperienced in attacks such as this, though. The nearer he got to me the faster his nerve was leaving him. I easily side-stepped the spike whilst grabbing his wrist with my right hand to pull him off balance. I then delivered a palm-heel strike with all of my weight behind my left hand, driving it into his jaw, just beneath his right ear. The loud crack announced a broken jaw and instant coma.

One of his greasy pals stooped to pick up the spike so I stamped on the greaser's hand and silenced the mad screaming with a downward punch behind his ear, knocking him out. I turned to face his other pals but it was all over; the screws were on my case, blowing whistles and surrounding me. I didn't struggle as two screws grabbed an elbow each. Two more screws to my front were itching for me to resist so they could use their truncheons.

'*Mira!*' shouted Hassan, pointing to the steel spike in the sleeping hand. '*Ustedes más ciego que un topo.*' ('You're as blind as a mole.') My Arab friends argued my innocence and the screws reluctantly let go of me. Gratefully I watched six Arabs arguing on my behalf. Nobody was disputing the fact that I'd been attacked, because the attackers were comatose and the other gypsies had slunk away.

The screws tried to revive the attackers, but face-slapping and rubbing the backs of hands will not undo my handiwork. The screws were getting worried now so I brought them back round

THE TEETH OF THE BEAST

with an ancient kung fu technique I had learned many years ago.

The attendants from the *enfermería* arrived to take the gypsies away for treatment. The oily turd was crying out in pain as the entourage moved off the wing. Hassan offered to buy me a coffee so I strolled across to the *economato* with six Arabs all talking to me in various tongues.

Hassan gave me a plastic cup of coffee, strong and black, which seemed to ease the pain in my teeth and gums. He then introduced me to his pals, who were all quite well dressed in clean, fresh clothes and polished shoes. Tribak and Hassan translated the Arabic for me and we were all getting along like a house on fire when a big, greasy fat bloke appeared and started gobbing off in rapid Spanish, poking his forefinger into Tribak's chest. The big gypsy was getting increasingly aggressive and I knew that threats were being made. Hassan told me that he was the brother of Broken Jaw and I needed to be careful from now on because the fat gypsy would most certainly stab me when I went into the showers or the lavatory.

Fatboy poked his finger at me, shook a fist and jerked his thumb towards the lavatories. He then made a throat-cutting gesture by drawing his forefinger across his Adam's apple. I responded by grabbing his Adam's apple and a fistful of windpipe then savagely slamming his head and shoulders into the concrete floor with a leg-sweep and reaping throw. I immediately yanked him upright into a sitting position and slipped behind him to apply a choke-hold, using my left forearm to crush his windpipe and block the carotid arteries, causing rapid asphyxiation. I released the pressure to keep him conscious but kept the choke in place as I ordered Hassan to tell Fatboy that I would kill him and any other member of his tribe if they came anywhere near me. Fatboy grunted that he'd understood me so I pulled him to his feet and foolishly kicked his arse towards the lavatories, thereby opening the wound in my own arse.

I thanked Hassan and strolled alone around the *pateo* wondering what the hell was going on around here. I hadn't yet been here 24 hours and I had major problems already.

'Hey, man, you're fuckin' deadly.' It was Dutch. 'We've all been waiting to see who gets at you first.' He started laughing. 'I won two bets,' he said. 'The first one was that the gypsies would get to you first and the second was that you would still be standing if it kicked off.'

'Well, you can buy me a coffee and a Kit-Kat,' I laughed.

'Where the fuck did you learn to move like that, man? I've seen some fast fuckers in my time but not like that. You must be a professional. What do you do?'

I hesitated to answer this question because I'd have been making a rod for my own back if I told him the truth. 'Oh, I'm just a bit handy, Dutch. Nothing to brag about.'

'Don't gimme that shit. What's those Jap tattoos on your arm?'

'They're Chinese, actually. They were done years ago in Hong Kong. Silly, really. I wish I'd never had them done,' I lied.

'Well, I don't fuckin' believe you. You can tell me any old bollocks but I know you are too much of a handful for these fuckers in here.'

'You sure you're from Holland, Dutch? I reckon you're from fucking Runcorn or somewhere.'

We were laughing as we joined the *economato* queue, and I was looking forward to another coffee. Out on the *pateo* there were metal tables and benches screwed into the concrete where blokes were writing letters amongst groups of chess players, but there was plenty of room for Dutch and I to sit and chat.

The inevitable happened. 'Why are you in here?' asked Dutch.

'A long story, my friend, but I suppose there's plenty of time to tell it.'

I told him that I owned a minibus that had been used to transport half a tonne of hashish from Fuengirola to Burgos, where it would have been loaded onto a truck to continue its journey to Rotterdam, but was intercepted on the outskirts of Madrid.

'The police give you a hard time?' he asked.

So I explained about the beating and kicking and the pistol-whipping – all done when the handcuffs had been applied. I showed him my broken teeth and the missing fingernails. My hands were now a mottled black and yellow colour and my thumbs were badly swollen.

Dutch was silent for a moment, then said, 'Beware of the dentist. He just yanks everything out. Those teeth that are broken off at gum level will cause a problem: he'll simply rip the fuckin' gum out. If you can't pay him, forget it; he'll fuck your mouth up for good. Ask Bing – he's one of my mates – the dentist fucked him good an' proper. You can meet him later. He couldn't eat for a fuckin' week or more.'

The news about the dentist dismayed me because I needed treatment. My problem was that the jagged edges of a couple of broken molars keep cutting the edge of my tongue and the bruising inside my mouth and gums was still tender.

Dutch was telling me about various screws and bullyboy prisoners when my name was called on the tannoy. 'Kreestoffer Chancer – *medico*,' echoed the sound system.

'That's you, mate, for the *enfermería*. The quack wants to see you,' said Dutch.

Two screws awaited me at the big iron gate, one of them slapping his truncheon into the palm of his open hand. They looked at me as I approached.

'Kreestoffer?' said the tall one, slapping his truncheon.

'Yeah,' I replied.

'*Venga*,' said the short one, pointing his stick through the gate, telling me to get in front of him.

We walked in silence through umpteen iron gates and echoing corridors, and around the control tower bathed in sunlight from the skylight high up in the superstructure of the dome, looking only half as sinister as it did the evening before. It still resembled a giant Dalek, though, and somehow appeared even bigger than before as our footfalls echoed across the shiny black-and-white-tiled floor.

We entered another corridor and, several corners and iron gates later, I was ushered into a large office where women wearing spectacles and crisp white coats were waiting to deal with me. The screws stood like sentinels at the door, arms folded, caressing their truncheons while I sat at a metal table with all things medical strewn across it. A woman dressed in starched whites strapped my arm just below the bicep and tried to explain in Spanglish (Spanish and English mixed) that she was about to take some blood. She then tapped lightly on a vein in the crook of my elbow and inserted a big, thick needle. Six phials of blood were taken and labelled, then a woman with a stethoscope beckoned me to her little room just across the way. The screws followed me across the room but the woman ordered them back to the main door.

She told me to undress and lie face down on the narrow bed covered with green tissue paper. She showed no surprise when she saw my bruises and swollen testicles. She pressed my ribs until I jumped with pain, informing her that she'd found the damaged one. She called in a nurse to strap my ribs. She then called in a male nurse to sort out my arse after she had checked it. He cleaned the wound and told me to wash it with salt water every day before I put ointment on it.

The doctor looked into my mouth with a lot of humming and haahing then looked at my hands. I was given an antiseptic mouthwash, ointment for my arse, a box of painkillers and antibiotics, and an injection of antibiotics into my right buttock. Apart from the labels on the phials of blood, no other writing was done: no notes, no signatures, nothing. I now realised there would be no medical evidence concerning my ill-treatment by the Spanish secret police: the scurrilous, cowardly bastards.

I arrived back on the wing just in time for lunch, so I joined the queue that had formed in front of the *comedor* gate. There were possibly 100 prisoners in front of me and I reckoned about 150 shuffling around the gallery floor. Everyone was now locked in the gallery in readiness for the midday meal before being locked in the cells for the afternoon siesta.

I checked the white-tiled wall for phlegm and snot before I put my back to it, standing sideways in the queue. I had strange men on either side of me and I was unguarded and exposed, but far from defenceless. The queue suddenly moved forward as the gate opened, leaving a gap between me and the front section. Nobody tried to get past me to the front. As if I had leprosy, everyone stayed back. The queue was four men wide up ahead. I was the only one in single file, then behind me it was four abreast again. I made it unaccompanied and unmolested up to the servery, where this time there were several prisoners dressed in whites. They were ladling soup, a main course and a pudding into the indents in the *bandejas*.

The first server ladled soup for me then dropped a bread roll into it, splashing it across the tray into where the pudding would sit. The next bloke served me fish with soggy salad, and his mate dropped a freckled banana into the little puddle of soup in the pudding compartment. I picked up a plastic cup and went over to the running tap where everyone filled their cups. I made my way over to the English table to sit alone under the gaze of hundreds of eyes. Even the blokes eating with their backs to me twisted their necks for a quick look. I pushed my food across the table and then got up and sat on the other side of it to face the blokes behind me, giving them all a fair share of my mug.

I tasted the soup but I couldn't figure out what flavour it was; I imagined it was old newspapers boiled in sour milk, or maybe wallpaper paste. I abandoned the soup and tasted the fish, but the stink was too nauseous, which actually pleased me because my nose was broken and partially blocked so I now knew my sense of smell was not impaired. I settled for the oily salad, the bread roll and the soggy banana.

I saw Tribak making his way from the wog tables over to me. He took some abuse from the frog table as he passed but it seemed not to bother him. Sitting opposite me, he told me to join him and his pals when they left their table because he felt the gypsies could try to ambush me between here and the cell, especially on the landings or the stairs. I thanked him for his concern and agreed to move when they moved. Again the frogs abused him as he walked by their table: he didn't even look at them.

Paranoia was playing havoc with me now as I imagined steel spikes in the hands of lurking gypsies in corridors and stairwells, waiting to plunge them into my kidneys. The wog tables started to clear so I moved through the rows to join Tribak as he went to the servery with his empty *bandeja*. Hassan and his countrymen fell in behind me as I walked with Tribak along the corridor and up the stairs. I realised that I was clenching my fists and my triceps were stiffening. Adrenalin was flowing, giving me tunnel vision. I immediately started breathing deeply to get a handle on my adrenalin and turn it into something positive: a well of super energy.

It was a long way to my cell. I had three more flights of stairs to go up, then a long walk past umpteen open cell doors along the landing. On reaching my landing, I stayed next to the handrail. It was a long way down from here, especially at the beginning and end of the landing because the safety net didn't stretch to the ends of the gallery.

Trepidation increased with each step I took. Each cell door was a potential ambush site because they opened outwards onto the landing, thereby causing an obstruction whenever they were left or swung open. I glanced to the lower landings to see several gypsies glaring up at me, three of them giving me the ancient throat-cutting gesture. I casually give them the finger, defiantly hiding my true feelings. Cat-calls and abuse followed me to the end of the gallery, where I safely entered my cell.

I tried to act unconcerned as Tribak and Hassan offered to 'watch my back', but right now I felt quite vulnerable so I thanked them both and tried to think my way out of this problem. Gypsies are tribal; hence the collective threat towards me, so I decided to find the head man and persuade him to call off the dogs, 'or I will rip your face off your greasy fucking skull!'

I had come to the conclusion, correctly, that the only way to survive this evil place was to respond to any threat that came my way with focused, violent aggression. I could not rely on my cellmates for constant protection, so I had to project an aura of invincibility, coupled with ruthless maniacal violence towards anyone who wished to harm me. They had to realise that if they didn't see me off with their first attempt, they would regret it forever. Courage and reckless abandon to the odds was no guarantee of survival, but, combined with many years of skilful martial-arts training, focused violence would see me through, or I would be injured, crippled or even killed in here.

I decided that, for however long I had to stay in this place, my reputation would be my shield. I had a head start because the screws had already got me down as *'peligroso'* – dangerous – thanks to the secret police putting it on my file. So now I would develop and strengthen my Bushido mindset as I lay on this prison bed mentally rehearsing the various crippling martial-arts techniques that I knew I would be forced to rely on during my years in hell.

I had taught martial-arts classes every day for years, right up to the day of my arrest, so my level of fitness was higher than average. As a martial-arts teacher I was a purveyor of violence; I taught people how to respond to violence, both defensively and offensively. However, I had never wilfully hurt another person outside of a self-defence situation. I had never used a pre-emptive strike nor initiated an attack on another person until the Carabanchel swallowed me up. Now I was forced to respond violently to all assaults, be they physical or verbal, in a most dramatic, bone-crunching style, because every verbal assault I received developed into a physical altercation, normally with me taking the short odds because there was always more than one attacker. I nurtured new and radical thoughts, which were out of keeping with my normal principles, in order to become ruthless, undiscerning, unflinching in my quest to survive. I remembered an old saying: in the land of the blind, the one-eyed man is king. I had to use my advantages. The Carabanchel was also a jungle, and the king of the jungle is the lion. There were many lions in this jungle, but the one with the sharpest fangs was the dominant one. I had no wish to dominate anyone, but I had to sharpen my instincts to repel the perpetual stream of bullies.

Intimidators abound in here because machismo is an all-consuming cult amongst the Spanish, especially the gypsies. Manliness is displayed by an aggressive, haughty expression and a strutting gait, which only indicates to me a massive deficit of intelligence. Spontaneous acts of physical agility abounded, like doing handstand press-ups and walking on hands across the yard, oblivious to the snotty floor. There was also an abundance of pretend fighting, shouting and *torero* (bullfighting) posturing directed at passing *payos* (non-gypsies). This childish behaviour increased the sense of oppression suffered by men who were not assertive and lacked fighting skills. The gypsies sought out the meek and weak to intimidate and rob. They constantly gibed other inmates, looking for a weakness. It didn't take long for me to see what the score was around here. I'd been here for nearly 24 hours and I'd had to defend myself against three gypsies already.

My future looked grim and painful, but what the hell! I'd go down fighting. I mentally resolved never to submit to bullies and intimidators, never to turn the other cheek and to make any aggressor pay dearly. I would think Bushido. In the quietness of my cell these thoughts cluttered my brain and robbed me of sleep as my cellmates softly snored, not quite in unison, but not unpleasantly. Thoughts of my difficult and dangerous road ahead dissipated as my mother came to mind: the old lady with so much common sense – much more than I'll ever have. I saw her wise stoical expression, behind which lay all the love in the world: a mother's love. I felt the urge to write to her but I hadn't the means. Tribak would have given me pen and paper but I was reluctant to wake him so I closed my eyes to find my wife's face looking back at me. It was etched with heartbreaking sadness, plunging my mood to painful depths. I was suffering from the self-inflicted mental torture of prison: the deep ache of sincere remorse.

Why couldn't I think of other things? Why couldn't I wrench my thoughts away from my loved ones? The big stone remained firmly in my chest, and lucid thought dissolved into tears of sadness as the wailing siren dragged me from my reverie – ending siesta.

Heavy steel bolts crashed back alarmingly on the lower floors, releasing prisoners into the yard for a two-hour break before the evening meal at about half past six. (The sound of crashing bolts will live with me forever.) Screws were screaming for everyone to get out as they pulled back the heavy doors. My cellmates quickly splashed cold water on their faces then waited for the screw to open the door.

Hassan told me to be careful and that he would watch my back. I thanked him and explained that I would defend myself vigorously and bollocks to the consequences. My cellmates were quite concerned about this but we were interrupted by the bolt crashing back and the door opening to reveal a screaming prison officer with a face like a well-smacked arse, all pink and puffy. The English-speaking thug, who I later found out was called Don Francisco, screamed abuse at us using the words nigger and cunt in his tirade. 'Cunt' was spat at me with a supercilious glare.

'Your English is good,' I ventured, as we trooped out of the cell.

Hassan closed the door and crashed home the bolt, nodding for me to walk ahead of him behind Tribak. Don Francisco had opened the last two cells on the landing, which I knew contained gypsies, but I didn't know if they were family or friends of my problem gypsies. I had to assume that they were.

A single Arab was between myself and six gypsies, any one of whom may have wanted to slide a steel spike into my kidneys. I stopped walking and leaned my back against a cell door and Hassan drew alongside me as the gypsies passed by in single file. Not one of them looked at me as they passed.

'Relax,' said Hassan. 'No problem.'

My fists were so tightly clenched that my few remaining fingernails were digging into my palms. 'This is no bloody good,' I thought to myself. 'I've got to be loose, fluid like water, not stiff like treacle. I must beware of getting uptight, and take more control of my adrenalin; it is my ally, my superpower, so stay focused.'

We continued down the stairs and through the corridors onto the *pateo*, where the sun of the early-summer afternoon baked the prison yard. Hassan and Tribak joined the queue for coffee as I strolled around the yard. I guessed there were about 200 men strolling around out here, with another 100 or so spread between the television room, showers and *economato*, and a long queue waiting outside the telephone cabin that was situated in the yard near the entrance to the dining hall.

I could see a familiar face in the telephone queue and he was waving at me. As I got near, I recognised Paco, one of the men who was arrested with me. He flung his arms around me in a manly embrace.

'It's good to see you, Chancer. I spent the night in *galería siete* [wing no. 7]: a fucking terrible place. I was banged up four to a cell! Which cell are you in here? Is there room for me?'

'No, Paco, I'm in with two Algerian blokes and there's no space for anyone else.'

He frowned as he said, 'Antonio is with me; you know: the man from Galicia. The others will be coming to this wing as well today.'

'I don't know the others,' I said, as I tried to remember the faces of the men who were arrested with me. They were all strangers. Paco and Antonio had been the only ones I'd known, so these others meant nothing to me.

'Do you have your wife's telephone number?' said Paco.

'Of course I do, but I don't have money to buy a phone card. I've got fuck all.'

'Don't worry, I will get you a phone card tomorrow and some money for coffee and things,' he said, smiling all over his face.

'I need a writing pad, envelopes and stamps,' I said rather gruffly.

'OK, I'll get that for you before dinner. Here, take this money and get yourself coffee and biscuits.'

Being Spanish and knowing his rights, Paco had obviously managed to hang on to his money. But because I was a *giri* and unable to speak Spanish, I'd lost everything except my passport.

'Thanks. See you later,' I said as I walked over to the *economato* and joined the queue, where I stood for all of five seconds before the first beggars accosted me. There were just so many of them: big men, little men, all with the same black, greasy hair and dark features, all not quite understanding the meaning of the word no; all smiles and friendly faces until I refused them, then a bit of simpering followed by looks of daggers when they finally realised they were barking up the wrong tree.

I bought a coffee and a Kit-Kat and walked back on to the *pateo* where I sat at one of the metal tables to enjoy my snack.

'Hey, Engrish!'

It was Chinky, a Chinese bloke who I was locked up with in the holding cells before I went to the magistrates' court in Getafe, on the outskirts of Madrid.

'Hello there, Chinky. How're you doing?' I said across the table into his cheerful face.

'Not bad. You got money for coffee?'

'Yeah, here, take this,' I said, giving him the loose change from my pocket.

'You won udder one?' he said, nodding at my coffee.

'Yeah, why not?' I said, laughing at his chinky English.

He came back five minutes later with fresh coffee and sat next to me.

'You got aggro with gypsies, Engrish – not good. Gypsies come behind with knife, but I watch your back.'

'Thanks, mate, but I don't want you walking behind me all over the fucking show, do I?' I said, taking a swig of coffee to caress my teeth.

'No,' he said, 'but it better if I know when you in shower.'

His last remark reminded me that I'd wanted a shower before dinner but I'd forgotten my towel.

'Tomorrow morning, right after breakfast,' I said.

We had just finished our coffee when out of the yard gate strolled a most beautiful girl dressed in a black miniskirt and white blouse showing legs up to her armpits and jugs like Jane Mansfield's. She carried a plastic bag and towel and walked past everyone into the shower block followed by a crowd of Spanish blokes. Chinky and I strolled over to see what the score was and witnessed several spicks wanking as they ogled the beautiful face, breasts and legs that framed the hairy dick of the transsexual under the shower who was coyly lathering his big tits whilst slowly pirouetting in the shower stall.

A large, muscular gypsy strode naked from the opposite shower to join the transsexual, who immediately squatted and took the spick gypsy's tool in his mouth and vigorously sucked it until the gypsy pulled away and went back to his shower, beaming all over his shiny face as his dick slackened.

A queue quickly formed, led by a Negro who I later got to know as Tupak. I'll never forget the size of his schlong as he waved it in front of the transsexual's face. I thought he wouldn't get it in his mouth but he did. Chinky was laughing hysterically as we left the shower.

'You see everything here, Engrish. It better here than Wanchai in Hong Kong,' he laughed.

'Oh, I don't think so, Chinky,' I said, as I had a flashback of the Yankee Fleet Club and Mai Ling's Pisspot Shack. Oh, sweet memories.

We strolled around the yard chatting about Chinky's case. He explained the various methods he had used in his lifetime of smuggling heroin: how he worked successfully for years until he became involved with a Spaniard, then everything turned to rat-shit because his spick partner grassed him to save his own arse – how unusual!

I dislike people who deal with heroin, but I liked Chinky. Maybe that was because he was Chinese and his people had been using heroin since the British began trading in great quantities with them in exchange for tea many years ago. I could see he was not a user of smack because he was healthy, lean and hard. There was an alertness about him that a junkie could never attain, which made him a good choice for watching my back.

The screws came out to herd us into the dining hall for the final meal of the day. Paco joined us in the queue to tell me he had spoken to his wife, Consuela, who was on her way now to tell Susan what had happened to us. Panic flashed through me as I pictured Susan's face when the information had hit home. I wondered whether or not I should have told her first; then I thought it might have been better coming from Paco's wife, who could probably have answered any questions she may have had about Spanish prisons and the possible things that were likely to happen. Susan would have been frantic wondering where I had been for the past four days, but now she would know. Oh, bloody hell, the pain of it all . . .

Paco said, 'I'll get you a card tomorrow so you can speak to her.'

'Thanks, Paco, you're a pal.'

Paco moved off to see somebody further back in the queue as Chinky said, 'He no pal – he fucking spick – never trust spick.'

Time would tell that Chinky was right.

The crowd surged forward as the screw opened the gate to the dining hall. It wasn't long before I had my metal tray loaded with some kind of meat stew that had a vague smell of putrefaction about it. I also had three slices of Spam, a boiled egg, a bread roll and a tiny tub of yoghurt that had gone out of date the day before.

I made my way to the English table to sit alone, with the conversation I'd be having with Susan the next day playing on my mind. Suddenly Chinky appeared before me.

'How about me sitting on Engrish table? No problem, I fuck off when udder Engrish peoples come.'

I looked around to see dozens of hostile eyes staring at us, many of their owners shaking their heads.

'Sit down, Chinky. Welcome to England.'

Widespread muttering broke out around the dining hall, but the gypsies were the loudest, with lots of '*giri*' and '*chino*'.

Ignoring everyone, I started to eat my dinner. Before long a giant appeared before me, holding his dinner tray.

'Do you mind if I join you? My name is Jake,' he said. 'I'm from Belgium but I lived in England for a while.'

'Sit down, Jake. Nice of you to ask. If I was as big as you, I wouldn't have bothered asking.'

Jake laughed heartily as he sat on the bench next to me holding out his massive hand for me to shake.

'Chancer,' I said. 'Nice to meet you.'

Jake was a big, strapping fellow adorned with slabs of hard muscle; obviously a dedicated bodybuilder. He spoke English as well as anyone I went to school with and his repertoire of jokes was limitless. I'm glad Jake joined me because he became a good pal over the next six months.

He had been a doorman and bodyguard for a girlie-club in Brussels but in a weak moment he'd buggered off to Spain with the considerable amount of money that was in the safe. The Spanish police had arrested him at a railway station in Madrid with all of the money in his suitcase, but now the police were saying that he must have hidden it somewhere. Hmm . . .

We finished our dinner and made our way into the gallery, where the cells had just been unlocked. I was explaining to Jake about my problem with the gypsies but he had watched it all unfolding from the beginning. Realising that he knew about it before he joined my table warmed me to him: he was an ally.

After the evening meal there was lots of activity in the gallery; many inmates visiting their friends in various cells. The screws allowed half an hour before locking the cells for one hour, then the cells were unlocked for about 20 minutes so that everyone could go back to their own cells in readiness for *recuento*, the body count.

My cellmates were out visiting their friends so Jake and Chinky were in my cell when the screw came around. He locked them in with me. Jake explained that the screw would unlock the cell in an hour's time and then everyone would return to their own cells to be locked up for the night. Jake warned us about various screws who

41

were bullies and about the problems involved with using the telephone. The telephone was controlled by a screw who took your identity card and logged the phone number in a ledger. He then took your phone card and dialled the number, passing you the handset through a tiny window. So he was inside his hut and you were outside, trying to have a conversation at the head of a noisy queue. All the time you were talking, impatient bastards would be yelling for you to finish so they could use the phone. When the screw had decided you'd been on long enough, he'd shout for you to finish, then, two or three seconds later, he'd pull out your telephone card and pass it, with your identity card, back through the little window. If you were in conversation with your lawyer or a loved one, it didn't matter to the screw; he'd end your chat by yanking out your phone card, and if you hadn't finished yet he'd take special pleasure in it.

You would never know how much credit was left on the phone card. So, unless you timed yourself, your next phone call could be shorter than you'd planned, and the screw would not allow you to continue with a new card: it was too much effort for him to pull out the spent card and replace it with a new one. Also, if the screw dialled a wrong number or the line was engaged, it counted on your weekly allowance of three calls; unless you were a spick queer or paedophile – they seemed always to be on the phone. Consequently, using the telephone was always stressful.

The screw returned to unlock my cell and Jake and Chinky were replaced with Tribak and Hassan. We were then locked up and counted, so I settled down to write letters to Susan and my mother. The prison seemed to hum as it settled down for the night. I was in the middle of transcribing my heartfelt words when suddenly a long, drawn-out cry pierced the drowsy atmosphere. Accompanied by syncopated clapping and cheers of encouragement, Spain's worst singer was bursting his blood vessels and everyone else's eardrums reaching impossible trebles during his attempt to slaughter a gypsy love song.

Somewhere below my cell I could hear the tinny twang of guitar strings being tightened into tune, then the strumming of several chords in an attempt at finding the slaughterer's key. They eventually came up with a combination of frantic strumming and staccato, hoarse screaming that seemed to excite their fellow tribal members, who contributed by joining in with and ruining the syncopated clapping.

My love of Spanish music went into a terminal decline that night, as did my love of all things Spanish. This process was accelerated by the innate racism of Spanish prison officers and inmates. The screws' venom was levelled at *giris* and gypsies and was also infecting the boot-licking inmates who mirrored the burning hatred of the screws in their own black eyes. Spending time in their charge has poisoned my mind forever. I promised myself that when I got out of this rat-hole, I would piss in every Spanish reservoir I saw and batter senseless any gypsy guitarist I heard.

The din continued for over an hour, with songs from various different rasping gullets. The morning would see several sore throats and lost voices, with lots of hoarse congratulations and false praise about the wonderful singing: the bastards lied to each other all the time. Eventually I fell into a fitful sleep. My mind, plagued with guilt and visions of Susan, could not shed the mantle of distress, even in sleep.

The coming days tumbled into each other as I came to terms with my situation and became accustomed to the routine of things around here. I had telephoned Susan three times this week so my distress had dissipated somewhat and I was now sleeping better. Knowing that Susan was managing the house and creating enough income from her holiday lettings to survive gave me tremendous relief.

My family in England had sent me money via the British consul, so I could now settle down and concentrate on other things, such as my trial and keeping fit and healthy in this germ-laden pit. My first purchase was a soft toothbrush and tube of Colgate toothpaste to help get my gob right. After what Dutch had told me, and my own, rapidly gained experiences, I'd decided never to let a Spanish dentist anywhere near my mouth. I used a tiny nail file to grind off the sharp edges of my broken teeth and, in so doing, strained the muscles in my face by forcing my hand deep into my mouth to get at the jagged bits. My cheeks felt as though I had just inflated a barrage balloon in there. Anyway, it was worth it: I could now move my tongue around without slicing the edges. Many prayers and thanks go to the Great Lord of the Universe for bestowing upon me a high pain-threshold and a mouth big enough to get my hand into. When I was put in this dark place, I thought the Lord had abandoned me, but I soon discovered that He hadn't forsaken me: far from it. From where did the presence of mind and strength of character come? How did I get through years of cruel Spanish imprisonment and survive countless attacks on my person to emerge unscathed physically and mentally in the real world? Prayer and meditation were my keys to survival; I prayed daily for strength and He gave it me.

If you're a mad bastard, hardman or incurable villain (excluding nonces), I've got something to tell you. When you're in prison, you'll end up turning to your Maker in the silent, lonely hours of the night as you lie in the hopelessness of your cell. Your tiny world will stifle your thoughts, but, because you think there's a shard of hope, you'll offer a prayer. You try it tentatively at first, because you need to overcome your own misgivings and the way you've scoffed at others who haven't hid their beliefs, but you venture forward with your stumbling prayer, defeating your own shallow, self-inflicted embarrassment that you yourself planted in your soul. Tell me otherwise and I'll call you a fucking liar.

THREE
FINDING MY FEET

I had avoided trouble for several days and the end of my first week in hell was drawing near. My little celebration party was slightly shafted, though, by falling prey to a gypsy ambush in the shower stalls. They had been clocking my every move for nearly a week, so they knew I liked to shower straight after breakfast.

The 20 or so shower stalls were always occupied by Europeans just after breakfast, so I knew something was about to happen when Dutch shouted through the steam, 'What the fuck are spick gypos doing in here?'

I quickly moved out of the shower stall to grab my towel from the wooden bench, where it lay with my clothes. Six gypsies had entered the big room, leaving two at the entrance to act as lookouts, so they were eight in all with possibly twenty more loitering with intent out in the yard.

Jake stepped naked out of his stall to slam his massive fist into the nearest spick face with a resounding crunch as a nose and cheekbone cracked from the immense impact. Chinky wrestled the spike out of the hand of Nito, one of the chieftain's lieutenants, then slammed it downwards into Nito's shoulder, breaking the collarbone as the spike tore into the flesh.

As quick as lightning I thrust my rigid fingers into the nearest pair of Spanish eyes, sinking them nearly up to my knuckles. I then did exactly the same to my next target, who was positioning himself for a thrust into my kidneys with his *pinchou*, which was fashioned from a bone taken from a leg of lamb. The long, sharpened bone dropped from his grasp as my stiffened fingers plunged into his eye sockets. I scooped up his evil bone and buried it in his left buttock, forcing an agonising squeal of pain from the gypsy rat. With one hand over his eyes and his other hand clutching his arse, I silenced him with a very hard punch into his throat, dropping him like a senseless corpse: two more to go!

Jake and Chinky set about Manolo, another mindless thug notorious for his violent bullying. They battered him into unconsciousness as I dealt with Carlos, the tall, skinny gypsy who thought he was Lee Van Cleef and twice as hard. His dark eyes were wild with anger and fear as he lunged at me with a sharpened broom handle, which was about a metre long. I parried his thrust with my right forearm then stepped in to deliver a palm-heel strike with my left hand that landed just beneath his right ear with a satisfactory crunching sound as the jaw hinge was wrecked under the impact of my 230-lb frame.

I picked up the broom handle and discovered human shit smeared around the point. There was also a groove carved about an inch back from the point, packed with shit. I placed the tip of Carlos's dirty weapon just behind the tongue of his tennis shoe, then drove it down into his instep, twisting it so the shit was dislodged in the wound.

Pandemonium ensued as we grabbed our clothes and punched our way through the invading crowd of reluctant heroes trying to get in on the act so they could grass us to the approaching screws. I clocked that the barbershop door was ajar so I dashed in amongst the queers and quickly dressed, making sure my arse was to the wall in this faggots' hangout. I treated them all to my demented stare as I dressed, each of them knowing they were uncomfortably near an English lunatic. I threw my bag and wet towel at the barber with a growl that he understood perfectly well to mean, 'Look after my kit, you spick poof, or I'll rip your fucking head to shreds.'

I marched out of the barbershop and set off jogging around the yard. Chinky and Jake were sitting with the chess players and Dutch's group was in the *economato* queue. There was much head shaking and many concerned expressions on Spanish faces around the entrance to the showers as the screws and busybodies came and went. The orderlies from the *enfermería* arrived and took away the wounded heroes.

I slowed my jog to a stroll so that I could look with hatred into each pair of hostile eyes that caught my gaze. Not one spick held my challenging stare as I strolled around the *pateo*; my lunatic image was taking shape. I had to promote and maintain this uncharacteristic stance to survive in this dreadful place.

I expected to be collared by the screws for the shower incident, but nothing happened until the following day when I was called to the wing office where Don Rafael awaited me. He was the chief screw, the *jefe del modulo*. Nobody liked him: not the screws or the prisoners, but I came to respect him and we got on well. He spoke particularly good English with a Nottingham accent.

'I read your file, Chancer. I see you are a martial-arts instructor. What grade are you and which style do you teach?'

He was sitting at a large table-cum-desk, which was cluttered with newspapers, porno mags and overflowing ashtrays. He pointed to an empty chair opposite him.

'Sit down,' he said. 'Smoke?'

'No,' I said, crinkling my nose at the disgusting stink of the ashtrays. With an angry sweep of his arm the filth and shite on the desktop clattered to the floor, making the other screws jump and look nervously at each other.

'Stinking fucking pigs,' he shouted. '*Fuera! Trabajad!*' he roared, as his underlings slunk out of the office.

'The laziest fuckers on the planet,' he said, looking unblinkingly into my eyes. 'You are ex-military, aren't you?'

More a statement than a question. I nodded, saying, 'Yes, 12 years as a professional.'

'Good! I did 12 too. Did you have anything to do with the French Foreign Legion?'

'No, but I had a friend who served as a Paratrooper with them. He became a warrant officer class one in the British Army and we were good pals.'

Amazingly, Don Rafael knew my good friend, so we talked

about him for a minute or so, then I told him he had been killed. After a few seconds of silent respect we chatted on. We talked for ages in his office then he called the prisoner from cell no. 6, who was the gopher for the prison officers. He was at their beck and call day and night and was regularly shagged and beasted by whoever was on duty, especially the night shift. He arrived and was promptly sent off to get coffee and biscuits for us. Don Rafael told me he had lived in Nottingham for several years, hence his East Midlands accent.

'I'm not saying English girls are sluts,' he said, 'but I shagged myself to a frazzle in Nottingham. I wish I'd never left there; I had the time of my life in that city.'

As we chatted, other screws came into the office and politely talked in undertones to each other as they tidied the cupboards and the everyday shite of idle prison officers. The servant came back with the biscuits and the screws told him to clean the office floor without disturbing Don Rafael, but first to go back to the *economato* for another tray of refreshments, so I ended up having two helpings.

Don Rafael fired a load of instructions at his screws, then said, 'Come with me. I'll show you the gymnasium.'

Several iron gates, stairs and corridors later we arrived at the gymnasium. There were lots of weights and bodybuilding machines arranged around the place, but more interesting to me were the heavy punch-bag robustly hanging from its angle-iron bracket and the large stack of judo mats piled up in the corner.

'How often can I come here?' I asked, breaking Don Rafael's concentration as he punched the heavy bag.

'If you teach me some really good combat techniques and give me some private lessons whenever I want them, I'll see to it that you get a job in here.'

For the first time since my arrest I felt good about something. 'When do you want me to start?' I said, suddenly feeling confident and proud because I was good at my trade.

He looked at me knowingly, realising he would do well out of the deal. 'Next week,' he said. 'I'll bring you a tracksuit bottom and maybe a judo top. I think there's a black belt lying around somewhere.'

'No, don't get that. Just an old sweatshirt will do. I will be a target anyway without wearing a black belt.'

The gym was quite big with a high roof supported by steel trusses. It was kept clean and had a good supply of fresh air from the opened fire doors, which led out onto a yard that was used for basketball training and other games that couldn't be played in the gym. As the chief screw punched the bag, I quickly checked the condition of each judo mat. I couldn't believe my luck: the *tatami* (mats) were perfect and sufficient to cover the large area allocated for martial-arts training.

All of the gym orderlies were tough and each one specialised in some kind of sport. They maintained a strict discipline and supervised the various bits of apparatus that were dotted around the place. Strict equipment control was essential in here because of the many iron bars and odd bits of weightlifting kit that could be used as a weapon.

Two of the orderlies came out of the gym office, curiosity getting the better of them. They spoke simultaneously to me in an aggressive manner. Not understanding a word, I nodded at Don Rafael. '*Abla con el*,' ('talk with him') I said, without stopping what I was doing. The bullish manner was absent when they spoke to Rafael the screw; now we had a servile attitude as he reprimanded them and explained the situation. Had they been wearing caps, they would now be wringing them in their hands. I witnessed much Spanish sycophancy during my time in prison: another reason for my low opinion of the nation.

After they'd gone, Don Rafael said to me, 'These nosy bastards wanted to know why you were looking at the judo mats, so I told them that you will soon be working in here as an instructor; not as a cleaner, like they are. You need to remember that because they will have you cleaning the shithouse. Don't let any of these fuckers put on you in here. Look after your own kit and don't get involved with anything else. If any fucker other than a screw tells you to do something, tell 'im to fuck off. Come to me if you have a problem.'

I wondered what I had done to deserve this stroke of luck, so on the way back to the wing I asked the screw for the reason I was called to his office today. He told me that I was the talk of *galería cinco* because I had floored the most notorious gypsies on the wing, and his hatred of spick gypos stemmed from his childhood.

'No matter what the circumstances are, you can never, ever trust a gypsy,' he muttered with enormous hatred in his voice. 'There are two things in life I can't stand,' he said. 'And that's a prejudiced man and a gypsy.'

I laughed at his joke but I would learn during my stay in Spanish prisons that the spick gypsy is most certainly not the scintillating, sultry flamenco dancer much loved by visiting tourists. Oh, fucking hell no! That silly notion vanished with their heroin smoke.

That evening Don Rafael moved me to an empty cell and told me to carefully choose a cellmate during the next two days whilst he was on duty. Alone in my new cell that night I revelled in splendid isolation and eventually slept like an old crocodile until the wailing siren awoke me in the morning.

I did not relish the idea of sharing my cell at all, even with a chosen inmate, but I knew I had to pick somebody quickly before the other screws bunged a spick in with me. I certainly couldn't be doing with that. I thought about choosing Chinky or Jake, but then fate lent a hand in the form of Kennedy: a face from the past.

FOUR
STRENGTH IN UNITY

Kennedy was originally on another wing but because he had punched the lights out of a spick who had stupidly called him 'nigger' he was transferred to mine. He called himself Richard, which was not his real first name, no more than Kennedy was his real surname. He was a short, muscular man from Trinidad, about 40-ish and balding. He had a cheeky black face and a dazzling, white, toothy grin that went practically all the way around his head!

He was the most experienced mariner and skipper of everything that moved on water. From jet-ski to blue-water craft, Kennedy had sailed them all. Our wakes had crossed more than once, so we knew each other quite well and I didn't think twice when he asked if he could share my cell.

I introduced him to Jake and Chinky and, of course, he dined at the English table, which upset the spicks. In their eyes he should have been given a nosebag or maybe a trough; he definitely should not have been allowed to dine at the elitist English table: way above his station.

Kennedy's reputation as a global skipper and *traficante* meant that he soon had various VIP inmates paying their respects, regardless of his colour. The word quickly spread that I was also a skipper and probably Kennedy's partner in crime. The two of us also became associated in the spicks' mind when a group of them discovered why he had been moved to this wing. Now they wanted

51

to kill him because a Negro had had the effrontery to strike a Spaniard: such is their racism.

Chinky overheard a plan to ambush Kennedy during his next visit to the lavatory, so he immediately told me to warn my cellmate. I decided that this was the time and the opportunity to form our group and let it be known that if any one of us was victimised, the aggressors would have to deal with a group response from the lunatics on the English table.

The four of us were strolling around the yard when I made the proposition. Each of us eagerly agreed that, for our personal protection, we should present a united front: thus was born the *Mezclado*, which is the Spanish word meaning 'mixed'. The other inmates would soon come to know and fear us by this name; and our first action as a group was about to be felt as Chinky pointed out the gang of spicks who were conspiring against Kennedy.

We made our surreptitious way towards them and, in less than a minute, were amongst them. Kennedy confronted the ringleader, who was completely taken by surprise as Kennedy explained the consequences of any future activity against the members of the English table. We knew this message would quickly do the rounds and even reach the screws that day. But, to make our point, and to further my reputation as a lunatic, I grabbed the bollocks and windpipe of the biggest member of the group and laid him on his back with a swift pull-and-push technique that is quite effective with big men.

I gave him my demented glare and spat the word '*Peligroso*' at him. Under no circumstances could he possibly not know he was in the hands of a lunatic as he lay voiding his bladder over my wrist and hand as he endured his near-death experience. His facial expression revealed his inner feelings as I choked off the scream that was expanding beneath my grip. His eyes bulged with terror as both his hands pushed and pulled in his futile effort to break my grip. Panic was coursing through him as I quickly released and stepped away from him. Then he gasped and, taking laboured, painful gulps of air, pulled himself onto his hands and knees and then to his feet, assisted by his nervous *compadres*.

A crowd was beginning to gather as we four quickly moved away, dispersing as we went, heading in different directions across the yard. We were secretly bound for the *economato*, for a well-deserved coffee.

'Why the fuck did you rough up the big fella?' chuckled Kennedy as he joined me in the queue for coffee. 'He thought he was gonna fuckin' die, didn't he?' he said boyishly. 'I thought he would have stuck his spike in you but he seemed to forget he had it.'

'That's because I had a fistful of neck nerves in one hand and his bollocks in the other,' I said. 'The pain from crushed gonads combined with a crippling choke usually paralyses big blokes.'

'It would paralyse little fuckers too, for fuck's sake! You're gonna have to teach me some of that shit.'

'I will,' I said. 'I'm getting a job in the gym if Rafael the screw is as good as his word.'

Kennedy looked thoughtful for a moment, then said, 'I was going to get you a morning job in the *zapatería* next week.'

'What the fuck's the *zapatería*?' I said. 'And how the fuck can you get me a job?'

'It's the prison workshop where shoes are made. I can fix it so you can do mornings in the workshop and afternoons in the gym. You get good money in the workshop and it gets you out of this fuckin' yard,' he said. 'Also, I'll introduce you to some good people who will smooth things for a nice ride through your bird; I'll tell you all about it tonight when we're in the cell.'

I knew Kennedy was well connected but I was well impressed when I learnt he had one of the top officials of the prison in his pocket. Amazingly, he would soon be in my pocket too!

Dutch ambled up to me in the queue to give me some money. 'A pack of Marlboro ciggies, please, and get me a coffee with yours. There's enough change to buy yours too, you mad English cunt!'

I gave Dutch my quizzical look. He responded with, 'Don't give me that innocent shit; I know what you're fuckin' up to. King of the fuckin' wing: that's your fuckin' game, ain't it, you scheming bastard.'

'No, mate,' I said. 'I just want my own space: no snivelling fucking spicks poncing off me, then trying to knife me when I don't cough up; no fucking tuppenny-ha'penny gangsters trying to put one over on me. No, mate, I just want to do my bird unmolested in this fucking spick shitpile.'

'Well, I don't think anybody will bother you now . . . Unless he's as fuckin' crazy as you are.'

I felt good about my recent exploits; I had achieved the required image without too much pain and effort. My next objective was to get the job in the gym and perhaps the job in the *zapatería*. That night in my cell Kennedy explained his relationship with 'Pablo', the high-up official. My recollection of the actual explanation is somewhat hazy, simply because of the sheer number of personalities involved, but I do remember how intrigued I was to hear about the broad network of people from the government, police and the judicial system whose fingers were in the international drug-smuggling pie.

Two days later I started work in the *zapatería*. The foreman was a South American by the name of Oscar Bonilla, who treated me with respect. He wondered how I'd got a job in his workshop because he was the 'hire 'em and fire 'em' in here, and here I was being shown around by Kennedy, who seemed to be able to roam freely around any of the workshops without hindrance from foremen or screws.

Kennedy showed me a worktable situated at the back of the workshop, furthest away from the big entrance gate.

'This is your place of work, so don't allow any fucker else to use it. See this door 'ere,' he said, indicating a padlocked door in the corner, adjacent to the table. 'You will be able to make phone calls in there shortly. Pablo has given us a mobile and it's hidden on the other side of that door,' he said, nodding towards it. 'There's a duplicate key hidden in your worktable, so when coffee-break happens, we'll nip in and you can call your wife.'

I couldn't believe my ears – a mobile phone hidden next to my cobbler's table and I hadn't even seen a shoe or a boot yet! The foreman, Oscar, was hovering nearby pretending to do something, so Kennedy called him over and formally introduced us, telling him that I was a friend of Pablo's, so he should make sure I was well looked after. From that moment Oscar treated me like the Pope; I had coffee brought to my table every morning and my workload was minimal.

STRENGTH IN UNITY

Approximately 20 men worked in the *zapatería* and they were all from South America. There were several workshops in wing 8 and Pablo controlled them all. The metal shop was predominantly Spanish, with a spick foreman called Ricardo: a contract killer, and one of the few spicks who became friendly with me. The *carpintería* had a kraut foreman in charge of a mixed bunch of carpenters from everywhere: but no spicks. The print shop was solely for Spanish inmates, with a spick nonce as foreman. I later discovered that he was the sickest of paedophiles: a necrophiliac who beasted his child victims until the stink of decomposition necessitated burial before somebody else got a whiff. This horrible Spanish beast was a real monster, possibly 6 ft 2 in. tall and 250 lb of hard muscle, resembling Popeye's pal, Bluto. He was also the general foreman who controlled the movements of inmates employed on wing 8: a most vicious bully whose reign of terror ended when he met me.

Coffee break soon happened, so Kennedy quickly unscrewed a cleat from the bottom of the workbench and removed the key that was hidden behind it. I noticed Oscar had positioned himself at the entrance to the workshop and was keeping nicks for us. Kennedy quickly unlocked the padlock and freed the hasp-and-staple door catch to gain entry to the dark corridor beyond. We swiftly entered and pulled the door to behind us. I couldn't see much in the poor light but Kennedy lifted some old file covers on a shelf and picked up a mobile phone. He turned it on then fiddled with it for a moment before asking for Susan's number, punching it in as I spoke.

'There you go; it's ringing. I'll be outside; you've got five minutes,' said Kennedy as he ducked out of the corridor, closing the door behind him.

I was so excited to be calling Susan without having a baying crowd of spicks surrounding me, I felt I'd won the lottery. The silence of the corridor was absolutely marvellous. I could hear Susan's voice without the usual straining and having to poke a finger in my other ear to block out the noise. Her comforting words and positive attitude reminded me how much I admired her.

All too soon Kennedy popped his head around the door and whispered, 'Sorry, bro', you gotta finish now – tell 'er same time tomorrow.'

Feeling on top of the world, I passed the phone to Kennedy, who switched it off and held the door for me to get out and lock it. He then hid the key behind the cleat, saying, 'I'm taking this back to its owner, but don't worry; it'll be there again in the morning.' He strolled nonchalantly out of the *zapatería*.

I couldn't believe my luck. And I got an even bigger surprise the next morning when Pablo himself came to the workshop, took me to his office and let me use his office phone to speak with Susan again. What the fuck was going on around here?

Time always passed quickly in the *zapatería*. It was much better than being in the yard, pestered by begging spicks, but I had to persevere with that for part of the day until I got the job in the gym. One of the perks of working in the *zap* was that we didn't queue for our food with the inmates in the yard; there was a door leading into the dining hall straight from the workshop yard, so we privileged workers were allowed in first.

I was eating a stew of lentils (with meat of an unknown source: possibly pig, but I wouldn't bet on it) when Kennedy sat next to me with a worried expression on his face.

'What the fuck's up with you?' I said as he started to fish around in his stew for something edible.

'I need to ask a massive favour of you and I don't blame you if you refuse, bro'.'

'Oh fucking hell! What the fuck is it?'

'I want to bring somebody else into our cell. Don't fret! He's a great bloke and he'll make life much easier for us. You will like him and he will be a great help in the future.'

I could see by the pleading-spaniel expression that he had told whoever it was that there wouldn't be a problem moving in.

'Who the fuck is it – the Director?'

'No, you cunt!' laughed Kennedy. 'But he is well connected in the prison and we'll get all kinds of good things when he moves in. What do you say?'

The earnest look in his eyes hid any guile, but then I didn't expect any deception from my friend Kennedy, who, in my eyes, could never be a whillywha: a wheedling cajoler.

'You haven't told me who he is yet, you prick!'

'Oh yeah. His name's Enrico and he's the richest and most influential South American you'll ever meet.'

'So why the fuck does he want to move in with us?' I said sharply.

Kennedy's brain was in overdrive now as he tried to explain the whys and wherefores of the enigmatic Enrico. I could see he was holding back on something, but I decided I would find out soon enough if I consented to his request. Kennedy was not good at hiding his feelings, so when I agreed to let Enrico join us, his face was a picture as he dazzled me with all of those big, white teeth.

'Where is he now?' I asked, expecting him to be lurking nearby.

'He's in *ingreso*, the reception block.'

'What the fuck's he doing in there?' I said, somewhat puzzled.

'Oh, it's political; he's been in there for months. He was a government minister but somehow he siphoned off millions of dollars and shot over to Spain to spend it,' said Kennedy, grinning broadly, proud to be acquainted with such people.

'How did this rich, clever fucker get caught?' I asked, wondering how a bloke with so much dosh ended up in this fucking pisshole.

Kennedy warmed to my inquisitiveness, knowing curiosity always kills the cat.

'Well, nobody seemed to bother about it until they had a change of government; then somebody decided to fuck him.'

Then, in a more positive tone, he said, 'But I don't think he'll be here much longer, because there's new elections this year and the outcome looks set to be a highly desirable one for him.'

Kennedy's prediction turned out to be spot on: Enrico walked just a few days after the winner of the new election took office. But right now he was moving into our cell.

That afternoon we made up a third bed, but there was no room for it alongside us so Kennedy's bed had to be made into a bunk.

'I think I'll let him sleep below; he's older than me,' said Kennedy thoughtfully.

'You suck-holing nob-licker,' I said. 'You'll be asking me to move so's he can have my fucking bed.'

'That did cross my mind actually, so . . .'

'Get fucked!'

Everything was prepared for our new guest. The cell smelled

sweetly of pine disinfectant and Kennedy's poncey lotions: a bit like a whore's boudoir. Well, a very little bit. A screw unlocked the cell, shouting and cursing, but I noticed that he didn't actually look at either of us as he stomped off to open the next cell. Either my reputation was getting to some of them or there was something happening that I didn't know about yet.

Kennedy gave the cell a final check and then bolted the door as I made my way downstairs. The four of us met on the *pateo* and started walking around with the flow of the throng. We were sharing general chatter when the Tannoy crackled, 'Kennedy – *oficina ahora.*'

'That'll be Enrico. I'll call you if I need a hand with his kit.'

'What fucking kit?' I said angrily, as Kennedy started to laugh.

'This man's got everything: a telly, cooking kit . . .'

'Fucking cooking kit! What the fuck is he going to cook?' I said, rather gruffly. Kennedy was beaming all over his shiny black face as he put his hand on my shoulder and treated me to his sincere, knowing expression.

'Listen, bro', you won't be eating in the *comedor* when Enrico gets organised. You'll enjoy fresh food brought in from the street.'

I was amazed by this news and I thought it best not to say any more in case Chinky and Jake got pissed off if it turned out they weren't included.

Kennedy trotted away to the office and Jake said, 'Who the fuck is Enrico?'

I explained that he was a big-time South American who was held in *ingreso* but he was coming here today and was sharing my cell.

'I heard about him in the papers,' said Jake. 'Does he know what he's in for, joining you fucking two?'

Chinky started chuckling. 'He know he safe in your cell. Der's maybe 60 South American spicks on dis garrery: but he want be wid you. He cook more dan food, Engrish. Take care; I no truss spicks.'

Though we all laughed at Chinky's lingo, I admired him because his English was far superior to my Chinese. *Kung hei fat choy* (the Chinese New Year blessing) is about my limit.

I don't remember how many laps of the yard we did, but it wasn't long before Kennedy appeared with a middle-aged man of medium height with short-cropped grey hair and manicured nails. He was quite the most elegant prisoner I'd yet seen, with his pilot-style, short-sleeved shirt in olive green and slightly darker-shaded chinos belted around the waist with a plain brown leather belt matching his brown side-zipped boots.

I could see his eyes through the Porsche sunglasses but he removed them anyway when Kennedy introduced us. His handshake was unexpectedly firm, as was his spoken English: clipped but not quite patrician with no hint of an American or Spanish accent. His steely grey eyes were unblinking as we eyeballed each other.

'Thank you for allowing me to join you, Christopher. I will repay your kindness in due course.'

Before I could reply, we were surrounded by a horde of South Americans trying to pay their respects; the first of whom was Oscar Bonilla, who practically genuflected. They were all fawning as though he was the archbishop of Bogotá in mufti.

'I'll catch you later,' I said. 'Your *paisanos* want to see you now.'

I stepped back to allow the circle of boot-lickers access to His Holiness and the four of us strolled away to leave Enrico with his fans. We hadn't gone far before Enrico came running up to us, shouting at Kennedy. He was slightly dishevelled and pale-faced.

'Don't ever leave me alone again; you said I would be safe with your friends. My enemies are everywhere! A moment alone is sufficient for one of them to stab me!'

All the confidence of two minutes ago had evaporated as he positioned himself between Jake and me.

'OK, let's walk,' I said as we strode off briskly to put distance between ourselves and the perplexed South Americans.

Oscar Bonilla intercepted us on the far side of the yard, all apologetic and serf-like in front of Enrico, who was clearly embarrassed. Kennedy put his arm around Oscar and took him to one side to give him a load of bullshit. He caught up with us as we joined the *economato* queue for the first of the thousands of coffees and cakes Enrico would buy over the next few months before he gained his freedom.

The time soon came for us all to be herded back into the wing to queue for the evening meal. Part of the meal was chorizo, a smoked-pork sausage resembling a barbecued turd, served with a ladle of lentil stew flavoured with flesh of dubious origin. Enrico wrinkled his nose at the stink; then, as we exited the service area, threw his *bandeja* into the waste bin.

As we were heading for the English table, several South Americans called to Enrico to join them but he simply waved and smiled, then took his place at the English table. A piqued spick threw a bread roll at Enrico but unfortunately for him it hit Jake's head, causing much hilarity on the thrower's table. In less than 30 seconds, Jake had pounded the head of the idiot and was sat eating again. The two screws on duty remained totally oblivious, as they had their hands full monitoring the servery, where fights often broke out over the measly size of the portions that were slopped up.

I then noticed that Kennedy had only bread and fruit on his *bandeja*.

'You on a diet?' I said, nodding at his metal tray.

'No, there's grub in the cell.'

'What kind of grub?'

'You'll see when we go up just now.'

'I can't fucking wait. Let's go now,' I said, but then I realised Chinky and Jake hadn't finished their meals.

'Hang on a minute, we'll all go up together, like normal. No sense in changing things for a bit of grub.'

Jake looked up from his eating. 'Thank fuck for that, there's a table full of hostile spicks over there.'

I noticed that Enrico didn't take offence at his countrymen being called spicks. It would have been hard luck if he did because there were no niceties in this pit.

'Not worry 'bout dem,' said Chinky. 'Dey brave fighters when dey 'ave guns.'

I don't know whether or not Enrico was cringing inside, but his face indicated nothing. He nodded in the direction of the nignog table, saying, 'There's a dozen niggers on that table over there. Are they a problem?'

Kennedy thought the reference was to do with him, so he said,

'No, dem's African niggers; I'm a Caribbean nigger. De only problem wid dem is dey are racists.'

'They seem not to bother anybody,' I said. 'The clogs don't bother anybody either. The krauts and frogs get abusive with the blacks and the spicks, but nothing worth writing home about.'

I filled him in with the layout of the international tables and the geography of the wing. We then chatted about which of the screws were twats. I realised it was impossible to conceive of any one them not being a twat.

Jake chipped in with his usual warped sense of humour, 'The krauts and frogs are fully paid up members of SPONGE; that's why they don't like the coons and spicks.'

'What da fuck's SPONGE?' asked Kennedy, taking the bait.

'The Society for the Prevention of Niggers Getting Everything,' laughed Jake, as the table erupted with laughter.

Kennedy, splitting his sides with glee, spluttered, 'Dat's a fuckin' new one on me. Wait till I tells my ma. She'll laugh 'er fuckin' 'ead off.'

The table settled down to the business of shiteating.

Enrico had been in prison for months but had been holed up alone in *ingreso*, thereby avoiding the dross of Spain. I asked him why he moved from the quiet of *ingreso* to the bedlam of *galería cinco*. He told me that he knew Kennedy and when he was told that Kennedy had moved in with me he decided to leave *ingreso*, on the proviso that he could move in with us.

'But you don't know me,' I said, knowing that there was more to this than met the eye.

'No, but stories about the crazy Englishman are talked about every day in *ingreso* and because you are a skipper and a friend of Kennedy I decided that if I could join you in your cell I would really get to know you because I have some lucrative cargoes to move and I need to know the men who work with me.'

Kennedy nudged my elbow. 'We'll talk about this in the cell.'

'Yeah, OK,' I said, thinking that if there's any better way of getting to know a man than sharing his cell, I've yet to hear of it.

Chinky and Jake finished their grub so we emptied our *bandejas* into the swill bins and placed them on the stack. The stink around the filthy swill bins was truly obnoxious, but then, when I saw the serving staff smoking and coughing all over the food, I was not really surprised at the complete lack of hygiene. The Spanish authorities seemed unperturbed about the enormous health risks that prisoners endured in this filthy Spanish pit.

We had reached the ground floor and joined the shuffling throng for a five-minute stroll before going up to our cells. I was miles away when Jake snapped, 'Watch out!' I had completely forgotten about Jake's bread-roll incident and instead of being on amber alert, I was luxuriating elsewhere on the planet, strolling into a South American ambush.

Automatically, we had formed a cordon around Enrico, who was obviously shitting bricks and missing the loneliness of *ingreso*. Jake was the target but the South Americans knew we would defend him to a man; that's why six of them tried to surround Jake while the other twelve or so attempted to keep the rest of us busy.

Furious, focused violence is shocking to inexperienced street fighters; this was a massacre. Blood spurted all over the show as noses, throats and bollocks were fragged by pounding fists and boots as our galvanised aggression steamrollered the stunned South Americans in less than a minute. Three or four Spaniards were also decked for no other reason than being in the way; but they were not innocent bystanders, more likely opportunist assassins looking for a bit of glory.

After spending years of training with a heavy punch-bag, I had developed the most devastating head-butt and elbow strike, and I had become a most accomplished in-fighter; especially with choking methods and eye-gouging. I was now in my element amongst a gang of South Americans without their guns. Single head-butts or finger strikes into the eyes were enough to deck each spick I struck, especially as I fired my knee into their bollocks to make sure.

You always know when it is all over, so I hustled Enrico away from the mêlée and into the crowds of onlookers as the screws came crashing through the audience blowing their whistles. I had my arm across Enrico's shoulder as I forced our way through to the far end of the *galería*, away from the screaming rabble, to await my companions, who were not far behind me.

Jake was bleeding from a stab wound on the back of his hand and another on his chest. Neither was a problem, the perpetrator being much too nervous to deliver a meaningful thrust with his frontal attack, as this was exactly what he wasn't used to. With spicks you must always watch your back; a deliberate frontal assault from a spick would be like finding a Yeti turd: I've never seen one.

The angry screws wanted to bang everyone up immediately, so luckily we were all locked up before the grasses could squawk. The screws were too nervous to be bothered about grasses; their main concern was to get everybody locked up before more fighting broke out.

On entering my cell I was amazed at the transformation. There was a television placed on a small bedside cabinet at the foot of my bed and two reading lamps on a new table covered with a dainty tablecloth surrounded by three tubular chairs. Several cardboard boxes were crammed under the beds, and sitting on the shitter was a big plastic bag; but what grabbed me most was the bright red carpet that covered practically the whole of the cell floor.

'We ain't going to hear Herbie coming with that carpet, are we?' I said, referring to our resident cockroach who raced around the cell like a fucking VW.

Enrico was obviously struggling with his decision to leave the safety of *ingreso*; his face looked jaundiced. However, he still wanted to talk about the punch-up.

'I have never seen such viciousness, Christopher. Your method of dispatching people is so swift and brutal. Why did you burst that man's eyebrow with your head? He was already finished. He didn't even touch you. Why do that?'

His tone of voice was more a plea than a question; possibly because it was his countrymen who were pulverised.

'If I hadn't knocked fuck out of them, your future here would be even more bleak than it already is, so fucking get used to it.'

I took the anger out of my voice to say, 'I smashed his eyebrow so he would see the scar every morning and he will think to himself that he shouldn't go anywhere near the crazy Englishman without his gun or a box of grenades. Your countrymen want you for the handouts they can sponge; they wouldn't give a flying fuck for you if you was as poor as them.'

Kennedy interrupted with, 'Hey, man, der's tinned fruit 'ere and packets of spaghetti. Fuck me! Look at dis: der's tins of salmon and corn' fuckin' beef!'

He was like a child on Christmas morning.

We set about organising the cell and stowing Enrico's kit. He ended up in the bottom bunk with Kennedy smirking down on me from above.

'You brown-nosed cunt,' I stage-whispered to him as I lay on my bed to watch the television.

'I'll fix supper,' said Kennedy. 'It looks like we's 'ere for de night. Dem screws'll keep us banged up till mornin' now, so fuck it, let's eat.'

Enrico shifted onto his side, saying, 'There's fresh bread and a tub of butter in that box there; we'll need to eat that. I've ordered another for tomorrow. I've also arranged for new cooking equipment with Pablo, so that should happen tomorrow.'

'Just what is the story with Pablo, and what cooking gear are you talking about?' I said, as Enrico looked at Kennedy with a puzzled expression on his face.

'Have you not explained the situation with Pablo?' he said to Kennedy.

'Only about the telephone.'

'OK, Christopher,' said Enrico. 'Pablo is my personal friend. We have been friends for a long time and we do business together outside. I can have almost anything I like from him; no questions asked from the screws. He knows all about your and Kennedy's skills at sea and he has a stake in our future. So we must take advantage of his hospitality during our stay here.'

I didn't know it then, but a few months later Pablo and his family would be guests in my house in Andalucia, meeting visitors from South America in order to fix things for our future. Things started to happen for me now that I was involved in the Pablo–Enrico cartel.

We talked for hours in the cell that night about the various aspects of transporting tonnes of cocaine from South America to Europe, finally deciding that a 20-metre motor sailer would probably be the best bet to take the first tonne from Barranquilla to Youghal Bay in Eire. I fell asleep dreaming of being at sea on a beautiful yacht.

I awoke to cornflakes and fresh milk followed by a corned-beef sarnie, but I decided to go down to the *comedor* for coffee and to keep the English table English. Chinky pointed out that there were several empty places amongst the South Americans and that rumours were abounding about how the spicks and even the gypsies were going to see us off.

'Dey're all calling us the *Mezclado* now, Engrish. What you think of dat?'

'They can call us what the fuck they like, but I'll batter any of the fuckers who come near me.'

That was to be my last morning coffee in the *comedor*, because my workpass was waiting for me in the main office. That meant I had to go to work with the main workforce, who started before breakfast, so the first meal of the day was given to me at my workbench thereafter. But first I had to be escorted to the main office to get my pass. My escort was none other than the big nonce who was a kind of general foreman in charge of all the workshop personnel. He was a swaggering braggadocio, a peacock in high feather as he made his way through the tables to confront me and summon me with his finger to follow him out of the *comedor*. Kennedy translated for me, telling me to follow him to the main office for my workpass.

'*Ahora!*' the nonce snapped, turning briskly and marching away, giving me no time to clear my dining space.

'Leave dat,' said Kennedy. 'I'll take care of dat. Get after dat cunt coz ya don't know da way.'

I stepped out of the bench and walked after the hulking pederast, catching up with him as we mounted the stairs to the atrium level where the indoor control tower cast its shadow of bad karma across us as we marched past it, our footsteps echoing upwards to the ghosts in the dome. The screws opened the various iron gates to allow us through the corridors and up and down the stairs until we eventually arrived at a busy office where a burly prison officer beckoned me with a wave of his arm. The place was thick with smoke and stale sweat, which emanated from the worm-eaten elders of the 'past-it brigade', the veterans of the Falange – Franco's old mob – eking out the last of their time as clerks. They could each do with an undiluted carbolic-acid bath. I wondered how much collective suffering they had caused as they greeted the trusty child rapist as though he was one of their own out of uniform. The nonce made his first big mistake when he returned their greeting by shoving me violently towards the screw who needed my signature for the workpass. The screw looked momentarily alarmed, then surprised me by wagging his finger at the nonce like a schoolteacher chastising a pupil.

'*Tranquilo*,' he said softly as he handed me the pen to sign for the workpass, looking scornfully over my shoulder at the nonce. I signed the register of passes and then the second big mistake happened when I picked up the workpass. The big nonce yanked my elbow, making me drop it on the floor. He had a smouldering sneer on his face as I stooped to pick it up. He turned to grin at his decaying audience, so I used that moment to end any doubts he may have had about my ability to hospitalise him any time I felt the need. From my stooping position I drove my fist upwards into his bollocks, making him bend over forwards so his head was level with the metal handrail at the top of the stairs. I quickly applied an armlock to propel him forward and rushed his head into the steel stanchion from which the handrail started its descent to the floor below. The handrail rattled and shook as the clang of bone colliding with steel reverberated around the high ceiling. I forced his thick neck under the top rail and trapped it there with a chokehold and started to choke him out with a crushing upwards tug with my forearm against his windpipe. I pulled with all of my might and managed to get a bit more purchase by putting my foot on the bottom rail and really put tremendous pressure on the big thick neck. This hulking strong man who murdered little girls with gut-wrenching sexual acts thought he was about to die and promptly pissed into his trousers. The burly screw grabbed me from behind and started pulling me backwards, inadvertently helping me to strangle the shit out of the nonce. There was a sickening bubbling sound as the nonce fired the contents of his colon into his trousers, creating the most obnoxious stink, which wafted into the office making everyone gag. I released my chokehold and the screw shoved me down the stairs, waving me away. I made my way through the corridor to the first gate, where a puzzled screw asked me what I was doing there alone. After making him understand that I was from *galería cinco*, he escorted me back to the wing. Kennedy soon came to collect me to take me across to the *zap*.

'What da fuck you bin up to?' he asked. 'Dat big cunt is making a fuss about you breakin' his neck over at de office. Don Pablo had to shut him up to stop you bein' sent down da block. What da fuck 'appened?'

I explained about the pushing and pulling and how I choked the shit out of the nonce, then how the big screw pulled me off him and chased me away down the stairs.

'Dat was Don Humberto, who is a pal of Don Pablo. You're fuckin' lucky: he don't like nonces an' he's a karate freak an' he knows all about you. C'mon, let's get over to da workshop, outa da way. You can call ya' missus.'

That perked me up, but I was wondering what kind of reception I would get after yesterday's punch-up with the South Americans. Kennedy left me at the *zap* door, telling me he'd be back in a few minutes. I was alone, surrounded by South Americans in the workshop, but nobody came near me apart from Oscar Bonilla: nobody fancied a battering that morning.

Kennedy popped in to dig out the phone so I could have a chat with Susan. When I finished, he pocketed the phone and strolled away to Pablo's office, leaving me under the hateful, gutless eyes of the Hispanics. So there I was, everything hunky-dory, thinking that things couldn't get much better when Kennedy returned to tell me that Pablo said I could start work in the gym that afternoon. I couldn't believe my luck, though I knew I was setting a rod for my own back. I was willingly presenting myself as a target for all-comers, but I was mentally prepared and stoic enough in spirit to endure any pain – and any attacker would need to have an incredibly high pain threshold in order to survive my counter-attack. However, I was looking forward to organising classes and meeting fellow martial artists, who I knew would appear when given the opportunity of doing something meaningful and adding a shade of variety to their wretched lives. My instincts were that I would meet good men on the *tatami* who would become lifelong friends. My instincts were dead right, but all martial artists will agree that they have made more friends on the *tatami* than they could ever have made in the pub.

FIVE

BUSHIDO

Before starting work in the gym I decided to use the phone in the prison yard. The duty screw that day was Ignatio the Horrible, so I guessed I wouldn't have much time to speak, especially as I had clocked him drinking from his Evian water bottle, which everybody knew was full of vodka. Every time he was on duty he brought in vodka and books about armoured fighting-vehicles which he buried his face in, dreaming about glorious battles in the Western Desert and on the Russian front. He knew more about tanks than Erwin Rommel ever did. As the first bloke in the queue talked on the phone, he was lost in his pictures of armoured fighting-vehicles. At last it was my turn, so I stepped forward as the first bloke laid down the phone and ambled away from the hatch.

Ignatio the Horrible was inside one of his beloved panzers. I talked to him but he couldn't hear me as he sent bursts of heavy machine-gun fire scything through the Russian hordes on the Eastern front. His Tiger tank was ploughing through ragged infantry lines as he poured fire down on them: his heart filled with the glory of it all. Through the heady fumes of battle and cordite, a voice was trying to reach him, asking permission to use the field telephone in order to speak with the allies in England, *por favor*! There was an icy detachment about this cretin; a cold, inner emptiness that raised questions as to what was actually going through his scrambled brain as he peered into my face through the turret of his tank wondering if I was friend or foe. At last, recognition, as he realised it was the Englishman and not a Mongolian-featured rag-head from the Steppes: thank fuck Chinky wasn't next. Ignatio the Horrible, a Spanish prison officer: a more cruel man I've never met.

I finished my call just as Don Rafael, the legionnaire screw, arrived to take me to the gym.

'Come to the office when you've done here. I'm coming with you to the gym.'

He then spoke rapidly to Ignatio, plunging his spirits to greater depths, his face looking as though he really was going to the Russian front. It felt good that somebody could make this cruel bastard unhappy. Don Rafael was something of an enigma to his odious underlings, from whom he assiduously distanced himself. They didn't like him just as much as he didn't like them. He insisted on silence in the normally noisy office and was constantly sending them out on useless tasks, like checking the yard shithouse for dragon chasers. In their presence, he often spoke to me in Spanish, then changed to English in mid-sentence, changing again to German, completely confusing the earwigging screws, who kept up the pretence through their facial expressions of understanding every word. I could resolve the enigma: Rafael should have become a mercenary, not a screw. His leadership qualities showed, even in this pisshole. It was in the unflinching way he used his authority on everyone and in the way he used his fighting skills to arrest the many scrapping lunatics in his everyday life. He had an eerie coldness, an aloofness, but was still able to give me a surreptitious wink.

'That cunt Ignatio should be locked up in your fucking Broadmoor; he is truly a sick fucking nutter. The rumour here is that he shags his missus wearing a kraut helmet while she wears a Cossack hat and riding boots!' said Rafael, laughing heartily as we marched to the gym. 'I hear you're Enrico's bodyguard; I bet the nigger engineered that.'

'As it happens, you guessed right. Kennedy fixed it somehow.'

'Somehow my arse! Pablo fixed it, along with a job in the zapatería, and he told me today to put you in the gym, which I'd already fixed up for you anyway.'

The remnants of the previous gym session were being chased out of the showers by the bullying gym orderlies, who were pugnaciously forcing still-wet inmates out of the building in readiness for the next session to begin. A strict regime existed in the gym, and the orderlies were given carte blanche powers of control to keep order. Chaos and fighting were a daily occurrence in here and the orderlies took the brunt of the madness, rather than the prison officers, who didn't like tackling a madman armed with a dumb-bell or some other metallic object that could hurt them.

Three orderlies had just finished *recuento* – the counting of iron bars and weights before giving the all-clear to the controlling screws who held the previous session's inmates in an enclosure before escorting them back to their wing. If there was anything missing from *recuento*, they were conveniently placed for a body search before they left the gym complex. Twenty minutes or so would elapse before the next session began so the orderlies had time for a coffee.

The Spanish gym orderlies made a fuss of Don Rafael with the usual brown-nosing all around him, waffling and spluffing like enthusiastic children fawning around their favourite schoolteacher. It was painful to watch but Rafael knew the score; out on the street this lot wouldn't piss on him if he was on fire. He told the orderlies that my responsibilities were the judo-mat area and the teaching of inmates: nothing else. We all shook hands and tried to be nice to each other for two minutes, then I strode over to the stack of judo mats to inspect the floor of what I considered to be my patch. I then found the utility room where I filled a bucket with bleach, disinfectant and hot water and started mopping the martial-arts area.

Rafael could see that I was making myself at home so he left, calling over his shoulder that he would come back for me near the end of the last session before the evening meal. The gym filled with noise and a fresh batch of inmates as I unhurriedly continued the task of cleaning the floor. Nobody stepped on the wet floor, they all walked around it, looking at me curiously as they headed for their favourite bodybuilding apparatus.

Many eyes watched me as I unhitched the heavy punch-bag,

letting it fall to the floor so I could kick it over to the judo mats, where I then scrubbed it clean. A big man joined me as I soaped the punch-bag.

'There are many stories about you, Englishman, but to me you look just like a family man with children and possibly grandchildren. I believe you are more out of place in here than if you was on the moon.'

'That's right, my friend, but what's it to you?' I said, turning to face him. The man shifted to lean his elbows on the stack of judo mats, relaxing with his lower back against the pile.

'I will be your first student, so I will soon see what kind of *sensei* you are.'

'Not if you are in here for child offences, you won't.'

'Please, do not offend me. I am not Spanish.'

I could see the man was an experienced fighter; either that or somebody had taken a cricket bat to his face when he was younger. His demeanour was that of a confident hardcase, but there was warmth in his eyes and a friendliness that made me like him instantly.

'You can be my *uke* then,' I said, smiling at him.

'*Ukes* are normally small men: not big like me.'

'So you don't want to be *uke*?' I said mockingly. 'You don't like to be the guinea pig who gets chucked around in front of everybody else, eh? You think blokes will laugh at you? Not in my class, they won't. I promise you.'

He took the bait well.

'Nobody laughs at me, Englishman. They all know me in here,' he growled, looking about him.

'I don't know you, so who are you?'

He thrust his big hand forward for a handshake, which I vigorously returned as he said, 'My name is Ali Safave. I am Iranian.'

'Why are you in here?'

'Brown sugar. I move a lot of heroin but I got caught four years ago and I've been kept here in the Carabanchel since my capture.'

'So what's your sentence?' I asked, expecting him to say 12 years or something.

'I haven't had a trial yet; my case is quite complicated.'

'Why's that?' I said, shocked at how long he had been on remand.

'Because the shit was found in a diplomatic bag and several senior officials are involved, so I'm taking the burn because I won't grass the others. Besides, I'm being well looked after. My wife and kids went to Germany, so these dirty bastards can't get at them.'

I felt the injustice of it all but Ali seemed satisfied so long as his family were being looked after.

'I will join your English table if you like,' he said. 'I've had enough of the krauts. They make a lot of noise but they won't watch your back.'

'OK, join my table, but I eat mostly in my cell now. I'm sure the other blokes won't mind. Are you going to help me clean these mats?'

Ali helped me to drag the mats into the yard, where we scrubbed each mat clean as we chatted about our escapades. Ali had worked his way through the ranks of the heroin organisation in South-west Asia, where his business contacts and friends are legion. He started his trade as a mule, carrying various quantities of heroin around the globe. He inevitably became a trader after first becoming a debt collector and getting to know suppliers and buyers all over the place. He spoke fluent English, German, Spanish, Arabic and several languages from countries surrounding his homeland. Above all he was an extraordinary warrior who placed his family above all else. The people looking after them knew they would all die should they renege on the deal.

Over the next two years I got to know Ali very well, and a more honourable man I have yet to meet. His sin was peddling drugs but his way with the world was quite sincere. He would never steal or lie, nor would he harm another person without good reason. It wasn't in him to cheat, unlike the politicians and officials whose arses he was saving by not spilling the beans.

We dragged the *tatami* back into the gym and placed each mat in order to cover an area 18 metres long by 12 metres across. I still had several mats left over so I could expand if needs be. We then hung the heavy bag in a position whereby you had to walk across the *tatami* to get to it, so I had more control over it because men will always punch a punch-bag. A man with Aids would punch it and leave his skin and blood for the next man to unwittingly drive his fist into.

Everything was set for the first martial-arts lesson of my prison life. I was now prepared mentally and physically for the most dangerous job on the planet. I have always been a stickler for *dojo* etiquette so I asked Ali to bow before stepping onto the mat barefooted. I soon discovered that these important ceremonies gave a feeling of belonging to the inmates who formed the core of my combat classes over the years I spent in prison.

Fortunately, Ali was an exponent of hapkido, which is similar in many ways to ju-jitsu, so he readily took to hip throws and shoulder throws and he was familiar with the kicks, blocks and punches used in karate. I was teaching Ali a defence technique that I use to defeat a knife attack, when he said, 'We have quite an audience.'

'Yes, I know,' I said. 'My first batch of students will be wanting to join when they see this manoeuvre.'

Ali had armed himself with a plastic bottle, which he could use as a knife or a club, or even a bottle. I instructed Ali to stab me with an underhand lunge into my solar plexus, which he did with great enthusiasm. I deflected the thrusting arm and delivered a palm-heel strike just beneath his ear; not hard enough to concuss, but sufficient to shock the system. I then applied an armlock that could easily break the bones in his forearm and I emphasised this with an exaggerated movement and a loud *kiai* (shout). I then drove my elbow into his throat, pulling my punch before impact to prevent injury, then, with another armlock and leg-sweep, took him down and held him in a controlled position until he tapped out by smacking the mat with his free hand.

There are many variations to this technique and onlookers find it spectacular and effective, so whenever I needed new students, I'd use knife-defence techniques to attract them. By the time Ali was thrusting his bottle again I had 20 or more blokes standing around the edge of the mat.

Vito, a stocky, well-muscled Italian hit-man, kicked off his trainers; then, in accented English, asked, 'Please, may I step on the mat?'

'Yes, but first you must bow to show respect to the honourable martial art of ju-jitsu.'

This he did very stiffly, but nobody laughed or passed any comment. I then set about using the two of them, teaching them the technique and having them practise it between them in turn. Learning a technique and practising it over and over again is tiring and boring, so, when they could each perform to a reasonable standard, I introduced them to another technique. By the end of the session I had two men knowing and able to perform two effective self-defence moves to add to their mental armoury. The word spread like pox in a brothel and over the next few days I was inundated with potential Bruce Lees who wanted to learn something practical during their bird.

As well as my obsession with *dojo* etiquette I insisted that no nonces or rapists would be allowed on my mat. Consequently, I didn't teach many Spaniards apart from a few ETA terrorists and even that caused me problems because the screws didn't like it and banned them from my combat classes.

Not long after I started the classes, Vito came over to the English table and asked to join us. I asked him why he wanted to come to my table because he was already an established member of the wop tables. He said he wanted to improve his English and he was an outsider to them (wops), because his origins were in Sicily.

Everybody readily accepted Vito, even though he was quite surly and a ringer for Victor Mature or Sly Stallone. He carried plenty of hard muscle and his punching power was phenomenal. His thick, black, lustrous hair hung down to his narrow, well-defined waist. He kept his hair in a ponytail style and, unlike most men who wear ponytails, he didn't look stupid. Besides, only a fool would take the piss out of Vito, a cold-blooded assassin who considered his occupation to be most honourable.

I knew that this job of teaching martial arts would make me a target for the many young Spaniards seeking a reputation. I mentally prepared myself for the inevitable confrontations ahead of me. During quiet periods, especially in my cell, I would meditate and mentally practise the many techniques used in fighting scenarios, which I visualised in various situations. I resolved never to be defeated, regardless of whatever shock and pain was inflicted upon me. I cultivated a mindset of survival and automatic violence towards any threat to my well-being. For hours I would concentrate and focus on imaginary assailants and use my arsenal of devastating nerve strikes to bolster my resolve to remain invincible whilst in this disgraceful pit.

During the first two weeks of working in the gym I dealt with several nutcases who thought I was the prison punch-bag. My first problem was with an onlooker who decided to correct one of my takedown methods by walking onto the mat to demonstrate how it should be done. I told him to remove his shoes before stepping onto the mat; also, to ask to come onto the mat, rather than barge his way through my students to show me how to teach.

His *compadres* decided to egg him on with some name-calling and piss-taking comments. Before the situation worsened, I knocked him out with a single punch that he didn't see coming because he turned his head to leer at his pals just when I decided enough was enough. I grabbed his ankles and dragged him off the mat and continued the lesson as though nothing had happened. He regained consciousness after a few minutes of face slapping and hand rubbing from his pals, who continued giving me daggers with their glaring looks as they tended their idiot.

I quickly got fed up with their *torero* posturing and threats so I went over and flattened two more of them. One hard punch into each throat was sufficient to deck Lee Van Cleef One and Two, while the rest of them fucked off smartish.

The realisation that you are a target for the scum of Spain makes for sobering thought and a constantly aware attitude to daily life. Grasping the nettle of the danger that lay all around me abolished any shred of squeamishness and primed my ability to explode into focused violence like an anti-personnel mine in response to pressure, regardless of who was applying it. My unflinching stance, devoid of hesitation or self-doubt, prior to launching any attack, called for rigid self-discipline, which was a natural and necessary product of the diabolical conditions of this despicable pit called Carabanchel. The only comparable situations that I could think of were that of a doorman working the OK Corral nightclub, or maybe a samurai contemplating *seppuku*, the honorific samurai name for hara-kiri.

BUSHIDO

The decision to teach martial arts in prison necessitated a grim training regime to maintain the level of fitness required to perform endless ju-jitsu and karate techniques and really shine as a teacher of truly tough students. Also necessary was a constant state of awareness to repel the sneak attacks from the many Billy *el Chicos* (Billy the Kids) who felt the need to boost their reputations by seeing me off.

My daily rituals of exercise, meditation and evening prayers gave me the backbone to survive and eventually reappear in the real world apparently unscathed, mentally and physically fitter than when I was first swallowed by the Spanish judicial beast. To be constantly beset with peril I had to beware of becoming permanently callous, so I reminded myself during prayer or meditation that my piss-and-vinegar vitriol was not intrinsic and I could not allow it to take root in my psyche or I would have to get a job as a lighthouse keeper when I got out.

My high profile in the Carabanchel put me at risk and protected me at the same time. The fact that I stood out like racing dogs' bollocks made some people want to have a go, but when I wrecked the faces of various wing champions who'd tried it on, the deterrent was wide-reaching and effective. I'd stuck my head above the parapet and not only managed to keep it on, but to claim the scalps of any would-be assailants along the way. The attacks dwindled; so much so that it was only the new inmates who felt the need for instant stardom and a shattered eyebrow and, of course, to lose his bet. But there was no stopping those bereft of reasoning: the raving psychopaths.

A huge anthropoid face loomed head and shoulders above the spectators as its owner barged his way through to get at me. I recognised instantly that it was Jomo, the Algerian necrophiliac whose preference was dead children. His eyes were bright with madness as he stumbled onto the mat then adopted a wobbling crane stance as he squealed in a piss-take of Bruce Lee, or maybe it was Mr Myagi of *Karate Kid* fame.

The spectators' nervous laughter and the beast's squeal changed their tone somewhat as my right foot slammed into the kneecap of his supporting leg with my *kansetsu geri* kick. My target was the

77

patella – the actual kneecap – and I drove into the base of the femur and the head of the tibia bone, creating the most unforgettable pain. I followed through with a crunching stomp on his pubic bone then a tremendous punch into the centre of his mandible, impacting the jaw hinges, ensuring the lights went out for a few minutes. I rounded off his lesson with two very hard punches to each eye, merely to remind him never to adopt the crane stance in front of me ever again.

I had a passing thought that a group of happy children were looking down from a little corner of heaven that day, giggling at that heinous wog turd. Jomo was a fearsome bully with a reputation for mindless brutality. His size and strength combined with his madness made him a terrible foe, and that was why I then decided to give him a bit more: just so he didn't forget who to avoid.

A couple of his henchmen had revived him sufficiently to sit him upright on his arse on the floor. I punched them both out of the way then grabbed Jomo with a wristlock to yank him viciously to his feet. He jerked instantly to full consciousness as the nerves and bones in his wrist screamed a message of pain to his dizzy brain, extracting a shriek worthy of a place in a Hitchcock film. That scream was something else: it twisted the guts of my audience, their eyes popping with shock. I'll never forget that scream; I'm proud of it. You should have heard the next one, too, as I controlled the wristlock with my left hand, raising it high to expose his vulnerable sheet of ribs, enabling me to rocket several tremendous punches into them in order to break a couple. I then gave his upper arms the good news by punching so hard into the humerus bone that I thought I'd broken it. No wanking tonight, matey. Finally, I punched his bollocks; grabbing and squeezing them to nothing.

'It looks like I've missed all the fun,' said Don Rafael, striding across the gym towards me. 'You couldn't have picked a more evil *bastardo* than this one; I wish I'd got here earlier,' he said.

Any other prison officer would have had me down the block (solitary) in no time, but Don Rafael loathed all of his nonce wards, especially those who preyed on children. He liked and respected me, and I do believe he was the only screw I met who wasn't a xenophobe. Rafael the screw organised the removal of Jomo the child corpse despoiler, then took me to his office for coffee and a chat. He got rid of the lounging screws in true martinet style, bawling them out with quick-fire instructions to go hither and thither in search of dragon chasers.

Stinking tobacco smoke hung in the air, and he wafted it out of the open door with an enormous Spanish fan, the type normally sold to tourists to hang as a wall decoration. He folded it and hung it on a hook behind his desk, then dropped all the overflowing ashtrays into a wastebasket and flung it out into the corridor, where it noisily clattered and spilled across the stone floor. The arsehole in cell no. 6 would clean it up soon, immediately after he'd finished getting our two cups of coffee from the *economato*: café americano for me and a thick brown brew (café solo) for Rafael.

'Pablo asked me how you were getting on in the gym yesterday.'

This statement prompted me to think Rafael was fishing, but then I thought there was probably more to it than mere angling.

'Oh yeah, what did you tell him?'

'Only that you're enjoying yourself. But what intrigues me is why he wants to know if you're playing with brown sugar. He's got a few of us looking out for you in case you're dealing or taking heroin. Why's that, do you think?'

'How would I know?'

'Don't gimme that shit. He'll drop you like a turd the moment he hears you're playing with brown sugar or Charlie. Him and Enrico has got you and that black-arsed Kennedy lined up for something on the out.'

I wondered if any of the other screws thought the same.

'I don't know what he has in mind but if it means an easy ride with perks to help me through this pisshole, I'll go along with anything they want.'

'Right, then I'm gonna give you a tip. Touch fuck all. Have nothing to do with dealers and junkies. If you need to earn some cash, I'll get you some booze to sell. How do you like that?'

'Fucking great! I wouldn't touch brown sugar anyway, so there's no need to waste energy in that direction. And Charlie is a closed shop with the South Americans. But what do you want out of the deal?' I said, wondering what the fuck was going on around here.

Rafael leant forward across the desk with his hand around his jaw. 'I want to come with you when you get out. I know your future is full of adventure at sea and there will be buckets full of *dinero* and I want some of that life and you can give it to me. Carabanchel closes this year and some of us are not welcome in other prisons, so I'm taking the handshake.'

'Good for you, but I don't know how long I'll be locked up for yet,' I moaned.

'No matter what happens, you will not do more than two years. You will be looked after by Don Pablo and some of my pals, so don't worry about your time. You'll get away with murder so long as you don't touch the drugs. What do you say to having me on board?'

His eyes searched mine for any hint of doubt.

'You'll do well,' I said as he thrust his strong hand out for me to shake. 'You'll get rich and have more adventure than you can shake a stick at,' I lied, remembering never to work with a Spaniard ever again.

But this was great! Here I was in Europe's most notorious jail and I was being looked after by a top prison official and my wing guv'nor: both looking to do business on the out. I needed to wake up. It felt like I must be dreaming. The university of crime, eh? Maybe that's why we had to call them Don, just like in Oxford or Cambridge. Without my Bushido attitude, I doubt I would have been in such a fortunate position in the guts of the beast called Carabanchel.

SIX
BUSINESS IS BUSINESS

Rafael the screw was true to his word and delivered vodka and gin in one-and-a-half-litre plastic bottles. I had to ask whether or not it had been diluted between shop shelf and plastic bottle. He laughed and said, 'No, but it's the cheapest I could find.'

Fair enough, I supposed; I didn't expect anyone to come back and say, 'Hey, you cunt! That wasn't fucking Gordon's gin.' But I didn't want to hear the word 'water', because that's the fucking kiss of death in this game.

I set up shop in my equipment store in the gym and carefully selected my clientele. There were blokes in prison making obscene amounts of cash because prisons were the biggest one-stop drop-off location for drugs on the planet. You could buy puff, Charlie, smack and all kinds of psychedelic substances in any shithouse on any wing in any prison. The shit comes in with the screws or up the fannies of visiting wives and daughters. Regardless of how it comes in, it is always there in abundance. A scarcer commodity was booze: not hooch brewed on the wing, but the genuine article from the street, which of course meant that it was more sought after and, therefore, more expensive.

I sold vodka and gin in half-litre water bottles at *diez mil pesetas* (approx £40) a go and I was always out of stock; I couldn't supply the demand and that was just doing business with clogs, krauts and wops. I didn't sell to the spicks. Spanish blokes approached me asking for booze and I would challenge them aggressively with, 'Who's the lying *giri* who told you I have booze to sell?'

I dropped several customers for yapping to spicks, so eventually my business developed into a closed shop, opening only for wealthy Europeans: no spicks or nignogs – they had fuck all money anyway.

One outstanding customer of mine was a 6 ft 4 in. clog from Rotterdam by the name of Peter du Kuyper. He was a puff dealer of great standing, both in Morocco and in Holland. He supplied the Carabanchel with bales of puff ranging from nine bars (low-grade shit normally bound for Blighty) to *tbizla* (the highest-grade puff, produced for royal tables). Peter worked a team of screws and, I believe, a doctor and a couple of nurses.

Peter made loadsadough and I gorralot for my booze. At first Rafael started his shift by bringing me three litres of vodka, but it quickly ratcheted up to nine litres a shift. Obviously there were fluctuations in demand because of prisoners gaining freedom or being moved to another jail, but generally everything went well. So did Don Rafael because we shared the profits (weighed heavily in my favour, of course).

It had become necessary for Don Rafael to move me to another cell, next door to Kennedy and Enrico, in order to do the booze trade. This was great for me because I spent a lot of time gobbing off and dining at Enrico's groaning dinner table. Then, at final bang up, I was alone in my cell, able to read and write in silence or gawp at my new television.

Very often Don Rafael would visit me to let me use his mobile phone to speak with my Susan, then we'd shake the chandelier telling each other stories about the desert and the jungle. For some strange reason he started to warn me about not giving credit for booze one night. I assured him that would never happen and then we talked about the desert again. I would never give booze on credit to anyone but later I started to lend money to people because I became the bank. I'll tell you about that shortly.

Every business has its problems and mine was no different. Whenever an item of gym equipment got stolen, the outgoing class was thoroughly searched. I had many anxious moments wondering if the contents of plastic water bottles would be discovered by the *cacheros*. *Cacheros* are the specially trained screws used to search cells and bodies. Part of their selection profile must be madness with a blend of guile and indecency, because I didn't meet one who didn't want to peer up my arsehole or study my crotch in order to wank his tiny brains out later.

My cell always had some kind of prohibited goods stashed in one of my pugs (hidey holes). But I provided a distraction by always having homosexual and straight pornographic magazines lying open in my cell, especially resting on my case of plastic water bottles that all contained vodka or gin. Glossy pictures of naked young men always did the trick as lascivious eyes devoured the sheen off each page, successfully diverting their attention from the real goodies beneath them.

I sometimes had bankrolls hidden in my mattress, which I would pass to Rafael in order to post to Susan, who was struggling alone in our *finca*. There were bills to pay and she had to eat. 'Oh Lord, please don't punish her for my sins.' Thoughts like these were the real thumbscrews that fucked your head when you were locked up.

Nothing was ever found in my cell or on my person and it soon became apparent that I was moving about the prison without the customary body and bag search. I transported my booze and cash in my sports bag and for the rest of my time in the Carabanchel I didn't get a spin. Other players were quick to notice these things so it wasn't long before I was approached to transport drugs from my wing to the gym and vice versa. I was having none of that bollocks, so I was swift and aggressive with my refusals because I didn't believe for a moment that surveillance on me had ceased. Besides, why would I chance putting the kibosh on my own enterprise just to mule some greasy bastard's smack? No way, José.

So when Manolo, the half-kraut, half-spick ape from Majorca, came on heavy for me to mule his shit to the gym so his pals on other wings could sell it, I had to call on the *Mezclado* to watch my back because Manolo had quite a team behind him. He had done all his organising before approaching me, obviously thinking I was a dead cert to mule for him, so when I told him to fuck off, it was slightly more than a disappointment. The cocksure bastard had even got the word out to the other wings that the smack was on its way.

'You'll take my smack tomorrow or you're fucking dead,' he said as I queued for coffee in the *economato* crowd. The *Mezclado* were strewn around the prison yard, unaware that Manolo and four of his tastiest *hombres* had collared me.

'Tomorrow it is, then,' I said as I searched his cold, grey eyes looking for signs of life. Nothing, just like the dull gleam of a shark reflecting malevolence. I looked at the others: their adrenalin subsiding, their cruel, greasy faces transforming into glittering smiles oozing false camaraderie – typical fucking spicks. I reckoned it wouldn't be long before their shiny white teeth and sparkling eyes would feel the crunch of my remorseless knuckles.

'You will not regret your decision, English,' he said, sounding weird with his patrician accent. 'I'll weigh you off nicely each week; I'll even send your money to England if you wish, or maybe you have family here?' he enquired.

I wondered where he had learnt to speak English in such an aristocratic style. But I wasn't about to ask a half-breed fuckpig like him how he spoke like a person of breeding.

'No,' I said as I turned to face the *economato* to order a tray of coffee for my gang.

I could feel the dozens of eyes peering at me as I found Chinky and Jake.

'Tea up!' I called as I joined them. 'Get the others, Chinky, their coffee will go cold.'

Chinky blithely scrambled to his feet and darted away, knowing the whereabouts of each of the *Mezclado*. He would soon be back. The eyes that were on me were green eyes, jealous eyes, envious of the fact that I had a liaison with Don Rafael, the chief screw, who was never well disposed to the fawning shiteaters contaminating his working day. I made no attempt to hide our friendship; it was quite overt and, to all intents and purposes, was because we were martial artists.

By now several blokes knew about the phone calls on Pablo's phone so there was plenty for everybody to guess and gossip about: not that I gave a monkey's fuck about what any of these scumsuckers thought. Nevertheless, I knew that outside of the *Mezclado* I had no friends.

BUSINESS IS BUSINESS

I could now afford to supplement the English table with extras and treats from the *economato*. I didn't do this to keep my friends sweet: they were already sweet. But I was the leader of the *Mezclado* and I needed to be doubly sure of their loyalty and muscle for when I opened the bank, which was my next venture.

The one opening that needed filling on our wing was that of the moneylender: there were no loan sharks. I decided to oil the cogs of the currency market in order to make life easier for my band of international villains, for they would be an integral part of the business. The *Banco del Mezclado* was about to open, but first I had to put Manolo the fuckpig back in his pen.

By now I had bought the *Mezclado* several bits and pieces, most notably expensive weightlifting gloves and bag gloves for punch-bag training. Supplements like creatine and multi-vitamins were truly appreciated, but what they really enjoyed were the bottles of water I gave each of them. They all knew I was bang at it with the booze but there was never a query or a step over the mark regarding my antics. For whatever reasons we each respected the other and we stuck together. So now I had them all in a huddle to deal with the fuckpig. The plan was simple: tomorrow I would slaughter the fuckpig while the *Mezclado* malleted the rest of the herd.

The only opportunity for Manolo to pass me the packet would be at lunchtime in the dining hall before the afternoon bang-up. I would be in the *zapatería* all morning and in the gym later in the afternoon. Unless he expected me to keep it overnight in my cell and deliver it the following day, it would have to be exchanged at lunchtime. I explained to the blokes that this was a great opportunity to show the rest of the wing what happens when you annoy the *Mezclado* because this would set the scene for opening the bank. I then told them I wanted to open the bank this week.

Chinky was perplexed because he thought Manolo's money was easy gains with no aggro. I then explained my dilemma regarding surveillance. Besides, I wanted fuck all to do with smack.

One of the perks of running a prison bank was that a lot of blokes paid back their debts with street money brought in on visits. Normal Spanish currency, apart from coinage, was not allowed in prison, so the prison authorities issued the *ficha* in lieu of Spanish bank notes. The *ficha* was actually Mickey Mouse money issued in 500pts and 1,000pts plastic cards about the size of a credit card. Coins up to 500pts were permitted, but you couldn't have more than 10,000pts on your person at any time: it was an offence. Money sent into the prison by your family (normally via the consul), was paid into your prison account; out of which you were paid weekly up to the maximum of 10,000pts. If you were a Beechams or a Glaxo, you wouldn't take *fichas* for your drugs, and nor would the *Madrileños* who supplied the heroin from the street. So the dealers had big problems paying their suppliers because street money was so scarce.

Shit came in; real money had to go out. *Fichas* were as useful as a chocolate teapot and I was about to rake in bundles of street money which I would then sell on to the dealers for Mickey Mouse money which I would then dish out to the *Mezclado*, my happy band of international business partners. It worked like this: if I lent you 2,000pts, you paid me 3,000pts the next time the golden eagle shat: pay day. You could pay me back with forbidden street money if you wished, because if you were caught with street money you would go down the block (solitary). I then sold 3,000pts of street money to the dealers for 4,500pts of Mickey Mouse money, out of which 2,500pts of profit went into the pot to be divvied up when there was enough to make everyone feel good.

The *Mezclado* became moneylenders and bailiffs all in one week and everybody was happy. There was money available for drugs; there was money available for Mickey Mouse money, so everybody got pissed, stoned or chewed the clouds as our pot overflowed.

The following day I went to the *zapatería* as usual and had a chat with Susan using Don Pablo's office. Susan was in good spirits and her strength of character gave me a boost, which I needed just then because I had been concentrating too much on the pending punch-up. I had visualised a thousand times how I was going to batter the fuckpig before falling asleep the previous night and had awoken thinking about it.

Manolo was a big man, possibly 300 lb of mixed fat and muscle with which he intimidated everybody around him. Hence, he was the leader of his gang, which he ruled by favour, fear and cruelty. His arms and legs were massive, as was his shaven head. My strategy was to blind him first then attack his throat and bollocks before choking him out.

I was purposefully late arriving in the dining hall, so the *Mezclado* were all sat eating and waiting for me. I grabbed a *bandeja* and loaded it with some diabolical shite that the cooks had knocked up and went to my table.

Jake greeted me with, 'That ugly bastard has been shitting bricks. He must have thought you weren't coming.'

Ali chipped in with, 'It must be a big bag of brown sugar. They're all nervous and checking the screws.'

Just then one of Manolo's greaseballs got up from the table and surreptitiously made his way over to me, thereby heralding to all and sundry that something was up.

'You know Paco, *tiene un bigote y es muy alto?*' he asked with his hand held above his head to indicate how tall Paco was. 'He give you *paquete* on *escalera*,' he stage-whispered, pointing to the steps leading up to the gallery out of the dining hall. '*Si?*' he asked as every spoon and fork hung suspended between gob and tray awaiting my answer in the silence of the moment.

I clocked the duty screw wearing a bemused expression on his face, obviously guessing what was going down: probably correctly. I then looked over to Manolo, who was on the edge of his seat anxiously awaiting my response. Everything seemed to be happening in slow motion, though I know the incident lasted just a few seconds.

I had another look at the screw and nodded my head at him, indicating to the greaseball that he was clocking us.

'*No se preocupe, olvida todo!* Forget it! Fuck off!' I snarled. '*Eres* fucking *estúpido. Mira!*'

I swept my arm in front of me, showing him the motionless forks and spoons suspended en route to the gaping faces all around us.

'*Mira el tambien,*' I said, pointing to the astonished screw who couldn't stop himself from responding by moving a few paces towards us. '*El saber todo!* He knows! Every fucker knows! *Adios*, you cunt!'

Pure hatred was etched into the oily sneer as the lip curled to spit spick obscenities at me. I made a fast dummy move as though to attack him. He stumbled backwards, cursing, then turned to slink back to his table to report to Manolo, who already knew the score.

Manolo had been trading smack for so long here that he must have thought he was fireproof. His business operated openly in the lavatories, so everyone knew about it, although he personally did not handle any shit. Other traders were not so open, simply because of the threat from Manolo. He assumed that the turf was his alone. The problem this caused for Manolo was that his competition grassed him at every opportunity. He successfully distanced himself from the shit and the money, always using his lieutenants to store, trade and bank. His minions would pay key visitors for the incoming shit and do all the handling, cutting and packaging. Manolo merely kept track of things in his little pocket diary and battered defaulters with his own hands if the defaulter wasn't too big.

He was grassed a million times but was always clean as a whistle. Lots of blokes were in fear of Manolo because they thought he had friends in high places and could operate with impunity. He didn't have a friend in the world; he was just a clever, lucky bastard who realised he would be grassed by his countrymen every day, so consequently organised himself around that problem. His bloated face puffed and blew like a toad's gizzard as he blurted obscenities at his underlings.

The moustached, lanky Paco was sitting in the far corner of the dining hall on one of the gypsy tables out of harm's way when the *cacheros* struck. Two teams came rushing into the *comedor*; one team surrounded the English table, the other ensnared Manolo's table. I didn't give a flying fuck about Manolo's table, but I got the wind up in case one of my blokes was carrying: we expected a punch-up today, so somebody may have been tooled up.

Each of us received a scan with the metal detector and then our bags were rummaged: nothing. A cry went up from Manolo's table as the spicks scuffled in order to rid themselves of their forbidden weaponry. Chivs, spikes and blades clattered to the floor to be kicked away, but the *cacheros* were too quick and experienced for that pushing-and-shouting palaver, so everyone except Manolo went into the bag; he being the only person without a weapon.

88

BUSINESS IS BUSINESS

I watched as he glanced across the *comedor* at Paco; at least his smack was safe: or was it? I somehow didn't think so. The *cacheros* seemed to be satisfied with finding weapons; drugs weren't mentioned. I guessed we were grassed for weapons because Manolo's team was prepared for aggro. The grass must have guessed that we would also be tooled up so I was thinking the *chivato* (grass) was one of Manolo's monkeys and Manolo must have been thinking the same.

If Manolo had been caught with a weapon, Paco would have been left alone with a big bag of smack. Hmm . . . I wonder. Nah, a spick gypsy wouldn't grass his pals for a shitload of heroin, would he? You could bet your fucking life he would! A spick gypsy would grass his fucking granny for a spoonful of sugar.

My crew took it all in their stride: no scuffles, no protesting, just plain old silent hatred emanating from their eyes – cunning eyes, glowing eyes, deadly eyes mirroring lethal thoughts to all things Spanish, especially men. The silent message was clear to each *cachero*: fuck you, you greasy dirtbag.

The *cacheros* moved quickly away from the English table to help their colleagues with the spick tables, where the aggro was bubbling up nicely. Lots of shouting and shoving was happening now as the teams herded Manolo's gang out of the dining hall. Innocent bystanders with too much to say were being yanked into the herd, destined for the block, dragged screaming and protesting to solitary confinement. Manolo was standing alone next to his empty table. He turned slowly with a hateful sneer to face Paco, who wasn't there. He had fucked off sharpish during the mêlée, the confusion veiling his premature departure.

Whistles blew and sirens wailed, heralding an early bang-up, crucially robbing Manolo of his chance to instantly interrogate Paco, who now had all afternoon to cook up excuses and denials and possibly point the finger at someone else. Screws poured into the dining hall shouting and bashing tables with their truncheons, forcing prisoners with unfinished meals to leave them and get out of the *comedor* and into their cells. Latecomers had it the worst; the kraut table made lots of noise because some of them had been working late so had only just got their food and were indisposed to leave. Their resentment showed with their mounting anger as the dispute was settled with a few flying spuds and a flurry of truncheons.

Does the denial of food and beatings with truncheons constitute torture and violation of moral integrity? I reckon the screws knew that the Carabanchel would be closed before the next visit of the Council of Europe Committee for the Prevention of Torture and Inhuman or Degrading Treatment or Punishment (CPT). So bollocks, *'Viva Franco!'*

Within the European Council Criminal Code 1995, under the heading 'Torture and other offences against moral integrity', the Code promotes penalties of up to four years' imprisonment for the violation of a prisoner's moral integrity and six years for torturing someone. Punishment is also available for the use of unnecessary vigour. With regard to Spanish prisons I can safely say the Code would have been put to better use if it had been written on toilet paper. The CPT next visited Madrid on 22 November 1998: the Carabanchel had closed by then.

We were rushed up the stairs and locked in our cells. Then came *recuento*, the head count. Teams of *cacheros* arrived to search inmates and cells, so there was the continuous noise of crashing cell doors and screaming, pedantic, rectum inspectors. The stress of apprehension was rolling around like a cannonball in my chest as I waited for my cell door to crash open to reveal the leering face of whatever odious twat wanted to strip me naked in order to gawp up my hole.

I need not have worried; the *cacheros* missed me out. The sounds of searching and abuse died down and the gallery settled into a late siesta. I was just dozing off when Don Rafael quietly let himself in.

'It's a fucking good job you told Manolo's man to fuck off. You was being watched and if you'd taken the packet you'd have been fucked,' said Rafael, rolling his eyes.

I didn't correct him by telling him that Paco had the shit.

'How come we were only searched for weapons? They certainly weren't looking for smack.'

'That was because the info received was specific about *pinchous*.

Don Pablo was looking at you through the outer servery hatch, alone and unseen. He knew different; he knew you had been lined up for a pass. So did I,' said Rafael, wearing his Dick Tracy face, all smug and superior.

'If that's the fucking case, then I was being set up,' I said indignantly.

'Oh no, the word was out on the other wings about an imminent delivery during the early evening, which meant a different avenue for the incoming heroin. The usual method of moving drugs around the prison is in the breakfast trolleys in the mornings. The prison kitchen workers are from every wing in the prison so the shit normally comes into the kitchens then gets moved to the various wings.'

'If every fucker knows that, why is it allowed to happen?'

'Because there'd be fucking riots and the place would become unmanageable without drugs. Imagine how many fucking suicides there'd be. Besides, we know exactly what's going on and who's who, so everything's controlled and happy.'

I thought for a moment and then asked, 'How come the *cacheros* didn't give me a spin?'

'Oh, that's because they know you've got fuck all, so they didn't waste time on you.'

'How the fuck do they know I've got fuck all?'

'Because I fucking well told them, that's why.'

He pulled up a chair and sat opposite my bed, plonking his big feet on my mattress, then folded his arms and said, 'Right, tell me a story.'

Maybe he knew, maybe he didn't, but the alarm bells clattered to life as Quasimodo, the adrenalin god, jumped on the bell rope.

'What kind of fucking story?' I said, my acting skills exceeding that of any Academy Award winner, Oscar or BAFTA. Kiss my arse, De Niro. You couldn't match this as long as your arse faces downwards.

'Tell me about Enrico's plan. What are we getting involved with when you get out?'

My instincts told me to give Don Rafael something to dream about, so I decided to do just that and skate around any awkward questions he may have asked.

'Let's get something straight, Rafael,' I said, wearing my best Henry Kissinger expression. 'When I get out of here, I work for me. Nothing is written in stone around here. I won't know the dates or the destinations until some time after my release. All I can tell you about that job is that it is long distance and we'll be millionaires when it's done.'

'So how long after your release will I have to wait before I join you?'

I rehashed my Henry Kissinger mush and paused in feigned thought. 'Immediately. You will join me the very week I get out because I'll need money straight away. I'll work Morocco to Spain using fast, rigid inflatable boats which we call RIBs; you call them *barcos de goma* or simply *gomas*. We'll do three or four trips then relax in North Africa for a few weeks until something crops up.'

I studied Don Rafael's face as he tried to conjure up the Errol Flynn image of himself dashingly cutting through the surf, creating waves of high-spraying whiteness at the bow and a wild, foaming wake. Should the dream turn to reality his fucking backbone would soon disintegrate with the crump and thud of the hull pounding the wave tops.

It was not in my interest to ruin his image of things by telling him the truth about crossing the Mediterranean Sea with a tonne of shit in a little rubber boat; about the stab of fear when another vessel is sighted; about the pouring of petrol into fuel tanks as you bob about like a cork in the swells; the incredible weariness caused by many adrenalin-filled hours coping with a changeable sea for which the Mediterranean is notorious. No, I'd let him dream on about his romantic adventures on the high seas.

'Will we be sailing near Gibraltar? I've never been there, you know. I'd like to see that part of my country.'

The faraway look was still in his eyes as I said, 'Bollocks to that fucking dump. Apart from the high street there's fuck all there and everything is run by wogs and Jews, so unless you speak gibberish, Gibraltar's not for you.'

He laughed heartily at my joke and then asked, 'Are you serious?'

'We won't be sailing anywhere near that fucking place. Besides, it's too risky. The short journey between the La Linea part of the

Spanish coast and the Tetouan area of Morocco is well patrolled by both navies and there's too many fucking loonies running the show down there.'

Thinking about what I'd just said reminded me about the Sbali brothers, Mustafa and Mo – just about the only two players with any sense of honour and probably the only team never to have lost a cargo in that cesspool end of the Med. I dismissed them from my thoughts as I said, 'Anything west of Malaga is fucking kamikaze work.'

'I thought that's where everything happens,' said Don Rafael, with his big eyes questioning me.

'You'd think that because every fucker from down there is in prison,' I said, beginning to relax now as I realised this wasn't intended to be an interrogation. 'All the effort against smuggling is down there,' I added. 'That's where most of the patrols are: west of Malaga.'

He was slouching in the chair with his feet on my bed, twiddling his thumbs with his chin on his chest, letting me know he had nowhere else to go this afternoon and he expected me to tell him about his future.

'So, where will we be working?' he said, shifting his arse to let fly with a cracking fart that seemed to break the tension I had been feeling. Now there's a paradox for you: an atmosphere-polluting fart helps to clear the air between men.

We were both smiling now, and I decided to tell him about business working out of Ras-el-Ma, Morocco, sailing up to the Valencia area of Spain.

'There's a job operating out of Ras-el-Ma near the Algerian border with Morocco. If we do that a couple of times, we'll have plenty of money to relax in luxury for a while, waiting for the big one with Enrico.'

'Where's it going to?'

'Sagunto, just north of Valencia,' I said, quite casually.

His eyes wide: 'Fuck me! How fucking far is that? In a fucking *goma*?'

'You want adventure and money? Well, with me that's what you fucking well get.'

93

CARABANCHEL

The puzzled expression on his face showed no fear but I knew he was concerned about such a long, hazardous journey at sea in a rubber boat loaded with a large quantity of hashish. There's a special kind of courage required for this job and Rafael would have been desperately plumbing the depths of his fortitude if he was ever confronted with the realities of this task, especially when he saw two tonnes of Morocco's best and the extra petrol lashed to the deck. I was thinking purely hypothetically now because there was no fucking way I was ever going to work with a spick again, even if he did have all the credentials.

'Don't worry, Rafael. We work only with a good weather forecast and I've done it before, so relax.'

I played down the angst of the job. I would never reveal the true hazards of smuggling cannabis resin in its various forms; certainly not while he was looking after me in here.

'It's fucking ball-aching work and we'll need a week in bed when we've done it, but the money's good.'

For the first time I saw uncertainty in his eyes; not fear, but a kind of bewilderment. I had to choose my words carefully now; I didn't want to frighten him off. He'd put himself in my web; now I had to keep him there.

'How fucking far is it?'

'Around 400 miles.'

'How long does that take?'

'Depending on sea conditions, about 18 to 20 hours.'

'How much cargo will we carry?'

'Never less than a tonne and a half; probably two tonnes, else it's not really worth it. It depends on what kind of RIB we have. Hopefully, we'll have a 12-metre job with twin Yanmar diesels and a fucking huge fuel tank. The last time I worked with these blokes I was refuelled at sea by one of their trawlers out of Alicante. Not a good idea because too many things can go wrong.'

Too late, I knew I had said the wrong thing. Rafael was hanging on my every word: he wanted an explanation. If any race of people can make a question mark with their mush, it's the Spanish. His face was a picture. It wore an expression of dumbfounded curiosity.

'What the fuck does that mean – too many things can go wrong?' he snapped.

'Well, it was your fucking countrymen that I had to rely on. No disrespect to you, but they are so fucking lazy it frightens me.'

'How the fuck do you mean?'

Not so snappy now.

'They can't maintain a sense of urgency. It wears off after three minutes. I was waiting for ages at the RV. They were late and couldn't have cared less. It does your fucking head in when you're waiting in a remote area of sea with fuck all on the horizon and an eggcup full of fuel swishing around the bottom of the tank. It calls for cutting-edge thinking and correctly deducing what's going on. I was on the verge of chucking the cargo over the side and heading for the Spanish coast. I didn't have much fuel but I might have made it. At least I'd have got to a shipping lane.'

'What happened?'

All concerned now.

'I caught a glimpse of something on the horizon and prayed it was them. It was, but they were two hours fucking late. I'd already guessed it had to do with the time difference between Spain and Morocco; that's why I hadn't dumped the cargo and fucked off earlier.'

'I don't know if I'd have thought about that, y'know: time differences and all that.'

'Oh fucking hell, don't say you're like the rest of your countrymen: unable to fucking think. You said you was in the Foreign fucking Legion. Here's me thinking I've got a diamond who speaks English like Robin Hood, speaks Spanish, speaks French and probably speaks Arabic, but can't fucking think.'

I said this in a jocular way so as not to seem disrespectful. I likely wouldn't have said it had he not farted five minutes ago.

He chuckled and said, 'Not even a prison officer could get away with talking to me like that.'

I realised how much ice had been broken between us; both ends of the spectrum had joined.

'Your future has fuck all to do with prison officers; you're coming back to the land of the living where your fortitude as a legionnaire will be put to better use. You will see that respect, as well as wealth and adventure, comes in truckloads when you have a reputation on the sea, which is where you're going with me.'

Don Rafael sat up and lurched forward to grab my hand in a strong handshake, to which I applied the Freemason's thumb. It didn't get a response, so I guessed all his years in Nottingham were spent perfecting his English in *Ye Olde Trip to Jerusalem*, a famous Nottingham pub.

'Right. Now tell me, what happened with this fucking trawler?'

'Oh yeah, fucking hell, where was I up to?'

I gave my bollocks a scratch, stretched, then clasped my hands behind my head on the pillow.

'Oh, right. The trawler drew alongside as somebody threw me a rope. I was making fast with the rope when some stupid cunt threw a *jarafe* of petrol down onto my deck next to the transom, where it burst open and splashed 20 litres of petrol all over my fucking cockpit.'

'Why the fuck did he do that?' asked Don Rafael, knowing that it was the most incredibly stupid thing to do; the expression on his face illuminating the fact.

'Everybody's brave until they get near the shit. The realisation of what would happen if they were caught now, near a couple of tonnes of shit, turns their bullfighting machismo into chicken shit. You can hear them farting, "poop, poop, poop", like fucking little chuffer trains, scurrying round the decks. You'd think it was fucking plutonium; not a harmless fucking weed.'

The incredulous look on Don Rafael's mush pissed me off.

'Listen to me. I've seen blokes cut and run, part-way through a job, when there's only been a few kilos to deal with. What do you think a couple of tonnes looks like to some cunt who's just delivering petrol? He thinks it looks like five fucking years in this pisshole; that's what he thinks.'

'But surely they know all that when they take the job on.'

Slightly exasperated now.

'Right, they do. But they still shit themselves when they tie up to me because they're frightened of patrols, helicopters and the thought that there's always a fucking grass on board.'

That changed his exasperation to resignation, because Don Rafael knew more about the wagging Spanish tongue than most, him being the chief screw in this fucking dump.

'Imagine what would have happened if that petrol had landed on the fucking cargo. All that effort for fuck all because the cargo would have been worthless.'

It was worth telling the story just to see Don Rafael's face.

'And guess what?' I said, laying it on with a trowel. 'The lazy, useless bastards wouldn't help me. They hand-balled each 20-litre *jarafe* of petrol into my arms and watched me struggle with each one across the fucking RIB.'

I paused for a moment before rubbing it in. 'But you'd never guess what the yellow, gutless cunts did.'

I'm sure he winced inwardly as I continued. 'When the last container of petrol was handed to me, they immediately cast off and steamed away, full throttle, to the west, taking with them my hot food and drink that had been put on board the trawler for me. They pretended not to hear my shouting nor see me frantically waving my arms above my head.'

Don Rafael looked a bit sheepish, uncomfortable at being a Spaniard just then.

'I can promise you that when you're working with me, there will be no refuelling from Spanish trawlers. In fact, you may as well know now: there will be only my Moroccan contacts on the African side, and on the Spanish side there will be my English, Dutch, German, French, Finnish or Italian contacts: you will never have anything to do with your countrymen. You will be Tony, from Nottingham. Even the English lads wouldn't guess you was Spanish, the way you speak with a Nottingham accent. Anyway, that's all in the future, which will be rich and rosy.'

Don Rafael was all ears, wanting to know more.

'So how did not having hot food affect you?'

'Oh fucking hell. By the time I'd finished pouring the fucking petrol into the tanks, I was exhausted and badly in need of a hot meal – especially as I'd been expecting it. I was really looking forward to eating a hot, juicy steak, which was what I should have been given. It was demoralising watching the useless wankers scurrying off with my food. I vowed then never to refuel at sea ever again, especially with Spanish trawlers.'

'What the fuck did you have to eat then?'

'Let's just say I was sick of fucking Mars Bars and Coca-Cola.'

'But everything went well, didn't it?'

'Oh yeah, fucking hell, I've never lost a cargo yet. My reputation in Morocco is top notch; that's why they all want me to work with them. I don't need fucking Enrico or any other cunt. I will always be in demand in Morocco,' I boasted. 'You stick with me and you'll never be out of work. You'll have money coming out of your fucking ears.'

Don Rafael's life had stagnated within the Spanish prison system since he'd left the military. Lots of blokes do that: leave the adventurous life of the armed forces then join the prison service in search of a second pension and a fat arse, awarding themselves a sentence of years behind bars, sharing the misery, and in most cases causing it. A self-inflicted wound to the inner self.

There were many small men who cast a large shadow in here, spending their time enjoying the power of their uniform. They actually preferred to be at work here, behind bars, wearing their suit of blue serge armour, than to be the absolute nobodies they were out in the real world. Some of them reminded me of those evolution charts hanging on museum or schoolroom walls. Words like Neanderthal and Homo erectus sprang to mind. Charles Darwin obviously missed this fucking lot: the Spanish prison system wasn't on his itinerary.

Don Rafael's saving grace was that he had served in the Parachute Regiment of the French Foreign Legion and he kept himself hard, fit and fearless. I was studying his face and I wasn't surprised to see the anticipated joy of adventures at sea. The notion of roaming the seas and visiting strange lands captivated his mind as the idea of shedding the shackles of his brain-numbing career revived his outlook on life.

He had a thousand questions but I knew he would control his enthusiasm by not blurting them out all at once, so I thought I'd tickle his fancy by projecting some images for him to dream about.

'I'll be glad when this is all over and we have a few trips under our belts,' I ventured.

'Why's that?'

Ears bristling, sitting up from his slouch.

'Well, when we're fixed up with enough money to take a breather, we'll take an apartment in Marina Smir, or better still, in Mdiq, at Zem Zem's pension, where we can relax and sort out the jobs, away from the mad bastards in Nador,' I said.

My thoughts drifted across the North African coast, following the remote beaches westward from Algeria to Tangier where I had many times silently beached my craft to rendezvous with the rag-headed phantoms of the night who silently loaded my boat.

'Who are the mad bastards in Nador?'

A concerned look on his face now.

'There are many people in Nador who know me for what I am – a reliable skipper. Once we have done a job out of Nador and the word gets out that François is back in town, the local pot barons will be clamouring for our services and we won't get a minute's peace, so we'll need a *pied-à-terre* to rest up in.'

'Who is François and what is a *pied-à-terre*?'

A puzzled look on his face now.

'In Morocco I am known as François and a *pied-à-terre* is a flat; an apartment, a bolthole, a place to think and plan, and Zem Zem's pension is really nice with a lovely beach. We can nip into Cabo Negro, where there's the world's best seafood at Restaurante La Ferma. You'll love it. Anyway, I thought you could speak French: you've never heard of a *pied-à-terre*?'

'Oh yes, but not the way you fucking say it, you cunt.'

A superior look now.

'Ah well, I've never lived with frogs like you have. Anyway, listen, you'll love it at Mdiq. We can get a couple of horses and explore the beach or just bugger off anywhere we like. I'm not going to tell you about the women, else you'll be here all fucking night pestering me for more stories.'

Don Rafael was hooked on the idea of working around North Africa. Being an ex-legionnaire, he'd experienced the *souks* and the *kasbah*, the backstreets and bars, the lurking excitement of being amongst squatting, jabbering rag-heads, the blend of apprehension and delight during a bar crawl. There's no such thing as a pub crawl in Morocco; Islam doesn't permit such establishments so you need a good, kindred-spirited rag-head to guide you in your search for booze. You can normally get a drink in tourist hotels, but when you live the life of the contrabandista, you must avoid such places. Being Jack the Lad in a tourist hotel is the kiss of death in Morocco: or anywhere else, for that matter.

'By the time we get to Mdiq, we will probably be finished with *gomas*. Some of my friends will have located me by then, so it's as well that we have our own accommodation and not be tied or contracted to any Arabs. We need to be independent.'

Don Rafael contemplated my words and realised we would be upgrading.

'So what will happen then?' he asked, with a look of anticipation.

I savoured the moment because I enjoyed having the chief screw right in the palm of my hand.

'One of my friends is from Holland – we'll call him "Dutch". When he discovers where I am, he will arrive by motor-yacht – probably a Colvic-Watson or a Fischer: a good, seaworthy craft. He will make me an offer that I will not refuse.'

'Why's that?' said Don Rafael, consternation all across his face.

'Because I have worked with him before and the job has been running problem-free for many years.'

The screw's face held an expression of awe as it dawned on him that he would be living on a yacht.

'Will I have my own cabin?' he said, mouth open.

'Of course. You will also have an apartment in Toulon, on the Riviera.'

'Why would I have an apartment in Toulon when I have a cabin on a yacht?'

'Because you don't want to be on it when Dutch's hash is being unloaded. The yacht's taken out of the water for repairs when it arrives in the French port, then the cargo is removed during the first night in France. She will stay there for three weeks high and dry, then we return and put her back in the water for the return trip to Morocco. It's a lovely life, Rafael, how do you fancy that?'

Don Rafael looked at my feet, and then at my face.

'We haven't mentioned *dinero* yet,' he said, looking for all the world like Alastair Sim doing Ebenezer Scrooge.

'I thought I'd tell you about the life first, just to see if it suited you; you being ex-military and all that.'

'You knew that before you started telling me about it. You know it fucking suits me; now it's time to talk *dinero*.'

'OK, my friend,' I said, as I stared into his big hard eyes. 'This is what it's all about – *dinero*.'

The poker player in him emerged as his eyes tried in vain to mask the excitement of a royal flush. He waited, expectantly. So I told him.

'I will pay you, possibly, seven million *pesetas* for each *goma* trip, depending on how much cargo we carry. If you work with me with Dutch, then you will get between ten and fifteen million *pesetas* each trip; again, depending on how much we carry. We will possibly do six or eight trips a year with Dutch, so you can work out your yearly income yourself. Right now, as a prison officer, you earn less than three million *pesetas* a year. So how does that grab you?'

The numbers hit the screw like a lottery win. He struggled to get his head around being rich beyond his wildest dreams.

'*Putre madre!* Fucking Jesus Christ! Are you taking the piss?'

His eyes were wide, as he knew that the figures were true-ish. So I barked back at him: 'What's up? Isn't that enough for a learner? Because that's what you are: a fucking sprog.'

He started to laugh and I laughed with him as he spluttered, 'It doesn't seem real. Where would I keep so much money?'

'Relax, Rafael. There are rules regarding money that we all abide by to keep our freedom and not let the police get their grubby hands on it. We risk our lives to earn our money; the police risk fuck all.'

I wondered how Rafael would react to the methods used by my friend Dutch. I then realised that it mattered not one jot what he thought: it would never apply to him. Nevertheless, I fed him some titbits to keep him on the end of my string.

'You will have small accounts in Spain and Morocco, but the bulk of your money will be in Cyprus and Liechtenstein, held in accounts organised by Dutch's accountants – in your name, of course. The accountants' office is in Brussels and any significant withdrawals go through that office.'

Don Rafael was thinking hard; the brow was furrowed and the thumbs were twiddling as he let out a meaningful harrumph.

'I don't have an account and I really don't know if I want one. I like to manage my own money.'

'Ah well, if you work with me you will need some kind of money-management system, so you may as well be fixed up by the professionals in Brussels.'

'I don't know if I want that.'

A hard, determined look on his face now.

Just then, the door flew open and in strode a short-arsed screw, all snarls and shaking truncheon. Behind him in the doorway lurched two of his kind – *cacheros*: the anal sniffer dogs of the Spanish prison system.

Don Rafael was primed and on his feet in a flash of fluid movement, capable only by men of outstanding fitness and by fearless warriors who are in a constant state of alertness. Lunging straight into short-arse, he turned him around and frogmarched him back through the open door, barging into the other two and somehow managing to close the heavy cell door behind him without too much of a clatter. I heard the bolt sliding across – locking the door to prevent what?

I relaxed as the voices receded from the cell door and the angry tones drifted into the nothingness of the whispering gallery. I was just wondering what the time was when the door swung open and Don Rafael reappeared.

'That parsimonious little shit gets right up my arse,' said Don Rafael gruffly.

'He probably would have got right up mine if you hadn't been here.'

We were now laughing our fucking heads off.

'What the fuck did he come here for anyway?' I said, all concerned.

'They came to give you a shakedown; said you had a big *paquete* of smack. A dipstick gypsy grassed you up; said you have Manolo's heroin. Don't worry, I've put those fuckers straight. They won't bother you again. They think I'm shagging you so you're my responsibility.'

'Oh fucking hell. What the fuck did you let them think that for? If that gets around the fucking prison, I'll have problems galore.'

'Don't kid your fucking self. That's the best fucking cover story you could wish for. No fucker dare come near you now so you fucking owe me. And what about my feelings? Me, shagging an ugly cunt like you when I have the pick of the juiciest transsexuals this side of fucking Singapore . . . You're taking the piss!'

We laughed our fucking heads off because if we couldn't grasp the funny side of things, we'd go stir-crazy.

'You know, I'll always be looking for that certain look on your fucking face from now on. Well, if I see it, you definitely ain't coming to fucking sea with me,' I chuckled, as Don Rafael pulled the chair back and slouched back into it, swinging his big feet across the bottom of my bed.

He settled down with his hands clasped across his chest. 'You was telling me about money and banks and accountants and Brussels and you was beginning to piss me off. Now tell me again about money.'

'When a fresh bloke gets a load of money, more than he's ever had before, he may do something stupid like buy a fucking Ferrari or a new house. Anyway, he may do something stupid, which brings everything on top. If you start throwing money around, people will start noticing. It only takes one green-eyed cunt to grass you up and then you've got a tail. The tail isn't interested in you; he wants the fuckers who gave you the money. Don't forget, the police know fuck all; they are clueless. They know nothing about any job or how anything works until somebody fucks up by being Jack the Lad, spending money that everyone knows he shouldn't have.'

I lay on my bed waiting for a response. Don Rafael twiddled his thumbs, expressionless. So I went on. 'One of the conditions of working with Dutch is that we use his accountant in Brussels. Our accounts get credited with the money on the day we dock in France. Not fucking weeks later when the shit's been sold – instantly. We have access to our money on that very day. Some will be paid into our Spanish accounts and some into our Moroccan accounts. The remainder will be split between the Cyprus and the Liechtenstein banks.'

Again I awaited a response: nothing.

'You can do whatever you like with your dough, but if you want to buy a house or something big like that, then you must be clever. You couldn't buy one where every fucker knows you. Besides, major purchases like that are best handled by the accountants. Let them earn their fucking money.'

'I don't know if I'll like that,' he said, grumpily.

'Well, that's no fucking problem; don't work with Dutch.'

He sat up jerkily.

I needed to keep Don Rafael on the end of my string, so I offered an alternative: 'When you've done a couple of trips with me on RIBs, you'll have learnt enough to work on your own. I'll see to it that you do. I'll teach you all there is to know about it. I can fix you up with plenty of RIB work so you can work alone, like I normally do.'

'No, fuck that. I want to stay with you and do the yachts and the big stuff.'

'Then you'll have to do as I do: work and become quietly wealthy. We can live like kings in Morocco while our pot of gold keeps growing in Cyprus.'

I was beginning to beguile myself now: I was falling for my own bullshit! I cast my mind back to previous escapades and the joys of travel.

'I would like a house in Essaouira on the Atlantic coast between Agadir and Casablanca. I will live there when the time is right. Life is good in Essaouira,' I mused.

'What's so fucking special about that place?' he said, drool all over his face.

'You'll see when we go there. I like ports and beaches and the beach at Essaouira is really big and the wind blows across it constantly. I've spent many hours wandering on that beach. It's a great place to explore. There's the ramparts, the *souks*, the harbour and lots of little cottage industries like wood-carving workshops and there's a seafood restaurant at the end of the harbour called

Chez Sam: a hangout for expats. I don't like the gossips – they're all fucking villains, coming it large, dropping names like Reggie and Ronnie and Mad Frankie. Fucking nutters, all of 'em, but the fish and the ice-cold white wine – mmm . . . that's what I like.'

The chief screw had his fingers pressed together as though in prayer.

'What do you do for kicks?'

I couldn't tell whether or not there was a sneer.

'Kicks? There's loads of kicks. What do you want? Smack, Charlie or *tbizla*, the best hash on the planet? What else? Fanny, little boys, big boys? You can play 'hide the sausage' in so many different ways in Morocco, it'll make your bollocks spin.'

He slouched there, tapping his feet together in an unknown rhythm.

'I can get that in this fucking place,' he said, scornfully.

'Fair comment, but I'd rather be in Morocco where I'll be free to do what I like. I'll have a Jeep or a Land-Rover and do the desert; fucking real off-roading like I used to do in the Army. Funnily enough, I like the desert. There's a place I know out in the sticks where you can fire a 50-calibre Browning machine gun and several other old weapons. The rag-heads set up a shooting range in the arsehole of nowhere and stocked it with Camel Corps weapons from the last war: old Desert Rats stuff and Afrika Korps guns. Some of it came from Tobruk, or so they tell you.'

I suddenly stopped talking and studied the faraway look on Don Rafael's face. I had him now; I'd found his Achilles heel: war, weapons and the desert. I carried on.

'Last time I was there, I got to fire a Mauser MG42. Y'know? It was fucking great. Some of those old guns have greater firepower than the most up-to-date ones. There's all kinds of shit you can bang away with on that old range.'

The chief screw looked at me then lied. 'I've seen enough weapons to last me a lifetime.'

'So have I, but I like to keep my hand in.'

Then I got all serious and snapped at him. 'Look, Rafael, in this fucking game you find your kicks where you can. Some blokes take Charlie or smack; others are permanently stoned or pissed between jobs. Well, I can't be doing with any of that old bollocks and I won't have anybody around me that does – you need to remember that.'

I let that sink in, then said, 'One day, I'll have my own yacht and maybe a decent RIB, because between jobs is all leisure time. I'll fill my days with what makes me happy. I'll be fishing, diving, off-roading, exploring, eating gourmet food and drinking the finest wines with my woman. At the end of the day I want to gaze up at the glittering universe to give thanks for another good day. What the fuck else is there?'

Don Rafael jumped to his feet, smoothed himself down and then stamped his feet, an old military habit often performed by ex-squaddies. He strode over to the door, turned and said, 'When you put it like that, there's fuck all else, is there. Do what makes you happy: that's it. I'm off. See you later.'

He silently exited my cell, not bothering to lock it because he would be back on the gallery in a few minutes to open up again. It was late afternoon. I lay on my bed wondering how that fuckpig Manolo would handle the loss of face, not forgetting, of course, the *paquete* held by the lanky Paco. I now knew the *cacheros* hadn't found it in his cell because he had grassed me to send them on a wild goose chase away from himself. I later found out from Don Rafael that the *cacheros* had actually found a badly hidden *papelito*: a tiny slip of paper holding a single fix of heroin. His plan was quite transparent to me: sacrifice a little bit, but not enough to get sent down the block for more than one night, especially if he also told the *cacheros* that I had the rest. Then he'd tell Manolo the *cacheros* had confiscated the lot, hoping that he would believe him. All this in order to salvage something out of his greasy endeavours.

That night Don Rafael visited my cell in search of more adventure stories, but I got in there first and asked him about lanky Paco. He told me the story about the *cacheros* finding a tiny wrap of smack in his cell and that he'd grassed me for the main packet. He didn't let on about Paco grassing Manolo, so I didn't say anything about Paco having the package that everybody supposedly knew about. The main point about that night was that Don Rafael entered my cell with his sports bag, which he carefully placed at the bottom of my bed. After first explaining about lanky Paco, he reached into the bag and produced two plastic beakers and a large bottle of Coca-Cola that was ice cold, with beads of condensation running down the outside.

'How do you like your Coke?' he beamed.

'Just like that,' I said, pointing at the bottle. 'Ice cold – lovely.'

'Well, I like mine like this,' he said, reaching into the bag and pulling out a bottle of Navy rum. 'Half and half. Half Coke and half rum. Fancy a drop?'

The Cheshire cat was grinning at me across the cell as he started to pour two large measures of rum into each glass. Then he splashed the Coke over them and handed me one.

'This is to me and you,' he said, raising his cup to touch mine. 'I feel so good about our arrangements for when you get out that I'm breaking my own rules. I've never drunk alcohol in prison before but I want to celebrate our future right now, so, fucking cheers. Here's to us and *dinero*!'

I felt slightly guilty as we toasted our future, because in my heart I knew that, of all the Spaniards in the world, this one was probably the only one alive today who would have come up to the standard required to be successful: doing the most dangerous job of long-distance smuggling in a RIB.

I knew that the day of my *libertad* would be the last day I'd have anything to do with Don Rafael. However, I had to sham this comradeship and maintain my budding relationship with this man who was so important to my well-being in this disgraceful Spanish pit.

Manolo was temporarily subdued. His henchmen were all down the block in solitary so he didn't have the troops necessary to back up his usual intimidating behaviour. Nevertheless, he was feared by many so he continued to strut as though he owned the place.

I made my mind up to move quickly and put the arm on lanky Paco, just as soon as he emerged from solitary, which would be any minute now. The heavy gate clattered open and the tribe welcomed him back into the fold. Lots of backslapping, handshaking and gleeful banter heralded the noisy return of the hero as they headed for the *economato* to beg for coffee. There they went, the dross of Spain, shouting and screaming at the blokes in the *economato* for coffee on credit, to welcome their hero back on the wing.

There was a mini riot going on now and the gypsies were banging the serving hatch and screaming obscenities and threats at the blokes behind the hatch. The screws were in danger of coming out at any second and closing the *economato* for the rest of the day, which would have been bad for the rest of us because today was Saturday and the workshops were closed, so everybody was on the wing, bored fucking shitless.

The *Mezclado* moved fast. Ali, Jake and Vito cleared the servery of dross, just like a snowplough barging through a drift. In seconds a new queue had formed, with me and Chinky at the front ordering coffee for our gang. The clogs, krauts and Basques had quickly moved in behind us, making the queue even more formidable.

No punches were thrown, but face had been lost. So now there was a gathering of gypsies at the far end of the yard: a lot of gypsies. The powwow had started and the daggers were aimed at yours truly; the fireworks would happen soon. I realised I had to act fast with lanky Paco so I awaited my chance.

We had our coffee and thrashed out various methods of dealing with the imminent threat from the greasy bastards at the far end. The debate ended amicably with the agreement that we struck first, creating a near-death experience for whichever back-stabber tried his luck.

Chinky had just bought us another round of coffee when I noticed Paco making for the lavatories. I didn't need to ask about watching my back: everyone knew as I quietly got up and headed for the stinking bogs.

My timing was perfect; I made my approach in mid-shit.

'Hey, *chivato*,' I said, looking at him squatting with his big feet on the lavatory seat and his arms wrapped around his knees. His grubby jeans were hung over the dividing wall; he didn't wear underpants. His cock and bollocks were hanging dangerously close to a thick smear of shite spread around the rim of the stinking shitpot. I know when to pick my moments.

'*Eres chivato, yo sabes tu abla con cacheros, mi amigo es cachero. Yo sabes tambien usted robo droga de Manolo, tambien cacheros descubrieron droga en tu celda.*'

My Spanish is quite crap but everyone understood me when I

spoke to them. Nobody laughed at me any more because those that did ended up on their arses caressing their bollocks, or woke up with a crowd around them. Image and reputation were everything in here, so respect was crucial if one was to maintain one's face in the Carabanchel – and I mean that quite literally.

Shock, embarrassment and fear hit the dipstick gypsy instantly as he jettisoned a mixture of gas and solids into the stinking pot. Adrenalin does that: fight, flight or shite, goes the old saying. For lanky Paco it was the last of these. He then froze in mortified horror; helplessly perched on the rim of the porcelain pot. The stink was making my nasal hair fall out.

I then made him an offer he couldn't refuse: my silence for half of Manolo's smack.

'*Sí, señor, comprendo. Ésta tarde?*'

'*Sí,*' I said. This evening would be fine.

This ploy with Paco killed three birds with one turd. I would have a nose in the gypsy camp (very important just then), a nose in Manolo's camp and a lump of money for the *Mezclado*, because Chinky would deal with Manolo's smack and nobody would be any the wiser.

I filled Chinky in regarding the smack and he was only too pleased to be doing something. He knew he had to shift it quickly before Manolo twigged; not that Manolo mattered to the *Mezclado*, but it's always best to get things done without the revenge factor.

I made arrangements for Paco to pass the smack to Jake, and then for Jake to pass it to Chinky. Nobody wanted to fuck with Jake. Everything went smoothly, especially as I ordered lanky Paco not to start selling his share until the following week. Chinky did well moving the shit and in so doing had snared himself some wealthy clients, so it was prudent to find him a supplier to continue his new business. I was instrumental in organising that.

Two of the *economato* blokes were in my combat class. One of them was an Argentinian by the name of Andy, the son of English immigrants. He spoke English with a Geordie accent, his parents having emigrated from Newcastle upon Tyne before he was born. He was a heroin addict, but nobody knew because he was never in the methadone queue and he never chased the dragon in the bogs.

He was incredibly lucky because his supplier was a friend of his who was one of the trustees employed to service the *economatos* on each prison wing. Andy was a closet junkie and only his supplier and I knew about it.

It was his erratic behaviour on the combat mat that had alerted me that something wasn't quite right with him. One day I hurt him with a wrist throw and he completely lost it with a display of tears and sobbing as he dashed away to the showers. Later, he caught me alone and apologised, then confessed to being a heroin addict. Outbreaks of distress and paranoia like this went with the territory. He'd tried to hide it from me before because he was afraid that I'd chuck him out of the combat class.

I put the arm on him to find out who the supplier was, so he told me about the trustee who went by the name of Costa, a Portuguese bloke who I already knew. But I didn't know he was a smack dealer. Don Rafael knew every smackhead and dealer on the wing, so the next time we had a chat I innocently dropped in a mention of Andy and Costa in relation to the gym and the *economato*. Had he known about them, he would have said something: but he didn't.

Without too much effort I persuaded Argie Andy to take extra smack from Costa with *Mezclado dinero* and then pass it on to Chinky for his clients on the wing. This deal put Argie Andy under the protection of the *Mezclado* and, to a certain extent, the rest of the *economato* staff as well. So what? Who cared? In for a penny, in for a pound. Besides, the *economato* staff were always giving treats to the *Mezclado*.

Business was booming, but constant alertness was getting me down. My cell was the only place I could relax. I spent every evening with Kennedy and Enrico until final bang up, relaxing and planning the job that was going to make us all rich. Then we would be unlocked and I would nip next door into my own cell to be banged up for the night.

Whenever Don Rafael was on duty, he would come to my cell at night to chat about when I got out. He always brought me something from the street like fresh fruit or toiletries. He bought me a new Gillette razor with refill blades and a tube of Nivea shaving cream, enabling me to throw away the prison-issue razor, a real luxury in here. But the real treat was the use of his mobile phone to speak to Susan. He would hand me the phone then disappear for ten minutes or so. When I spoke to her in the silence of my cell, the greasy phantoms disappeared and a feeling that I can only describe as ecstasy cocooned us, as though we were in each other's arms instead of being hundreds of miles apart. Bliss.

SEVEN
KENNEDY'S *LIBERTAD*

Kennedy and Enrico had been arguing in rapid Spanish as I'd approached their cell, but had suddenly stopped when they'd heard the footsteps. Following me into the cell was Enrico's gopher with a tray of food, so I thought the vexed silence was because of his presence. He laid the food down and Enrico dismissed him, but the silence rumbled on with coughs and harrumphs, indicating they were nettled by my presence.

'What's up?' I said, turning my head from one to the other as though I was watching a tennis match, waiting for the reluctant reply.

'Well, what the fuck's up?' I repeated.

Enrico started gobbing off in Spanish and Kennedy squirmed uncomfortably as I snapped, 'Speak spick at this table again and I'll shove it down your ill-mannered fucking throat.'

Kennedy touched my forearm and, in a stage whisper, said, 'I'm leaving, bro'. I get out in three weeks' time. We have a lot to discuss and Enrico is stressed because he doesn't know if you'll sign on for a new job. He's nervous about telling you.'

The muffled noises of the gallery seemed to fade away into total silence in the awkwardness of the moment. Meaningful glances ricocheted off each other, foreshadowing a momentous disclosure.

Enrico's face resembled a sad Boris Karloff as he said, 'I am sorry, Christopher, for speaking my mother tongue, but I am terrified that we should share a most dangerous secret. I fear your rejection and we will have pointlessly informed you, thereby compromising our mission.'

Enrico was obviously a man of breeding and a past member of his country's diplomatic corps, hence his skills as a patter merchant. Had he been born an Englishman he would undoubtedly have had a gob full of marbles and be minus his chin.

'OK, what the fuck's going on? I'm obviously part of this, else you wouldn't tell me about it, or at least you've considered me as being part of it.'

'Listen, bro',' said Kennedy. 'Pablo told me this morning that I'm out in three weeks' time and the *educador* [social worker] confirmed it an hour ago, so I'm out of here fuckin' pronto.'

'That's great news and I'm over the moon for you, but what's so fucking secretive about a new job?'

Kennedy's face showed a mixed expression of fear and doubt as he said the word 'plutonium'. I revealed no emotion as my heart momentarily stopped, farted into my pericardium, then caught up with itself.

'So, what's the big deal with plutonium?' I asked, bouncing the question off them as though it was an everyday occurrence to fuck around with radioactive fuck-knows-what.

Enrico instantly looked hopeful, my cavalier attitude taking the edge off the sharp apprehension felt all round.

'D'you know what it is?' asked Kennedy, quizzical, eyes popping out.

'Does a one-legged duck swim in circles? Fucking right I do; I was in the fucking Army for years, wasn't I? I know more about nuclear fucking weapons than you do about your knob end.'

Kennedy chuckled with relief as Enrico sighed heavily, the tension visibly leaving him.

'Before you tell me any more about this, you must realise I haven't got a trial date, let alone a fucking sentence. So I really haven't a clue when I'm going to get out.'

'We've discussed that problem,' said Enrico, 'and you will have an *abogado* [lawyer] who specialises in *fianza* [bail]. So hopefully your stay will be a short one.'

KENNEDY'S *LIBERTAD*

My head was spinning with the thought of getting a lawyer who would get me out on bail.

'If we can get you out, I will arrange for German papers for you: passport, driving licence, everything that you require, including captain's papers. But first we must discuss many things,' said Enrico, deftly slicing a piece of cheese, which he popped into his mouth with some grapes.

'Before we talk about work,' said Kennedy, 'we need to know there's no problem with me and my woman staying at your house in Coín.'

'No, that's not a problem. Susan agreed that you can have one of the holiday apartments when you get out. I'll have to tell her now that you'll be out in three weeks' time, you jammy bastard.'

'Great! I'll pay my way with her and I'll give her your share of any change I make on the side.'

My friend Kennedy was true to his word: he paid Susan for the roof over his head and weighed her off with several million *pesetas* earned with little rubber boats. Also, when I eventually got my *libertad*, he was waiting for me with a brand new RIB with 500 horses on the transom. He was a good man, and I missed him awfully when he got out of the Carabanchel. But, there was a lot of talking to do before he went.

Details and timings for the plutonium affair were on a need-to-know basis, and I didn't need to know. But the idea to employ me arose because Kennedy needed a trustworthy and capable mate to man the vessel that would be used to intercept a larger vessel on the high seas, possibly a container ship, then take the consignment to a rendezvous probably on the Turkish coast. I really thought the job was a bad case of wishful thinking and I didn't hear another word about it after saying to Kennedy that I reckoned we would be paid with bullets rather than cash as I couldn't see anyone allowing us to sail away, knowing what we'd know.

Enrico nailed me every day to talk about the Charlie job, especially about the arrangements at the Irish end. He talked endlessly about the packaging and the route through an unmanned border crossing into Ulster, then on to Larne to board the ferry to Stranraer and on to an isolated farmhouse in Somerset. He was

115

terrified of being left alone when Kennedy departed, so he pestered me daily to join me in my cell. I knew that Pablo would have him moved in with me on the day of Kennedy's release regardless, so I laid it on thick with Enrico that he could do so, but I needed to see some effort regarding my bail.

I didn't know it then, but lawyers were already trying hard, but unsuccessfully, to get me out on bail. I later wondered whether or not the presiding judge knew who was behind the scenes trying to spring me and was hanging back for a much larger smear of grease across his palm. The reason for this assumption was because two of my co-ds walked away on bail and they each had 12 previous convictions for drug trafficking! I had a clean sheet and *residencia* – a home to go to. EU my English arse.

On the day prior to his release, Kennedy dropped a bombshell.

'In August,' he said, swallowing hard, 'there will be a meeting about the Charlie job. Pablo and Enrico have asked for the meeting to be at your *finca* in Coín.'

'Oh, fucking hell. You're implicating Susan now, you cunt.'

'No, no, bro'. Listen to how it will happen. No fear about Susan; she'll know nothing, I guarantee that. Just listen first; it's part of your ticket out of here.'

'OK, spin the shit. I'm all fucking ears.'

We were strolling around the yard, waiting for Chinky to fetch the coffee. We went and sat in the precious shadow of the south wall. The shade wouldn't last long because the sun was creeping to its zenith, from where it would mercilessly broil us. We didn't have much time to talk: Chinky would appear at any moment. Kennedy was agitated.

'I need to know now because Don Pablo will not ask you himself and I'm away tomorrow.'

He swallowed hard and forced a belch. This meant, I'd discovered, that he was either stressed or bewildered.

'OK, you're on. Tell me the score.'

The teeth beamed at me in the sunlight.

'Pablo will book himself, his son and his Colombian bird in for two weeks' holiday with Susan.'

'They don't think it's a freebie, by any chance?' I said, caustically.

'Fuck no, they will pay in advance. They will also pay for two guys coming over from Cali who will stay for a week. Me and my missus will be there anyway, but, like Susan, my missus knows fuck all about it. The girl is Pablo's bit on the side but she's part of the family in Cali. Get me? Need I say more?'

'If Susan is compromised in any way, I'll kill you first.'

'Great! So that's it, then. I'll tell him in a minute. You won't regret this, bro'. I fuckin' love ya.'

Kennedy scurried away to give Don Pablo the glad tidings, in return for which I would get a smooth ride for the rest of my bird and a great effort would be made to secure my release, albeit unsuccessfully, but bollocks, I didn't know that then.

I called Susan to tell her about Kennedy's sooner-than-expected arrival at our house, explaining, as best I could without compromising anyone, the holiday plans for one of the Carabanchel's top officials. I told her that Kennedy would inform her of the details when he settled in. I didn't mention Pablo's rank or who he actually was: Kennedy could surprise her with that gem.

That evening was spent sorting the kit that he would take with him the following day, while I would inherit the rest of his stuff. A game of Travel Scrabble would come to provide me with many hours of heated debate over misspelt words tried on by various cheating bastards during my travels through Spanish pisshole prisons. He also left me a pair of handmade leather slippers, which had been promised to somebody else: the mischievous black bastard knew what would happen. A hard-faced kraut collared me a few days after Kennedy's departure, accusing me of purloining the slippers before he could get them. Kennedy owed him, so the slippers were his and if I knew what was good for me I should, 'Hand zem over now, Englander!'

The kraut was typical of big, heavy, strutting ex-boxers from the Fatherland: a red-faced, thick-necked, shaven-headed nazi who I decided to call the Angry Tomato. He was a ringer for Shemp, the bonehead in the Three Stooges, and was just as predictable. He dropped his left shoulder, indicating that a big right-hand punch was being launched. I parried the punch as his arm was still bent, effectively blocking it by striking his bicep with my forearm, causing him terrible pain. With my other arm I drove a tremendous punch into his fat gut, just beneath his sternum, putting out the lights. The moment he hit the deck I finished him with two very hard punches to each eye, just so everybody knew.

The day Kennedy left the Carabanchel was one of the saddest days of my life. I felt an emptiness unlike anything I had felt before; a colossal void was tearing at my innards, a sensational loss that I believe can only be experienced by men in prison. There was never a noticeable bond between us. We were always arguing and abusing each other, but to us this was pure entertainment. To this day, though, I have never understood why his departure was such a colossal tragedy to me. I can only think of it as one of the mental effects of confinement. I carried one of his bags from the cell as far as the control tower, where we hugged and wished each other good luck, and then he was gone out of the arsehole of this disgusting Spanish beast.

Dejected and feeling lonelier than the North Pole, I forced myself through the rest of the day and I'm fucked if I can remember how I occupied myself; but that night I experienced the worst-ever self-inflicted torture as I allowed myself to wallow in my own self-pity. I was sad because I had lost my pal, but I was happy for him in his liberty.

On arriving at our house in Coín, Kennedy thrashed his loins with his wife day and night for a week. According to Susan, when he wasn't in the swimming pool he was in his missus. I was to discover later, on my release, that this trait is common amongst newly released prisoners. Well, it was for me and Kennedy; it was either the swimming pool or the wife: in out, in out, shake it all about. It was tap water for cleanliness and maiden's water to compensate for the sense of loss.

Fortunately for Kennedy and his missus, Susan had one of our apartments empty. Normally, when I was around, I would help her with her holiday business. But now, with me behind the door, it was hard for her to look after three apartments full of holidaymakers, clean the swimming pool every week, look after her collection of exotic birds and keep 10,000 square metres of land spick and span. Oh, she did all the cooking as well! So while I was locked up she kept her business ticking over so as to stay self-sufficient. What a woman! Beautiful, industrious, caring and, most important of all, loyal.

Kennedy was working a RIB during his second week of freedom: need drives men on. Cash was in short supply and his contacts had all dried up or changed numbers during his absence, so he used my contacts to move some cargo. I gave him directions to find Mustafa and Mohamed Sbali, with a letter of introduction using passwords that only the brothers Sbali and I knew. This way they could be sure that he wasn't a police plant, who are in common use on the Costa del Sol.

To provide help in an emergency in Morocco, I gave him my contact number for Mustafa Kader, who was based in a little village near the sea. A working skipper is treated like royalty in these out-of-the-way places where tonnes of hashish are hand-balled onto the decks of fast RIBs by rag-headed phantoms of the night.

Kennedy did well by doing two voyages in five days, especially as he was carrying *tbizla*, the wondershit normally reserved for royal tables: dope par excellence, worth a king's ransom in Amsterdam.

True to his word, he gave Susan several million *pesetas* during his second week of freedom, so that made me feel much better, knowing she had a few quid in the bank. Fortunately, Kennedy gave Susan packages of banknotes to stash away for him, which she hid in the priesthole in our old farmhouse. I say 'fortunately' because his good fortune abandoned him one day when he landed in Melilla, where he was to recce an RV and a loading bay at nearby Mar Chica in Nador.

His flight from Malaga airport to Melilla was uneventful until the spick coppers clocked his black face and pulled him in for questioning. They took him into custody because the silly black bastard had forgotten his passport, though technically he didn't need it because the flight to Melilla was a Spanish domestic flight, so a passport wasn't necessary . . . unless, of course, you happen to be black.

The racist bastards threw him into Melilla prison, a stinking, roasting pit, where he stayed, totally distressed, for nine months. He was continually abused, threatened and mentally tortured, not just

119

because he was black, but because he frustrated the quarter-wit Spanish interrogators by keeping shtum.

The money stashed by Susan came into play now by paying thieving spick lawyers and sending him food and toiletries while he went crazy in that racist pisshole administered by the Spanish prison system.

Melilla is one of the Spanish enclaves on the North African coast. It is naturally more Moroccan than Spanish and, because it is a punishment posting for *Guardia Civil* and prison officers, anyone caught on the wrong side of the law there is truly in the shit. They like to send ETA prisoners there so they don't get family visits: it's too far from *Pais Vasco* (the Basque country). They don't care a shit that this is in breach of all human-rights thinking and EU rules.

The reason given for Kennedy's imprisonment was that he was in breach of *libertad condicional* rules by taking a flight to Melilla. In my opinion this is complete bollocks because, during my *libertad condicional*, I went through Melilla umpteen times. Ahh . . . but I have a white face.

Kennedy later told me that the police knew he was active on the high seas and they had bent the rules to get him locked up in Melilla prison in order to make him grass the Sbali brothers. He reckoned the Sbali telephone was tapped and there was a grass on the Moroccan side. The police were getting nowhere on their own accord but, thankfully, Kennedy had Caribbean blood in his veins, not Spanish, so the brothers Sbali stayed out of jail. The Spanish reckon the lowest of the low are Spanish gypsies; I reckon their police and lawyers share that status.

Kennedy's *libertad* had been quite productive, but Gabriel, the lawyer, then took a big lump out of his profits. My pal had spent many dangerous hours at sea, just to be had by a cunning lawyer who should have had him out of that Melilla prison in no time. Kennedy instructed Susan to pay Gabriel several million *pesetas* after Gabriel had promised him his freedom. Presumably this was spent on cocaine or in the casino near Benalmádena, because fuck all happened in Melilla. Kennedy was kept in that pisshole until the very last day of his original sentence, then he lay low at my place, awaiting my return. The next time I saw Kennedy was in the year

2000 when I joined him on the jockey seat of a 500hp RIB. 'Hi ho, hi ho, it's off to work we go.' Varrroooom!

Fate caught up with that lawyer just a couple of years later, when he was representing me on another nautical smuggling case. He was killed in a high-speed motoring accident whilst returning from Granada with his brother, who was also killed. Apparently, he had been on a prison visit to see another pal of mine, Abselam Endoueli, a real gent, an educated Moroccan with a Scotswoman for a wife. Unfortunately for Abselam and me, there was no record of either of us having paid Gabriel before his death. Fortunately for all concerned, his death was assumed to be no more than an accident, but the hot rumour was that he was shunted off the motorway by an East End face who got pissed off with his shenanigans.

EIGHT
PHYSICAL JERKS

A Japanese bloke arrived on the wing. He told us his name was John, so he became known as John the Jap. I called him Myagi, because he looked like Mr Myagi out of the *Karate Kid* films. He was fit and hard but his eyes were downcast and he looked completely lost on his first day. No wonder: the gypsies had clocked his arrival and were taking the piss by shuffling around him like geisha girls. Then he made the big mistake of buying them coffee when they put the arm on him.

He made his way across the yard towards my group, possibly because he'd clocked Chinky and thought he was a fellow countryman. As he drew near, the gypos fell away, backing off before they came too close to us. A couple of persistent ones tried to steer him away but he doggedly kept his course to present himself to Chinky, saying something in hissing Japanese, to which Chinky snapped loudly, 'Speak Engrish or die!' We all fell about laughing as we realised Chinky had read the slogan from the back of my T-shirt.

The bewildered Jap realised his mistake and cringed on the spot. Then, looking at Jake, who was the biggest man in our group, he asked, 'Are you all English here?'

'No,' said Jake, 'only him,' pointing to me, 'but we all speak English when we're together.'

'Ah so, very good, because this is my second tongue.'

123

'Your udder tongue lick dem fuckin' spicks' arses wid coffee. Why you do dat den come over here?' asked Chinky.

'Because I don't know any difference and today is my first day in prison, so when I saw your face amongst these European faces I decided to join you.'

'Which cell are you in?' asked Jake.

'No. 45, though I don't know where it is. My bags are over there in the office. They told me I can't go up until after feeding time.'

Jake looked at me saying, 'That's Didi's cell. He won't be pleased. He was only bragging this morning about having a single cell.'

Didi was a small, wiry Belgian who often joined us but preferred his own company.

'Tough shit,' I said. 'He's lucky to get Myagi here instead of some hairy-arsed Arab or a greasy fucking gypo. At least Myagi's clean and speaks English.'

Looking at Myagi, I asked, 'What're you in for?'

Silence reigned as we all peered through the harsh sunlight at him.

'Er, I don't know if that is any of your business,' he stammered.

'It isn't, and neither are you, so fuck off back to the gypsies.'

He stood there awkwardly as we all turned our backs to him and started gobbing off about all things Nippon. It was at that moment that Didi came running across the yard towards us. The screws had informed him of Myagi's existence and he was highly pissed off. Didi's command of the English language was exceptional. Though he was Belgian, he must have gone to school in Runcorn or somewhere.

'Hey, Hirohito, you fuckin' slit-eyed bastard. Get over to the screws' office an' tell 'em you want another fuckin' cell. You ain't coming in my fucker, you Japanese twat!'

Jake shouted something in Belgian at Didi but he didn't respond for a moment and, when he did, he said in English, 'I don't give a flying fuck what he's in for. I don't want him in my fuckin' cell.'

Turning on Myagi, Didi pushed him with both hands.

'Fuck off to the office now, you cunt. My grandfather and his brother were POWs on your Siamese fuckin' railway and was killed slowly by cunts like you.'

Myagi responded swiftly with, 'Many members of my family were killed in that war, not just my grandfather and his brother.'

'Yeah, but they were killed honourably, weren't they?'

'How can women and children be killed honourably?'

'Fuck you, you Jap cunt. Get over to the fuckin' office now. C'mon, move your fuckin' slack arse before I kick fuck out of it.'

Didi grabbed Myagi's elbow and yanked him into motion towards the office, Myagi reluctantly going along with him, allowing Didi to pull him all the way, displaying to all the world his pacifist principles. Didi won the war with Japan but lost the day to the sadistic Spanish prison officer Isidrio, who put Myagi in with Gilbert the frog and moved the most outrageous transsexual in the prison, Pu-Rambo, in with Didi.

Pu-Rambo was a big, thick-necked, muscular tripe hound, taken to wearing bright red lipstick and posturing like a rampant rhino. The piss-take with Didi would run for weeks, especially after their first night together when Jake asked to see how far down his shaft did the lip-ring go, to reveal how deeply he'd been swallowed. The lipstick on Pu-Rambo's face put me in mind of a beef tomato sat in the middle of a welder's bench. We all laughed about who was the pillow-biter: Didi or his cellmate?

Myagi settled in with Gilbert the frog and things were fine in the cell, but he was not welcome on the frog dinner table, so he made enquiries about the English table, or the *Mezclado*, as it was now known. Chinky told me he had been asking about dining with us, but had told him that I was boss of the table so he had to ask me. Myagi had a problem with that because I'd told him to fuck off the other day. Nevertheless, he made his approach to our table in his painfully polite, Japanese way.

'Ah, Chancer *San*. I have been told you are *sensei* in honourable ju-jitsu school.'

'So what?' I growled. 'What's it to you, Myagi?'

He stood to attention before me, then stiffly bowed with his hands by his sides.

'I am *shodan* in honourable Japanese judo. I am *kodokan* trained and qualified, *sensei*.'

I quickly got to my feet and returned the bow; much to the

125

amusement and interest of nearby onlookers, but with none of them making a sound.

'You surprise me, Myagi. You don't behave like a dan-grade *judoka.*'

'No, *sensei.* I try to live non-violent life. Judo is my sport, not my weapon,' he said, still standing to attention.

'That's probably very nice in Tokyo, but here in the Carabanchel you'll need to make use of it or suffer the duffing overs you're going to get. The gypos already have you targeted so you'll find out all about it in a minute. Anyway, what do you want with me?'

'First, I want join your school. Second, I want join your table.'

'Sit down,' I said, thinking furiously. I was excited about having a formally trained martial artist in my combat class, especially a black belt *judoka*, but he still hadn't told me why he was locked up in the Carabanchel.

'You know, Myagi, the word Bushido has several interpretations. Well, for me there is only one: the way of the warrior. The word belongs to your language, so you'll know better than me. Bushido doesn't allow me to consort with homosexuals, paedophiles, rapists and other foul bastards, who are everywhere in this Spanish shitbin; they are all around us here in this yard as I speak. So which category do you come under, Myagi? And please, do not insult my intelligence by telling me you are innocent.'

Blinking his slant eyes, he lowered his head to his chest and said into his singlet, 'Counterfeiter; copycat; craftsman. That's what I am, *sensei.* Please keep secret.'

'Show me your charge-sheet before you join my table and if I see you kowtow or buy another gypo a coffee, you're on your fucking own.'

'I'll show you my charge-sheet, but only you are to know my trade. Tell the others I'm an embezzler; that should satisfy them.'

Just then Ali arrived with coffee and biscuits, looking puzzled at the departing Jap.

'He wants to join our table,' I said, pre-empting his question. 'He's showing me his charge-sheet later.'

'What's he done?' snarled Ali, passing me an americano and two chocolate biscuits.

PHYSICAL JERKS

I could never lie to Ali, so I said, 'Keep it under your turban; he's a counterfeiter, but I'll tell the others he's an embezzler.'

I munched my biscuits and swigged the hot americano. My teeth and gums were managing much better by now.

'Guess what?' I said between swigs.

'What?' said Ali, gob hanging open expectantly.

'He's a fucking black belt!'

'The Shah's bollocks he is; more like a *shalwar* belt.'

'What the fuck's a *shalwar*?'

'Oh, sorry. That's Afghani for pyjamas,' said Ali, grinning like Bluto.

'Anyway, we'll soon see; he's joining the combat class.'

Ali choked on his *manzanilla* (camomile) tea.

'This I must see. When's he starting?'

'Next week's first session, depending what's on his charge-sheet.'

Ali chuckled between swigs of herbal tea: a big, powerful man, a killer of men, a true warrior, but he seemed amusingly quaint sipping his tea with his little finger outstretched.

'When are we going to start training?' he said, draining his teacup.

It was Saturday, so the gym was closed, which meant any training had to be done in the yard.

'Let me get this coffee down and we'll start jogging to loosen up. Then we'll do the blocking, kicking and punching routine followed by some hard sparring and blocking,' I said.

'Good. We'll get a good sweat on, ready for the showers before lunch,' said Ali, enthusiastically jumping to his feet, doing the Ali shuffle and laughing.

Training in the yard was always eventful; someone always wanted to take the piss or correct our techniques. The Spanish couldn't resist an opportunity to exercise their stupidity by insulting professionals like Ali and Vito: men with outstanding physiques and lightning-fast reactions to personal threats; men like Jake, the giant bouncer, capable of ripping the scalp and face from a skull; and then there was Chinky, Bruce Lee in disguise, ready to slice your gullet and pull your tongue through the slit before your eyes closed.

Chronic machismo drove these Spanish clowns into the ring

whenever we trained. When an oily dipstick insulted or even threatened the likes of Ali Safave, bravado was not the word to describe it, and this day would see another brutal end to our training session. We started with an easy jog, running clockwise around the yard with the flow of the strolling inmates. Several blokes joined in as we lapped the walkers again and again until there were possibly 12 or more blokes nicely warmed up, ready for some *chi gung* stretching routines. We commandeered the shaded area in the far corner of the yard and started our training schedule.

Week in, week out, this schedule seldom changed. Every Saturday and Sunday was the same, except for attack training: I varied that from day to day. We concentrated a lot on abdominal training: a great deal of time and effort went into sit-ups and heel-raising exercises. Tough abdominals are a must in the martial-arts world; even if your six pack is hiding under a layer of fat, you must keep those muscles constantly tuned up.

The training I devised was to promote flexibility and endurance, because combat training demands the ability to perform rigorous and physically demanding throwing, striking, choking, breaking, kicking, stomping, gouging, biting, punching and killing techniques in order to tear apart a fellow human being, regardless of how knackered you are.

I ended the fitness routine with a final blast of squat-thrusts, then went immediately into kicks, blocks and punches. Part of this training involved the kicking of each other's guts with a *mae geri* front kick directed at waist level. Your training partner would hold a rolled-up towel or jacket against his lower abdomen to absorb some of the clout as you drove the ball of your foot into him. It was during this kicking practice that the incident happened that ended the training session in such a memorable way.

Several groups of spectators had gathered at our end of the yard. It being Saturday, a lot of dragons had been chased, due to the weekend smack delivery in the welly-top fannies of the visiting wives and girlfriends. Oh . . . and mothers.

We were busy practising front kicks into the stomach when a spectator decided that a football-style kick into the bollocks would be more effective. So, full of dragon fumes and egged on by his *compadres*, he targeted Chinky's bollocks: Chinky being the smallest of us.

My Chinese friend was busy taking kicks from his training partner, a similarly built Russian called Sergie. Before I could intervene, the junkie had stepped between these very dangerous men and had his hand on Sergie's shoulder whilst trying to kick Chinky's bollocks. Sergie drove his palm-heel into the idiot's elbow joint, sending a wave of agony though the heroin haze that created the beginnings of a scream, which was choked off by the crunch of Chinky's right boot as it impacted the Spanish throat: no cock sucking tonight, José. That should have been the end of it, but the dragon's flame had ignited national pride and sent half a dozen *toreadors* to restore it. They rushed across the yard towards us but stopped short when the blood started spurting. The screws raced across the yard blowing whistles and waving truncheons but it was all over before they arrived.

Seven bleeding bodies lay moaning in the sunshine as we stood silently in the shade. The onlookers screamed blue murder and postured threateningly, knowing full well that should they step into the shade they would join their *compadres* bleeding in the sunlight. The screws could see how dangerous we were, gathered silently as a disciplined troop in the shade of the wall. It truly grieved them to know we were not at fault; we were not the problem. Their baying countrymen with their toothless-tiger antics were giving them grief, screaming and shaking fists in an empty gesture of revenge: complete bollocks.

The tumult had to be stopped pronto, so the screws turned on their countrymen, shoving and pushing them away from our area as we watched in silence. They prodded the gypsies and cajoled the *payos* as the walking wounded slunk away, helped by their *compadres*, but the gurney had to be called for the clown who'd attacked Vito. I'd witnessed the junkie taking a lunge at Vito with a *pinchou* fashioned from the leg bone of a pig. Like Carlos's broom handle it had notches cut into the shank filled with rat shit: a favourite gypsy embellishment. Vito parried the lunge with a reverse arm strike and attacked the elbow joint with a left arm *empi* (elbow strike) to break the arm. Keeping his grip on the broken arm,

Vito drove his knee into the clavicle, making an audible crack as the collarbone broke. Pulling the gypsy erect by his hair, Vito buried the rat-shit *pinchou* deep into the shoulder of the wrecked collarbone, then slipped his forearm under the chin to apply a violent, jerking choke, pulling him backwards into unconsciousness. He then slammed him into the floor of the yard, the junkie's head cracking noisily as it whiplashed into the unyielding concrete, causing further concussion. Vito quickly found his next target and delivered a *haito uchi* ridge-hand strike into the Adam's apple, followed by a savage knee-drop into the same part of the throat; then the screws arrived.

Vito's dark eyes had a look of satisfaction about them. His stance and body movement seemed serene and calm as he turned his back on the screws to slowly walk further into the shade, away from the insult of blue serge and grease.

I had a lot of respect for this unrepentant assassin, whose life stemmed from the primitive paternalism of the Sicilian hills before entering the arena of the international heroin trade. He had soberly and proudly honed his killing skills in order to earn the respect of those who employed him. Vito was of the rare breed of modern Mafia to whom loyalty meant everything; he would never question or attempt to justify any of his actions, simply because he was obeying the master whose hand he kissed. He was a man of few words, but to me, his *sensei*, he spilled a lot of beans; not just any old beans, but meaningful and memorable insights into the cold, dispassionate, brutal world of the debt collector, venturing fearlessly into the perilous dens of heroin users and dealers, where life means nothing. Love, to Vito, was some vague memory of the feeling he'd shared with his mother: no other had ever come close to that in Vito's life. His emotions hovered somewhere between fear and whatever he felt at the kill, though he would never show on his face anything other than a half-smile, regardless of what was going down.

Though his fieldcraft skills and his cunning put him in the top echelons of the Mafia hit-men, his simple weaponry made him a one-man hit-squad. I was amazed when he told me about his kit. The tools of his trade were quite basic and consisted of: a T-handled knife (which fitted in the palm of his hand so he could make a fist with the blade protruding between his middle fingers, enabling him to punch the blade into the target); a low-powered 9 mm Beretta (an old 1915 model), which he said was sufficient as he always stood next to the target when he fired; and a one-metre length of cheesewire toggled at each end, used for garrotting. Obviously, Vito was a skilful up-close predator.

He spoke always in monotones, droning on and on, but paradoxically thrilling me with his tales of exquisite planning, timing and execution. He was never boring, never boastful and never regretted a single day's work. His only vague brag was that he had Giuseppe Russo's genes in his blood (whoever the fuck he was).

Vito was the kind of man who sought education wherever he could. Hence, he deliberately practised his self-taught English whenever he spoke to me. Considering that I was the only person in his life ever to correct him, his English was especially good. He thought fate would take him to America; that's why he'd bothered to learn the language in the first place. Everything that Vito attempted to do was undertaken with intense determination. He became an avid student of the martial arts and wanted to learn the Japanese terminology, which, incidentally, sparked Myagi into organising a Japanese language class. It goes without saying that this was a complete fiasco.

Vito's pursuit of physical excellence was torturous to say the least. His bird was spent learning English and beasting his body into symmetrical magnificence. He was the most enthusiastic bloke in the world and taught me important lessons in my school of life. I feel I am a better man for having shared some time with him. He stayed with me for two years behind the high walls of the Carabanchel and La Moraleja prisons. *Ciao* Vito, wherever you are. Respect.

NINE
THE EVIL EYE

The man was in the far corner of the gymnasium sitting on the leg-press bench. His jet-black hair looked greasy, as though brilliantined, as his unshaven chin rested on his chest with his head cocked to one side. I noticed that he was looking at me, despite the angle of his head, because I saw the whites of his eyes as he swivelled them 90 degrees in my direction. He was no stranger to me; I had seen him in the gymnasium several times before: always alone, always silent.

He bore the hallmarks of a Spanish gypsy, but was seemingly aloof, as though he was a famous flamenco dancer, which he was not. He was completely mad. He had the striking looks of Banderas, the film star, which could melt the hearts of a million señoritas, but the gleam shining from his glittering eyes tainted the image of beautiful masculinity with the mark of insanity. These simmering, sensual looks changed to an expression of molten hate whenever they focused on anyone he didn't like, which was practically everyone. This must be how a magpie appears to a baby bird the moment before it is devoured: monstrous.

I could feel his gaze boring into me as I turned my back to him. I was grappling with Ali Safave at the time, so I said to him, 'What's with that cunt on the leg-press bench?'

'Oh, the Shah's bedpan!' he said. 'That man is cursed with the evil eye.' Ali tried to pull me off balance, then growled, 'Remember

133

what the Devil said: "If you bear malice to anybody, look on them with open eyes and pray evil for them in my name and you will get your heart's desires." They call him Brujo, which means sorcerer. *La ilah illalah.'*

I took Ali down hard with a leg-sweep during his moment of distraction, but he was back on his feet and into me like a whirling dervish.

'I see the evil eye caught you, my brother, or you would never have put me down so deceptively,' growled Ali, as he stomped on my forward foot, practically breaking it.

'Yeah, you're right, as usual. C'mon, let's finish and get a drink.'

We faced each other and bowed respectfully, then I dismissed the rest of the class with a communal bow so that Ali and I could sweep the mats and tidy up for the day. Everybody else was handing in various bits of equipment they had signed out, while others were in the showers and changing-rooms getting ready to leave. Ali often helped me to clean up at the end of the session, then we would go to the wing *economato* together for coffee before the evening meal.

We had stacked the *tatami*, swept the floor and then ambled in amongst the stragglers in the shower room. The sound of splashing water welcomed us to the shocking sight of Brujo shagging a young Colombian chap under one of the showers. We could see that the boy's ear had been partially bitten off and Brujo was eating it as he viciously thrust his scarred, misshapen cock into the youngster's backside. I was momentarily stunned as I witnessed the gnarled, mutilated dick of the madman disappear between the buttocks of the young, virgin arse. The blood from the chewed ear mixed with the shower water made it look even worse than it was, as several gawping Spaniards looked on in silence.

Ali and I moved as one towards the rapist then stopped in our tracks as we saw the wicked *pinchou* being pressed into the ribs on the blind side: another move from us and the boy would die on the end of a madman's dick. We watched helplessly as Brujo fired his contaminated seed into the youngster, then allowed his slackening, ugly cock to flop out and dangle under the cleansing shower water cascading over the unforgettable scene. He savagely grabbed the boy's hair and yanked him upright. Then, like a rabid dog, he bit into the half-eaten ear in readiness for another beasting. The agonising scream galvanised Ali and I into instant action, despite the glinting spike being pushed into the boy's ribs.

Brujo's attention was held by the toughness of the ear he was biting into, so he didn't see the knockout blow he received just beneath his own ear. Ali grabbed the wrist that had been pushing the spike into the boy's ribs and swiftly broke the offending arm. The young Colombian was unable to control his bowels and the contents fell to the bloody floor right next to the unconscious Brujo's face. The boy knelt and scooped his droppings into the open mouth of his despoiler, cramming it full of steaming shit, then, with studious urgency, pushed it down the madman's throat with his fingers.

As the last of the shit was packed into the gullet, Ali silently handed the boy Brujo's *pinchou*, then we all watched as he stabbed and slashed at the ghastly, mutilated cock then ploughed the spike into the perineum, the barse, that sensitive little bit between bollocks and arse. If Brujo didn't die that day, his crotch would remind him of his day out at the prison gymnasium for a long painful time. Brujo's beautiful face was next. The Colombian plastic surgeon was about to change its good looks forever and was removing an ear when the screws arrived to disturb this delicate operation. He quickly bit off the end of Brujo's nose as they yanked him off the shit-stinking face of the sorcerer.

We were all herded out and ordered to write statements accusing the Colombian of attempted murder. I wrote my statement in English, accusing the Spanish judiciary of allowing a convicted sociopath to mingle freely with remand prisoners, highlighting the fact that the Spanish were centuries behind the rest of Europe. I heard no more about the case, nor heard of Brujo or the Colombian ever again. Ali told me many times during the following year that he regretted not slipping the *pinchou* into Brujo's brain.

Creatures such as Brujo were rare indeed in South-west Asia (Ali's stamping ground). The people there should be forgiven for thinking that Brujo and his ilk were the stuff of primitive folk tales – a species no longer roaming the earth – not part of the everyday goings-on in a modern European prison, especially as the Spanish thought that it was Ali's part of the world that was primitive and cruel. Hmmm . . .

TEN
THE BLACK WARLORD

Tupak was a big Negro, a ruthless ruler of a downtown area of Madrid where he controlled all drugs, whores and blaggings. The biggest thing about Tupak was his dick, followed by his mouth, then his reputation.

I actually enjoyed talking to this son of an African chief who sported tribal scars around his face and along his enormous schlong, which he loved to display in the showers. Tupak deserves a few words here, not only for me to brag about seeing the biggest human dick in the world, but also to explain his, and its, reasons for being with me in the Carabanchel.

He was down to serve two years because a Spanish thief had grassed him to the Spanish Old Bill. The thief was employed as a waiter and was caught by the proprietor dipping the Jewish piano (cash register) and instantly sacked. Unfortunately, the thief knew about the proprietor being one of the many clients of Tupak, receiving a weekly packet of cocaine. So, being a Spaniard, he did the normal Spanish thing and promptly grassed his ex-boss.

Tupak never touched the shit – he had plenty of soldiers to do that for him – but he personally collected the cash every week from the bars and restaurants in his parish. He ran a protection racket, an escort agency and several brothels, sold every drug under the sun and milked his manor ruthlessly. So one would think this was the best place for him. That is precisely what the Spanish Old Bill thought and promptly arrested him on the word of a thieving waiter. There were no drugs or other evidence to link him to the crime: just his reputation. The Spanish restaurateur sold the cocaine to his customers, but he wasn't arrested. Only Tupak was taken downtown, charged and sentenced and here he was, flashing his gigantic conga eel around the shower block.

'When I get out, I'm gonna give dat judge's daughter a fuckin' big bag of smack, free! An' den I'm gonna pack my salami in 'is missus's minge. She'll be no fuckin' use to 'im after she's 'ad a ride on dis fucker,' roared Tupak, holding his pole proudly like a standard bearer on the Queen's birthday parade, the giant Walnut Whip looking angry on the end of his flagpole.

We always had a good laugh whenever Tupak came into the shower block. He should have been a blue-movie star; he wouldn't be in here and he'd be a millionaire now. Dutch always took the piss: 'You can't be much of a fuckin' dancer, Tupak. You get a hard on with that fuckin' thing an' you'll be standin' on one leg!'

'I only does the pole dance, smart arse, an' dancin' is foreplay. I only need to shake my knee an' the shakin' trouser snake brings 'em a-runnin', grinnin' like a wankin' Jap.'

'Ah so, leave me out of your disgusting arguments!' cried Mr Myagi, as the shower block erupted with laughter.

'The cunts can't stop us from laughing, can they,' chuckled Dutch.

Tupak was as fun-loving as any family man, but his family were the whores and henchmen who continued to operate his business while he was locked up. Every visiting session brought his lieutenants and top brass (female whore-master) to report on business and banking. His case was dried and dusted but his lawyer still came to see him to receive instructions regarding the goings-on in the street. His lawyer employed a clerk who could visit Tupak whenever necessary. The clerk was an ex-KGB executioner known as Ivan the Terrible, now living in Madrid. He was employed by Tupak to control erring gang members. His day job in the legal profession gave him unlimited access to the prison visitor's block; need I say more?

The day soon came when Tupak propositioned me to work for him.

'Gorra minute?' he said as he strolled by with two coffees.

I caught up with him and he handed me a coffee.

'Over there,' he said, nodding towards the shaded far corner of the yard. We strolled unhurriedly with the flow of the crowd until we reached the place where we could sit out of the sun's glare. The shade instantly shut off the niggling bite of the merciless rays and I felt comfortable and cool as we sat on the concrete slab that served as a bench on this side of the yard.

'I hate the fuckin' sun. Look what it did to me,' he said, holding out his hands and turning them over, showing off the jet-black skin on the back of his hands just like a little boy showing his mother how well he'd washed them. 'I have yet to see the man with a deeper tan than mine,' he laughed.

'It's not the blackness of your skin I worry about, Tupak. How black is your fucking soul?'

'Oh, please, man, don't say t'ings like dat. I hurt nobody,' he said, raising his eyebrows to expose the whites of his eyes to give an expression of innocence that only a Negro can achieve.

'Oh, so what the fuck is Ivan the Terrible doing in town?'

'Who da fuck told you about him?'

'None of your fucking business how I find things out.'

'It must be dat cunt Lewis on *galería siete*. 'E's one of my runners on da street, an' 'e's in your fuckin' judo class, ain't 'e.'

'Keep fucking guessing, Tupak. You'll never know how I know every fucking thing.'

We each took a swig of coffee, looking over the rim of the cup into each other's eyes, searching: for what? I could see no menace lurking in those watery brown pools: no danger, no trickery, just calmness. But looking into my eyes was a ruthless warlord who had somehow seized control of a downtown area of Madrid and was still controlling it with a mailed fist whilst being locked up here in the Carabanchel.

Tupak was clever and obviously not a man to cross.

'You see fairness in me, Chancer. I pay a fair day's pay for a fair day's work.'

His brow furrowed as I said, 'There's a lot more than work to be paid for, if you think you're doing something with me.'

'I know you 'ave da contacts an' all I've got is da money to pay for everyt'ing.'

'You want hashish, don't you?' I said, smirking slyly at him over my coffee cup.

'Yeah, man. I buy my gear 'ere in town. I've got several sources but I don't trust any of 'em. I reckon if dey gets rumbled dey'll give me up for an easy ride. Da same goes for da Charlie an' da smack. Dis place 'as opened my eyes, man. I did'n' realise 'ow fuckin' risky it all is till I met dis fuckin' lot. Everybody 'as been grassed by a fuckin' spick, an' 'ere I am dealin' wid da fuckers. All my suppliers are spicks. All right, dey's fuckin' frightened of me – da cunt what put me in 'ere will be dead by Christmas – but now dat I've seen dis, I mus' change t'ings. So now I 'ave a deal for you on de out.'

'Tell me all about it,' I said, as Chinky arrived with coffee and biscuits.

'The udders'll be across in a minute,' Chinky sang in his Cantonese lilt. 'We got anudder ploblem wid dem fuckin' gypos.'

Tupak harrumphed loudly and said, 'Do I 'ave your ear for dis, coz I'll talk to you later if I 'ave.'

I took the coffee off Chinky and said, 'Yeah, we'll talk tonight. Come to my cell for the hour's lock-in, we'll go through it then.'

'Great,' he said, 'then I'll tell you 'ow I keeps dem fuckin' gypos off my back wid Ivan the Terrible,' he chuckled, as he got to his feet and walked away. It struck me then that nobody from the gypsy camp ever went near Tupak.

Throughout the time I spent with Tupak the Warlord, he was never anything less than a gentleman and a man of his word. Tupak served two whole years with me, not ever getting into trouble and not receiving a single day's remission off his sentence. Such is life for a Negro in the Spanish prison system: racism rules here. The Generalissimo (Franco) is long dead, but the little man's big shadow still stains this pisshole prison, which was his favourite death pit.

ELEVEN
A REAL WARLORD

'I need a favour of you,' said Ali, passing me a coffee and a Kit-Kat. We were sitting in the early morning sunshine and it was Sunday; so there was no work today, just training and relaxing. Jake and Chinky arrived, creating a fuss about the hawking and spitting: part of the indigenous culture.

Vito chided Chinky about his own noisy nasal discharges, so a hubbub of lively banter was brewing nicely. Jake let fly with one of his trombone farts, setting the scene for some hilarious attempts at English profanity.

'What's the matter?' I asked Ali, between chuckles.

'I have a friend in the Bronx who is to be transferred to this wing tomorrow. He is Afghani and is having a hard time with the spicks.'

Ali sounded truly concerned, so I asked, 'What's the favour?'

'I would like him to join our table.'

'Oh c'mon, Ali, you know any friend of yours would be welcome.'

'That's nice, but he may bring problems because he has upset the spick police; that's why they put him in the Bronx and you know what the Bronx is like.'

The Bronx was well known to the prisoners of the Carabanchel. It was a cell that contained twelve beds in three stacks of four, with one concrete sink and a single concrete shitter. It was used to house prisoners who had done no wrong inside the prison, so it was not a punishment like being sent down the block to solitary confinement, but rather a big stick to be used by someone on the out to get their own back: like a pissed off judge or copper, or even the Diplomatic Corps, as seemed to be the case here. So I asked, 'What has he done?'

The *Mezclado* fell into silence as the banter ceased in readiness for a new story.

'My friend is mujahidin, a top man, a commander in the Afghani Resistance against Russia. He came to Madrid to do business with brown sugar, but was ripped off and grassed by his spick partners, who stole 80 kilos then had him arrested for possessing a few grams. He got six years.'

A buzz of indignation flared up, then died instantly as Ali Safave continued the tale.

'He passed the information to his family in Kandahar and vengeance was swift. The assassins arrived in Madrid to kill the spicks, then disappeared back to Afghanistan. The police knew it was a revenge killing by the mujahidin, but could do nothing. So my friend gets a hard time.'

'Why are they letting him out of the Bronx?' asked Jake, trying hard not to look too incredulous.

'I believe his family put a message through diplomatic corridors that it would be a good idea to treat him well, seeing as there's a few senior Spanish diplomats outside of Spain, if you know what I mean.'

Vito eyeballed Ali, saying, 'He must be an important man to have diplomats on his side.'

'He is,' said Ali knowingly.

'Then why was he trading heroin in Madrid?'

This was said with no animosity or suspicion, just a straight, meaningful question.

'His family own the poppy fields. They process the heroin and ship it around the world. The money was used to pay the Pakistanis for guns that the Americans had donated for free, but the Pakis made them pay. That was how it used to be. My friend speaks several languages so he'd take time off from the fighting in order to raise funds for the jihad. So though the Russians failed, the business continued,' said Ali, proudly.

A REAL WARLORD

In many ways Vito and Ali were alike, insomuch as they had each trod the primrose path and were unrepentant for their deeds. It seems a paradox that these villains possessed high moral principles and lived by an old-fashioned code of honour and chivalry that was scoffed at by modern man. These men would never betray their ancestors by cheating, lying or stealing; or being disloyal or dishonest in any way that would shame their family or their own conscience. It is difficult to get one's head around such noble sentiment whilst simultaneously using the word 'heroin'. I fear that unless you get to know such men you will never understand the paradox nor solve the enigma of chivalrous prisoners.

It is rare indeed to find the notions of honour, courage and concern for the weak in prison writing. But there I was, surrounded by such nobility, and the next day saw an addition in the form of Abdulla Habibullah of the mujahidin: an educated, courageous leader of daring warriors who faced the ignorant, cruel peasantry of the Russian army and the appalling, indiscriminate killers of the Russian air force for over ten years.

Russia, of course, ultimately failed to overrun Afghanistan, and therefore I'm not disputing the fact that the proceeds of the heroin industry were no longer needed to buy arms for the Resistance Movement. It would be foolish of me to attempt a guess at where all those millions are spent. But, for the sake of this book and because the man became my friend, I will tell you about a real warlord.

When I first clocked him, he looked quite diminutive alongside the hulking frame of Ali Safave. He was about the same size as Chinky, a different colour and a different eye arrangement. His eyes looked half-closed, but not quite the oriental squint. His nose was beautifully convex, sitting atop a thick, black moustache, giving him a look of serenity about as far removed from a killer of Russian soldiers as ET.

His first words to me were mumbled and sounded like, '*Assalamu alaikum*, Christopher *Khan*, blah, blah, blah, *inshallah.*' Then he said, 'How do you do, Christopher, so nice to meet you at last.'

His public schoolboy accent came as a surprise as we shook hands vigorously, then released our hands to touch our hearts to underline the honour of the meeting. Some wags say that this is to wipe off the shit from the hand of the infidel, so think what you like.

One unusual thing about him was the amount of hair growing on the top edge of his ears. It was hanging over in a fringe and was fine in texture in comparison with his thick moustache. He wore Western clothes, though a bit baggy and slack looking, and on his feet the ubiquitous leather-soled flip-flops (which looked like a hand-me-down from Mahatma Gandhi).

I was standing in the gaze of a very brave man whose wife and sons had been slaughtered by the trespassing Russian army and the more I thought about the gross injustice perpetrated by the leaders of that fuckpig of a country, the more it did my head in. Don't think that they broke the mould when Stalin died. On the contrary: more than one leader since has followed his genocidal leanings, leaving bloody footsteps all over the show. A pox on those jealous, grabbing bastards.

Abdulla met each member of the *Mezclado* and offered to buy coffee, but Jake and Chinky ushered him between me and Ali on the concrete bench then strode away to the *economato* for the group's coffee and biscuits.

Abdulla and Ali chatted across me in Farsi until I raised my hand and said, 'Speak English or fuck off.'

The two of them immediately sat back as Abdulla said, 'We were saying only good things about you, Christopher, so we used our own language to prevent your embarrassment.'

Abdulla was obviously alarmed at his faux pas so soon after meeting me.

'OK, nice, but when you're with me you speak only English, OK?'

'Yes, no problem. It will not happen again.'

All that day Abdulla stayed with me, joining me for our strolls around the yard and standing nearby when we were training. The inevitable happened the following day when I was in the *zapatería*: he was accosted in the coffee queue.

Apparently he politely refused to buy cigarettes and coffee for a group of gypsies and was being jostled when Jake and Chinky upgraded the jostle into a full-blown punch-up. Chinky told me later that Abdulla was a fearless and skilful scrapper with fast hands; several gypos were nursing poked eyes. I felt good about that, he must have been watching carefully as we practised *nukite* strikes yesterday.

'When we are in freedom, you must come to my house in Kandahar.'

I'll never forget those words from Abdulla and one day I hope to see his house in Afghanistan. We talked every day about the Russians or how to move heroin around the world. I vowed never to deal with heroin, but guess what grows next to it in Afghanistan? Yep! Afghan Black, the supershit hashish which keeps Canada and Australia happy. 'Kandy' is the mass-produced Afghan Black for the Australian and Canadian markets and comes from the Kandahar region: hence the name.

We made plans to break into the UK market with Afghan Black and spent many hours plotting and planning the methods and routes to move significant amounts of the Afghan happy herb to Britain. These included routes via Karachi in Pakistan, through the Red Sea and on through the Suez Canal, or along the camel route across Iran and Turkey and into the Mediterranean Sea.

We studied many ideas and plans because that's what prison is all about: meeting like-minded adventurers with the nous and guts to get on with it when the time was right. Due to the mountains of money derived from the wholesaling of heroin, Abdulla was prepared to purchase a craft of my choosing to sail from Karachi to the port of discharge. I spent many hours poring over motor-sailer and yacht specifications and sales blurbs, until eventually I decided on a cutter-rigged, blue water cruiser that required only a two- or three-man crew. My second choice was a ketch-rigged motor-sailer; a sturdy Fischer, capable of stowing three tonnes of Afghan Black without too much bother.

They were great plans, with detailed priority lists of tasks. The complicated web of logistics was made simple by concentrated preparation and planning in the Operations Room of prison, where time was plentiful and free from the distractions of freedom. We spent undisturbed hours poring over maps and charts brought in by pet screws, managing the glitches out of the system by constantly inventing possible problems and solving or finding ways to avoid them, gleaning information from Turkish and Arab inmates about movement control and hazards across Iran and Turkey. Thanks to my inquisitiveness and ability to communicate with fellow inmates, I discovered a route from Afghanistan through Iran and Turkey to the Black Sea and along the Danube into Europe. This may seem far-fetched, but I've spoken to blokes who have actually travelled various legs of this route, so it was feasible, especially as I had the contact numbers of people along the way. Without putting too fine a point on the detail, I can tell you that one of the routes I planned ended in a cider barn on the edge of Dartmoor in glorious Devon.

The irony of this choice was that the cargo would be Zodiaced into Smuggler's Cove at Holcombe, between Teignmouth and Dawlish on the south Devonshire coast. The only problem with unloading there was that, if easterly winds were blowing, a heavy sea could have been whipped up, which would have made unloading impossible due to the narrow space underneath the main London–Plymouth railway line.

'Smuggler's Cove, eh? Ooh arr, me hearties! Pass they fuckin' bottles o' brandy, Long John, us'll get pissed this night, an' fuck they Excise bastards in Teignmouth harbour. Aye, lad.'

Wishful thinking, if you like, but you never know your luck.

One of Abdulla's cap feathers was his transport expertise. He shifted tonnes of ammo and weapons around the Hindu Kush and all points west to Iran: Kandahar and Herat being his preferred stamping grounds. Now, of course, the camels and donkeys carry a different cargo, though the risks and hazards are still plentiful.

He told me he learned about transport the hard way, when his father put him with a bloke called Agha Gul who organised many mujahidin mountain convoys during the early days of the Russian invasion. Many of Abdulla's tales were wasted on me simply because I couldn't grasp the complicated clan differences of the mujahidin. They all supposedly fought the common enemy, Russia, but they were at each other's throats all the time. However, his contacts in Afghanistan and Pakistan were priceless.

Senior Afghan and Pakistani officials, both military and civil, turned a blind eye to him during the years of Russian trespassing, when opium-laden donkeys stumbled over the mountain passes into

Pakistan, heading for the processing plants at Quetta and Peshawar, where his relatives produced and packed the end product, which was then sent along the chain of relatives and friends to Karachi, from where it went all over the show.

According to Abdulla, the intervention of foreign powers during the struggle against the Soviets caused the opium floodgates to open. Frontier police, Excise officials and various government personnel were easily persuaded and paid off because they were helping the struggle against the Communists. Hurrah! You can tell that one to the Ayatollah.

I had just come out of the shower block and was strolling alone with the flow of the shuffling throng when a Moroccan bloke caught my sleeve and said, 'Your Arab friend *tiene un problema con el gitano en el servicio.*' It was a Sunday morning and the *Mezclado* were still in the shower block. I hadn't yet seen Abdulla, so I knew my 'Arab friend' was he.

I asked the Moroccan to run to the shower block to tell the others, then I dashed away to the stinking communal toilets in search of Abdulla. As I neared the entrance, I clocked two gypos keeping nicks (lookouts). They clocked my approach and readied themselves to block my entrance. I caught the tallest one with a *mae geri* front kick to the pubic bone, then poleaxed him with an *empi* elbow strike to the back of his neck as he doubled over. His mate stepped backwards to let me pass, so I dropped him with a very hard *uraken* back-fist to the philtrum nerve, just above his upper lip. I felt the teeth collapse inwards against my knuckles, instantly putting him in a coma.

I didn't spare them a second thought as I leapt into the stinking Spanish shithole, every nerve in my body tingling with apprehension as I searched for my friend Abdulla. The fumes of heroin hung heavily with the cannabis smoke, adding flavour to the shitty fog of this disgusting place.

I could make out a huddle of blokes in the corner through the spectators dotted around, silently watching the attempted murder of my friend Abdulla, who was in the corner with his back to the wall. In that millisecond of recognition, I could see contempt and determination in his eyes and his face contorted with rage as he

147

fended off blow after blow from the three greasy maggots attacking him. Blood dripped from his shirtsleeves, running out of the punctures in his forearms where the *pinchou* had penetrated. His ear was slashed clean through and hung down, waggling like a cockscomb. In that instant I knew they would kill him if he succumbed to their onslaught. I had arrived in the nick of time.

The nearest gypsy didn't know what hit him as I devastated his kidney with a tremendous punch that practically broke him in two. I grabbed the second gypsy by the hair, yanking his head backwards, then stomped his leg behind the knee, forcing him to kneel on that knee in order to lower his body, allowing me to bludgeon his nose and throat with my elbow. I grappled the *pinchou* from his weakening grasp and then drove it into his buttock, where I felt it strike a bone. I left it embedded there so I could attack his dirty hands. I snapped all the fingers and dislocated his thumbs, then wrecked each wrist, just so he would remember his day out in the perfumed palace of varieties: the Carabanchel shithouse.

Abdulla was busy taking apart his attacker when Ali Safave bounded into the stinking bog and dropped an innocent bystander with a pile-driving axe kick. I couldn't be arsed as he started punching his way around the shithouse. I thought 'Fuck it' as he battered protesting spectators who should have helped Abdulla.

Gypsy reinforcements arrived to overcrowd the dance floor, then Vito, Jake and Chinky rumbled in right behind them as Dutch and his clog mates blocked the door. The sound of pounding flesh filled the air as spectators and gypsies were punched and kicked into the shithouse cubicles, where they were beaten senseless to lie soaking in the piss, shit and snot of this heaving Spanish bog.

I thought momentarily about taking control of the situation but forgot it instantly as a long-haired nutter called Kiko came at me with his chiv – another ornamentally carved animal bone – which I deftly removed from his sleeping fingers after I blocked his lunge and slammed my fist into his throat. A quick inspection of the point showed three grooves packed with what looked like human shit, so I cleaned his weapon by stabbing it into his pectoral muscle, just beneath the nipple. I stabbed him at an angle, so as not to pierce his ribs, then gave it a smart twist to make sure the contents of the three grooves would be dislodged when someone removed it from his flesh.

We had just about finished when Dutch called a warning about the screws getting excited in their office. We were dispersed around the yard before they discovered the blood and shit in the toilet block.

Apart from thanking me for intervening, Abdulla never mentioned it again: typical mujahidin. In true Afghan style he sewed his own ear with a needle and thread with some help from Vito. He also fixed his other wounds himself and, to my knowledge, never once was treated by a Spanish doctor during all his years in Spanish prisons. He was not a big man, but in my eyes his stature put the Hindu Kush into the shade: a mujahidin warlord with the heart of a lion.

TWELVE
BEHIND THE DOOR

My cell was always noisy until Enrico switched off the television and said *'Buenas noches'* then went to sleep. I craved privacy and began to rue the day I allowed Kennedy then Enrico to share my cell. But wishful thinking occupies much of a prisoner's thoughts, so much so that the plus points are ignored. I told myself that I should be grateful for Kennedy and Enrico as my cellmates, rather than some sly, greasy twat like the creature living next door.

I remembered him asking to share my cell before Kennedy arrived. I had struggled to overcome my repugnance because the repulsive odour from this man was foul enough to stop a clock, and when he walked into his cell, the cockroaches ran out. His name was Rodriguez, a burly Spanish gypsy who was a member of the Madrid chapter of *Angeles del Infierno* – the Hell's Angels. I'd thought the Hell's Angels were very particular when selecting their initiates. Rodriguez was an example of how wrong I could sometimes be.

Just a bit further along the gallery, past Rodriguez's cell, was the end of the safety net for this level of *galería cinco*, which housed four floors of cells. The top floor (my level) was approximately 40 ft above the ground floor, providing a reasonably high diving platform for the blokes who wanted to commit sideways (otherwise known as suicide, hara-kiri, *Selbstmord*).

To comply with European standards, safety netting was strung between the opposing cell levels across the gallery. A sporting gap was left open, though, at the end of each level furthest away from the screws' office, to enable the serious kamikaze to jack-knife his way to oblivion. For the Carabanchel's non-suicidals, the safety net was also a lifesaver for anyone who got chucked over the handrails, normally for thieving. This was the busiest safety net in the world.

Rodriguez was a sociopath and a danger to everyone around him, so he was one of the lucky few who lived alone in a cell. At that time, I also lived alone in my cell, but that was because I had friends in high places – not because I was a sociopath.

It was the early hours of the day that I liked best, just after dawn. Of all the hours of the day or night, the hour that comes in the wake of the dawn is the most fresh, vigorous and enrapturing. I call it the zest hour. I would get out of bed early to do my breathing exercises before the air became clammy in the humid early summer. Carabanchel was the Devil's cooking pot in summertime, so I got my cool air before Satan turned up the heat.

The tenets of *chi gung* breathing and even the basic concepts of oriental martial-arts training are not going to be part of this story. But much of my time was spent as a practitioner, especially when I was alone in my cell and able to perform ancient exercises in complete silence.

This precious silence was broken every morning by the wailing siren; the exact same sound that warned Londoners during the Blitz of approaching jerry bombers. What an unnecessary fucking din to announce *recuento*. Following this were the resounding echoes of the crashing bolts. Screech, bang! Screech, bang! Screamed obscenities reverberated around the galleries, rudely piercing the slumber of those capable of waking, for the siren was wasted on the altered consciousness of the smackhead. It took more than an air-raid siren to jolt the neurotransmitters of the lobotomised heroin zombie. Rodriguez was also a member of this club.

It was just after dawn when I threw back my bed-sheet and swung my legs out of the metal cot. I checked for cockroaches before placing my feet in the flip-flops lying on the bleached vinyl floor tiles that were broken and cracked all over the show. In my peripheral vision I clocked a darting cockroach racing to the concrete shitter in the corner of my cell.

BEHIND THE DOOR

'Oh, look who it is,' I said to myself. 'It's fucking Herbie the Volkswagen.'

He was so big I could hear his legs scratching for traction. Now that's what I called a fucking beetle! I was sure this was Rodriguez's pet, sent in to steal from me, so I grabbed an old magazine to beat the juice out of him with, but he got into the crack in the corner behind the shitter before I got a clear swipe at him. As he scuttled his way next door to his master, I imagined him shouting, '*Hijo de puta!*' But it wasn't him shouting, it was the screw screaming at my next-door neighbour who was still stinking in his greasy pit. I could hear the screw frantically screaming and calling my neighbour a son of a whore and a steaming lump of gypsy shit. He was going to court that morning so an early call had been arranged for him, as was the rule here. The shouting became muffled as Hitler entered the cell to ruin Rodriguez's day out at court with his truncheon. The unmistakable sound of polished hardwood colliding with soft-tissue-covered bone travelled through the dividing wall between our cells as Hitler lost his cool on Rodriguez's head.

My early-morning session of silence then came to an end for the rest of the day with the sound of the awakened inmates' blaring tellies and radios. Some of them were yelling and cat-calling the lunatic screw who was now heading for the office to telephone the *enfermería* to alert the gurney crew to collect the attempted suicide on *galería cinco*.

I did my ablutions and finished by emptying a bucket of cold water over my head. Standing naked and dripping wet, I relished the invigorating dousing with cold water in the sultry heat of the early summer morning, one of the extremely rare joys of the Carabanchel. I vigorously towelled myself dry, then refilled the plastic mop-bucket in readiness for my next dousing. There was approximately another 40 minutes before *recuento* so I started my daily routine of callisthenics and martial-arts exercises before I emptied the bucket over my head again.

I carried out this early-morning ritual every day I was alone in my cell. It ceased whenever anyone else was banged up with me. Fortunately, I spent a lot of my bird alone, so over the years I spent in Spanish prisons, I kept myself fit and hard.

CARABANCHEL

Strange things happen to the mind when locked alone in a cell, but for me it was a relief to be separated from the dross of this cruel nation. My chamber became my safe haven where I could relax and daydream about the past; just lying on my bed thinking, mostly about my wife, Susan, lifting back layers of time and jotting things down in my journal to enable the future writing of books.

Umpteen things raced through your brain when the big metal bolt crashed home, locking you behind the door. Will the *cacheros* strike today? That loathsome bastard Hitler is on duty today; that sick queer Pepe is also on duty; and so on, with paranoia pecking away inside your head. Paranoia, in one form or another, was a daily occurrence in the Carabanchel. It was part of the architecture, built in, like the history of executions and the unmarked graves in this wicked limbo. That's why the Carabanchel was soon to be destroyed: not only to appease the EU club members, but to erase the past, just like the Germans did. Ex-Nazis keep quiet about their past, which ordinary krauts do their best to forget. But Spain's Carabanchel would be the same as Germany's Nazism: forever remembered.

Apprehension and panic would hit you when you heard the door bolts crashing open as the *cacheros* raided the cells. You never knew if you were on their list for a shakedown or ringpiece check. Other times, for no reason at all, a feeling of oppression struck to send your spirits nose-diving into an anxiety attack, which caused a unique type of stress. Whenever this happened to me it produced a feeling of icy coldness beneath the skin of my shoulders and back, while, simultaneously, a sensation of burning on the skin's surface raged across my back. This brought about a feeling of dread, an alarming heaviness akin to an anvil sitting on my chest.

I tried to embrace this sensation in an attempt to analyse it, but failed. It made me feel somehow worse and I just couldn't fathom it out. I never discovered what triggered it. I can only assume it had something to do with the unnaturalness of being behind the locked door: like all machines, we break if we're forced to work unnaturally.

Yet again, the means of repair came via the martial arts. Whenever I had a twinge of that peculiar sensation, I immediately knelt in my meditation posture and concentrated on breathing, combined with a purifying thought exercise that I learnt in Asia in 1966. This exercise effectively defeated the onset of that horrible feeling which only happened when I was alone in my cell.

I spent many hours performing stretching exercises in the cell, which was easier for me to do without the gawping Spanish inmates at the gymnasium. I started with rotation and mobility exercises to warm up, then went into a stretching routine to benefit all major body parts. I began my circuit training by first upending my bedding so I could use the edge of the metal cot for my step-ups exercise. I would then do sit-ups, squats, squat-thrusts, press-ups and many more military-type physical jerks to increase my fitness level. There was no groundbreaking stuff here, just good old-fashioned training that produced the likes of Tarzan.

Behind my door I had written the word Bushido, at which I gazed as I went through my routines. I had a trying time with that word, especially when I did an exercise called Big Bastards with the Clap. This was a combination of a star-jump, a squat-thrust and a hand-clapping press-up, which sorted out the big boys from the little boys. To a certain extent, my training was enjoyable, but in my situation I had to be obsessed, especially with endurance workouts, because there was absolutely no joy in bashing out Big Bastards with the Clap whilst training alone behind the door.

My routine was disturbed by the arrival of the gurney at my neighbour's cell, so I opened the Judas hole with the point of my pencil. On doing so, I couldn't see anything, but I could hear much better the mutterings of the orderlies and the unmistakable bellowing of Don Juan – the little Hitler of *galería cinco*.

The bellowing ceased as the gurney clattered out of the cell and came into view as it passed my door. I got a glimpse of the livid bruise on Rodriguez's forehead, just on the hairline of his widow's peak, then I stepped back quickly as Don Juan's cruel face loomed at my spyhole. My heart sank as I looked directly at the glittering eye. The cell-door bolt crashed noisily open, matching the crashing of my heart in my ears. Fear gripped my entrails as the door swung outwards, revealing the cruel little man with the big stick. My fear was not of the man, but of the consequences of his death, for I knew I would take his life in an instant should he attack me with his truncheon.

CARABANCHEL

I looked into the windows of this creature's dark soul: his cold, blue, evil eyes, unblinking in his hatred of all things foreign, including me. I was his lone English prisoner, whose mere presence in Spain was an irritant to his precariously balanced mind. His dark blue serge uniform was pressed in all the right places and the metal bits were all shiny, as were his black shoes. His bum-boy valet in cell no. 6 on the ground floor had done a good job with his kit, but Hitler still looked like a sack of hot shit.

His evil eyes looked right through me. It was as though he was trying to fathom out why I lived alone whilst his countrymen were packed three to a cell. I could read his thoughts: 'Who is this mysterious Englishman who has the privilege of living alone on my *galería*?' He would have remembered me being processed into the prison on my first day, battered and bleeding, wearing heavily bloodstained clothes, without a penny in my pocket. 'Look at him now!'

His eyes glittered menacingly as he stared into my face, spittle dribbling from the corners of his coarse mouth: the end result of his verbal abuse of the unconscious Rodriguez. Suddenly, his eyes softened as a half-smile cracked his headstone face.

'*Buenos días, Kreestoffer.*'

I swallowed quickly to wet my throat. '*Buenos díaz, jefe.*'

Jefe was the mode of address I conceded to, rather than the more respectful *Don*, which all suck-holing Spanish inmates called their prison officers.

The smile broadened, making him look like a mad Jack Elam, then he stepped back, slammed and locked the door and was gone. I stood in eerie silence wondering what the hell all that was about. Why did that little shit wish me a good morning?

THIRTEEN
TRADERS

Lewis was a fur trader – fur burger, that is: an importer of women whose only value to him was their pubic fur. He smuggled them into Spain from Poland, Hungary and Czechoslovakia to be used as dancing prostitutes.

He didn't boast about his exploits with the dancing girls, nor did he try to impress everyone with the crazy amounts of cash generated by his troupe of dancing shag-bags. But, in my heart, I knew this Cossack had a black soul and cared for nothing other than his own skin. For some unknown reason he targeted me to ingratiate himself with.

Claiming to come from Warsaw and to be of Cossack stock, this wily woman-trader didn't seem to fit the bill because he was frightened of his own shadow, very unlike the fierce, furry-capped adventurers of his supposed ancestry. He was an educated man, claiming to have an engineering degree from a university in Krakow. He spoke English with a BBC accent, German like Adolf Hitler, Spanish like Franco and was also fluent in French and Russian, but physically he was as weak as piss.

He flitted between the krauts and frogs at mealtimes, but never once approached the English table. Realising his gladiator credentials weren't up to scratch, he spoke to me and the others only in the yard. I don't remember how we met, or the first days of him speaking to us; it's like he just happened and was there around us, as if he'd been there all the time. He talked to me privately about his business operation and I remember being impressed.

Lewis first made his money by trading cars from Germany and women from Hungary with clients in Spain. Basically, he bought second-hand cars in Germany, then, with a car-transporter, moved them to Hungary, where someone fucked around with the documentation and number plates, making them acceptable in Spain, where they would be re-registered and sold to Spanish car dealers. While the cars were being processed somewhere in Hungary, Lewis was collecting the girls and arranging for them to rendezvous at a hotel in Budapest, where they would be secreted in the cars on the transporter in order to be trafficked across Europe to Spain.

He was only being held in the Carabanchel for a minor offence, until the police found out that he'd illegally taken a batch of young ladies to Portugal. This got under the skin of the lady judge at his trial, and she eventually had him extradited to Portugal. He got a much longer sentence there than he would have done in Spain.

Anyway, it turned out that his aim in befriending me was to recruit me to assist his wife by letting her stay in my remote *finca* with Susan on the Costa del Sol. His wife was a dancing teacher who organised and trained the imported girls and also managed the rotation of dancing shag-bags around the Spanish nightclubs ranging from Barcelona to Marbella and Madrid. It was a big, thriving business until Lewis had his collar felt. Somebody had told him that I would be out soon so he thought I might have been interested in caretaking his wife and business for the duration.

In the Carabanchel I watched Lewis deteriorate from the cocky whore-master that he was into a snivelling, disillusioned arse-licker, about as far removed from a Cossack as the Dalai Lama. He started associating with the nignog table and became pals with Edward, the Nigerian heroin smuggler, who ran the Bible class.

Lewis was becoming more and more desperate worrying about his wife and business; he had even convinced himself that he was innocent and everyone became thoroughly sick of his constant bleating. He was now truly ripe for the Bible class. Each evening Edwards's cell was packed with Nigerian lost souls, so enticing a white man into his cell for the daily chant and sing-song was a boost for Edward: he now thought the Lord had made him a missionary, so now he would convert the savage white man. You think I'm joking? You haven't met many Nigerians, have you?

Edward was a big bloke with an oversized head that was shiny, bald and exceptionally ugly. He wore a big, wide, constant smile, which must have caused much face ache. He was constantly nodding benevolently at all and sundry, expecting them to reach for his hand to kiss it. In his left hand he clutched a Bible to his chest, rather like a rugby player holding his pint of ale after the match. He greeted everyone loudly with much shoulder slapping, with vigorous handshakes and lashings of 'Praise the Lord'.

He must have thought the Lord would help him if he became a trader in souls, so he tried hard to reap the harvest of bent souls that the Lord had delivered unto him. I watched Lewis as he became more and more embroiled in Edward's Bible-whacking palaver. He eventually convinced himself that the Lord would make him a free man soon. I knew his mind had blown when I watched him shuffle across the snotty yard on his knees, hands clasped in prayer, looking piously to the sky. This was a penance that he said God had awarded him in lieu of a sentence here. God, being ever true to his word, didn't allow Lewis to be convicted here, but he did allow him to be extradited and given a big fat sentence in Portugal!

One day I was drinking coffee and chatting with Dutch when Edward and his choirboys came strolling by, as though in a procession. His big, booming voice assaulted my ears.

'Ah, Christopher,' he boomed. 'You must come to . . .'

'Fuck off, you ugly black cunt.'

Being so used to the brush-off, the procession shuffled by without breaking step. Nor did the smiles falter, but his slimy eyes were saying, 'You can see right through me, you white bastard.'

On they strolled, into the wilderness of the Carabanchel concrete.

I met Edward the following year when I was in Valdemoro, Spain's top-security prison. The day he was given a 12-stretch was the day the Bible sailed over the prison wall. Like me, the Lord can see right through these fuckers.

I was called to the visitor's block for a meeting with my lawyer.

In the waiting area I sat next to a bloke I vaguely knew who was from Bolivia. He surprised me by speaking to me in English.

'I wanted to speak with you before, but you are never alone. You are *patrón, capitán del barco*. You have yacht?'

I tried to grasp his character before answering. 'You speak good English. Where did you learn?' I said, looking into brown eyes in a calm, sad-looking face.

'In Bolivia. My mother is English.'

'Oh right, well at least I'm half-interested. What do you want?'

The sad face changed instantly into something wolfish as he swiftly checked for eavesdroppers. '*Muchos chivatos en esto shithole*,' he said, wildly glaring at nosy spicks across the room.

'Yes, I know. They all look like you,' I said jokingly.

'I am not Spanish; I am half-English and half-Bolivian. My father's bloodline is not contaminated with Spanish blood. He is pure South American Indian.'

I then noticed his jet-black hair, slightly flared nostrils and what I perceived to be Indian features: not Hispanic.

Looking into my eyes, he said, 'You may or may not know about the systematic genocide of the Indians. More than 90 million of my ancestors were slaughtered by this scumbag country. That is why I poison them with cocaine.'

'Whoa! Hold it there, Geronimo. You don't expect me to believe that shit. You do this for money, not some noble fucking cause.'

'Yes, I do it for money, but I enjoy doing it. I hope Spain gets burnt off the face of the planet. I despise these posturing primitives.'

I could see this man had some kind of axe to grind, but behind all that, there was the wish to get rich quick. 'What do you want with me?' I asked him.

Again, the wolf scanned the horizon. 'I have a good way of shipping the merchandise, but I have no yacht, nor *capitán* to guide it,' he said resignedly.

'And you think I can put a yacht at your disposal?' I said, smiling at him.

'Listen to my proposal then tell me to fuck off or work with me. But first I must know if you have a yacht that can sail across the world.'

'I have a yacht and I can sail any fucking where.'

'OK. I will sit with you in the yard on Sunday and tell you about my plan.'

'Good. I look forward to that.'

I had just a few days to gather some background information on my new Bolivian friend, who I'll call Alfonso, but I got nowhere. None of my usual Latino snouts could tell me anything about him. In the end I had to ask Don Rafael about him.

'What the fuck do you want to know about him for? He's no fucker, just another mule, probably caught with a belly full of cocaine condoms.'

'Just check him out for me. I need to know.'

Late on Friday night Don Rafael silently entered my cell. 'Here's the phone; call your wife, I'll be back in a minute.'

He handed me his mobile phone then disappeared, quietly pushing my cell door to.

I chatted with Susan for what seemed like ages, then Don Rafael slunk back into my cell. I said my cheerios and 'Love ya', then she was gone. A fleeting moment of sadness swiftly dissipated as Don Rafael held out his hand for the telephone, saying, 'I have news about Alfonso.'

He pulled the chair alongside my bed, then plonked his big feet on the cotton counterpane while delving into his bag for two cold beers. The ring-pull San Miguels hissed out their froth as Don Rafael said, 'He's a fucking trader! He moves Peruvian flake big-time.'

'I thought you said he's a fucking mule.'

'That's what I thought, but he's caught up with a firm in Galicia who were caught with three tonnes coming into La Coruña. He's implicated but there's not much on him. It's possible he'll walk, but he has enemies. He should never have come to Spain.'

'Then why did he come?'

'Someone told him his shit wasn't up to scratch, so he would not get his cut. His trip over here coincided with the arrest of the Galicians. He was lifted at the airport in Madrid. That's why I thought he was a mule.'

'OK, so he's a big player and probably not a bullshitter.'

'What the fuck has he got to do with you?'

'Fuck all yet, but we need to think about the future, Rafael, and you can't have too many contacts in this game, so I'm going to have a chat with him.'

Feeling fresh and cool after my shower on Sunday morning, I joined the rest of the gang for a stroll around the yard before Chinky and Jake brought the coffee and biscuits over. Alfonso loomed into view, nodding his head towards the shaded far corner of the yard. I winked acknowledgement, then peeled off from the *Mezclado* as we passed the corner to join Alfonso sitting alone in the shade.

'This will have to be quick,' he said, 'because I don't want anybody thinking there's something going on between us. There are spies all over this place.'

'OK, Alfonso, what's up?'

'Do you need a map, or can you imagine the area of operation?'

'Depends where it's at, mate. Where are we working?'

'Do you know the Dominican Republic?'

'Yes,' I lied, as I clocked the screws' office to see if anyone was interested.

'What about Guyana?'

'What about it?' I said, stupidly.

'Have you sailed from there before?'

'No, but I know where it is.'

'OK. There's a choice of ports for loading. There's a place along the coast from Georgetown in Guyana and the other port is in Bahia de Ocoa on the south side of the Dominican Republic. There's more profit working out of Guyana, so you might prefer that one.'

The wolfish expression on his face was making me feel paranoid now. I started looking for screws with cameras and aimed listening devices. Fucking hell! Looking at my feet, I said, 'What are we talking about regarding merchandise?'

'Guyana is pure Peruvian and Bahia de Ocoa is whatever is available at the time – but pure,' he said, opening his newspaper and holding it high in front of him. He had cut holes in it so he could see across the yard. Fuck me! I was paranoid now.

'Who am I working with in the Caribbean and where am I unloading?'

'You'll unload in the UK and if I'm still in prison when you get out, you'll be working with my mum and dad. All relevant info and contact numbers will be given to you when everyone is happy about you. Nobody knows about you yet.'

'So this is all pie in the sky just now?'

'Oh no, this is very serious business and if my stint in prison gets me a *capitán* who can do the job, then my time will not have been wasted.'

He shook the newspaper then twisted 90 degrees away from me so he could look directly at the screws, after first readjusting the holes. 'We'll talk again when you've thought about everything. Just tell me when you're ready.'

I decided to study my map of the Caribbean Sea and work a few things out before speaking to him again. I stood up to walk away, saying, 'I'll let you know in a couple of days, OK?'

'Yes. I will not tell my folks until I have another discussion with you.'

'See ya.' I walked away.

I had many meetings with Alfonso the cocaine trader, but we parted forever when the Carabanchel closed its gates: I went to La Moraleja prison, he went to Valdemoro prison. I was transferred briefly to Valdemoro to attend my trial in Madrid, but it's a massive, top-security place so it was no surprise that I didn't bump into him. If you ever get to read this, Alfonso, don't worry, mate, the contact numbers have been destroyed.

FOURTEEN
AUGUST

The sun drilled into us mercilessly; there seemed to be no escape from the cruel Spanish blowtorch. Starting with the early sunrise, the heat seeped its way through concrete and brick, turning the most simple task into a sweat-drenched chore. In my cell it was almost unbearable, even with Enrico's electric fan swishing around on full power.

I would bumble through my work in the *zapatería*, which was minimal. Then I would sit in Oscar Bonilla's little office to write my letters and switch on the electric fan that Don Pablo, the big-cheese prison official, had given me prior to his departure to my house in Coín, Malaga.

His going on holiday meant that there was no mobile phone in the *zap*, but fortunately Don Rafael wasn't going on holiday till September, so I used his mobile each day he was on duty. However, I need not have worried because Enrico soon produced a new mobile phone, complete with charger, compliments of Don Pablo, so the heat was compensated for by almost unlimited telephone calls.

Spain closes for August. The judiciary closes down completely, so if you haven't got *fianza* by the last week in July, forget it. Nothing happens until they all come back from holiday during the first days of September. Knowing that the judicial machinery had ground to a halt for a whole month while we melted in the oven of the

Carabanchel was so frustrating for remand prisoners that punch-ups happened constantly.

Heat and malevolence merged to form an August haze of violence within the prison walls. Players at the domino and card tables erupted constantly with rage as the sun pushed them over the edge. Redundant footballs were aimlessly kicked across the filthy yard by strolling inmates, then kicked back in annoyance by disturbed porn readers. Tendrils of hatred for all things Spanish had grown like a poison ivy around my heart by the end of this horrible month. The only thing I could feel glad about was that the telephone calls to Susan and my Bushido mentality had kept my integrity intact during this trying time.

Don Pablo and his party had arrived at my house on the Costa del Sol and were having a most wonderful time in my swimming pool and dining on Susan's exceptional culinary skills while I was roasting my bollocks off in his infamous pisshole, the Carabanchel. I received a daily report on the goings-on from Susan and Kennedy, telling me that the plans for the 'Big Job' had been accepted by the blokes from Cali and the plan would be put into action on my release.

Susan knew nothing of these plans, but she realised something was being cooked up because Don Pablo set fire to each piece of notepaper at the end of each meeting. She also told me how unpleasant it all was, having to host one of my keepers while I rotted in his hole in baking Madrid: she cried herself to sleep each night they were there.

Kennedy outlined the plans in a letter that he sent me, using our own peculiar code. I'd developed this from the Slidex system used by the British military. Apart from pick-up points, the plan was much the same as we had concocted previously: essentially to sail a minimum of one tonne of cocaine per trip from Trinidad to Bantry Bay in Eire, where it would be stored in an isolated farmhouse then ferried across the Irish Sea to be sold in London.

Bantry Bay had been selected as the port of entry simply because of the location of the farmhouse; but the decision was ultimately down to me because I had yet to recce the area and finalise the entry point. Because of the ingenious mode of transport, the cargo would be jettisoned into shallow water, then recovered by a Land-Rover with a winch. So my skills as a recce sergeant in a field squadron of Royal Engineers would once again come in useful.

This, of course, was all pie in the sky in order to keep my status while doing my bird. When I eventually got out of prison, I did my own thing and never once touched cocaine or heroin. This never crossed Enrico's mind as we discussed the plans for the Big Job night after night while Don Pablo was at my house. I had to show enthusiasm at all times and I must admit that my input had made this plan exceptional. I enjoyed the challenge in all the plans that I was involved with, but this one was excellent, with logistics and location details done to the last brass tack. The job priority-list took care of everything: supplies, comms, safe havens and emergency recovery, all dovetailing with scintillating precision.

Enrico's millions were bankrolling this job, so everything had to marry up realistically because Enrico was a most shrewd operator and nobody's fool, so I did not attempt to overestimate anything regarding costings. Besides, unless I was shanghaied, I was not going. And nobody could twist my arm on it because nobody knew when I'd be getting out of prison, or which prison I'd eventually be getting out of.

The sun was cracking the slates as the ETA blokes marched around the yard wearing sandwich boards sporting the Basque flag and slogans praising *Euskal Herria*: the Basque Red Net. They were marching in step with each other and chanting a dirge, just like a funeral cortège. If *Adagio for Strings* ever needed a lyric, then these were the boys to sort it. Their cause needs no comment from me, but I personally liked each ETA terrorist I met, simply because of their good manners, their ability to speak English, their self-discipline regarding health and physical training, plus their focused disregard for the Spanish.

Arregi was a blond, blue-eyed fitness freak who bore a monstrous grudge against the Carabanchel. He told me his sentences were thirty-three years for each of his two killings: a sixty-six stretch. Fuck me! I would put words to the *Adagio for Strings* if I ever got that. His hatred stemmed from the fact that his elder brother was tortured to death over a nine-day period of brutal interrogation in

CARABANCHEL

February 1981, here in the Carabanchel. Arregi's sixty-six stretch was awarded for killing two men who were instrumental in torturing and killing members of ETA.

I liked Arregi. There were no grey areas with him: he liked you or he wanted to kill you. Here he was now, marching with eight of his countrymen, proud and granite-faced with dark, damp patches of sweat weeping out of their armpits, rivulets dripping from each chin onto the Basque flag, making the colours run down the brightly coloured sandwich boards. The merciless sun beat down on them as they marched proudly around the yard. We watched with anticipation as the screws' office buzzed like a disturbed beehive. Prison officers were toing and froing and their numbers noticeably increasing, with larger specimens arriving carrying big sticks.

After about twenty minutes of marching, the screws started to come out of their office in threes to patrol the yard. In just a few minutes there were 12 screws patrolling the yard, with more to come, when suddenly Arregi and his soldiers took off their sandwich boards and inverted them, putting them on the ground like little ice-cream signs outside a grocery shop. On the reverse of the sandwich board was the Spanish flag, all yellow and red. They were arranged in a circle so that all nine men could piss on them simultaneously without pissing on each other. They zipped up, about-turned and each marched away, increasing the distance between them as they dispersed to the prison walls to mingle with the spectators. In the centre of the yard sat a ring of Spanish flags, steaming under the relentless sun. Nobody knew how the ETA boys had done it, but in the centre of the circle was a *tricornio*, the ridiculous dress hat of the *Guardia Civil*, sitting there with a large ETA turd nestling within. Atop the steaming turd was a toothpick sporting a tiny Spanish flag.

Whistles blew and black, shiny truncheons flashed in the sunlight as we were rounded up and herded to our cells, laughing our fucking heads off while the ETA blokes were separated and taken away. The screws treated the ETA prisoners like shit because they each came under the category 'FIES', which meant *Fichero de Internos de Especial Seguimiento*. This was a special class for dangerous prisoners, which was taken as a licence to treat them like animals. An animal's life in Spain is normally short and the end, when it comes, is a blessing.

ETA blokes often joined us for coffee. They moved around the international groups to practise their language skills. The krauts and frogs always had ETA men amongst them, while Dutch and his clogs never had them: no fucker speaks Dutch, do they? The Spanish prisoners avoided the ETA men; they were scared shitless of them.

August inexorably blazed its way to September, but not before another threat to my life was made by a horrible black bastard called Suleiman, from Mogadishu in the Republic of Somalia. He had borrowed *dos mil pesetas* and failed to pay it back, so Jake and Vito leant on him slightly in order to balance the books, so to speak.

Suleiman was a tall, slim, hard-looking villain with that East African blackness resembling coal tar and a hollow-cheek facial structure making him look poker-faced and hungry. He was rumoured to have murdered many starving natives of Ethiopia whilst wearing the uniform of some ragbag military outfit which he deserted to become a heroin dealer trading out of Turkey. His fortunes brought him to Madrid, where he promptly lost them along with his liberty when he was grassed by his Spanish kennel mates.

Actually I was surprised when he asked me for 2,000 *pesetas* because I knew he was busy trading smack: the Suleimans of this world are always at it. I was even more surprised when he didn't pay me back. I reckoned it was to do with a certain state of mind which often beset black Africans, especially with names like Suleiman. I put it down to a mixture of self-delusion and cheek, in so much as they thought that, because they were of noble descent, the necessity to pay one's debts was beneath them. They assumed a haughtiness that was usually corrected by a swift kick in the bollocks. Unfortunately for Suleiman, he thought the kick in the bollocks was the paying of the debt. So he was a wee bit pissed off when Ali Safave laid him out in the shithouse after first telling him how much the debt had grown. Suleiman awoke with a crowd around him and vengeance in his black heart.

I first learned of the threat when Ricardo, the Spanish hit-man and boss of the *metalico*, the metal workshop, told me that one of his lads had been asked to fashion a *pinchou* with shit grooves at the pointed end for a gypsy who was selling it to Suleiman. Suleiman was also trying to recruit a gypsy to use it on me. Later that day Ali confirmed this when he told me he'd heard on the grapevine that Suleiman was seeking a spike and someone to shove it into my kidneys. He was confident of getting the spike, but he couldn't get an assassin to do the job – my reputation was working well.

After my chat with Ricardo I asked him to put the word out that any gypsy who gave Suleiman the *pinchou* would be given it back, sheathed into his urethra, straight from Suleiman's rotten arsehole. This put the cat amongst the pigeons and was bound to get back to Suleiman, giving him something to think about in bed that night.

I couldn't be doing with threats to my kidneys, so the following day I went into the *comedor* at lunchtime to wait for Suleiman to sit at the nignog table. In the queue I watched him pick up a *bandeja* and fill it with rotten bananas and pig stew. So much for Islam. He threaded his way through to the nignog table, sat down and started to tuck in when I nipped across and placed a bone *pinchou* on his *bandeja* and said, 'You can borrow mine till payday.' I quickly returned to my table before he could speak. A black hand swiftly removed the ornate bone spike from view as the whites of the eyes did all the talking on the nignog table.

Just before lock-up that evening, Chinky brought me the *pinchou* and the money from Suleiman.

'I don't truss dat black cun'. He strike anudder time when we not ready.'

'We are always fucking ready, Chinky. Don't ever think otherwise.'

The bank was busy during August. There was a lot of good puff on the wing and heroin was in abundance. Pu-Rambo the transsexual had succumbed to a gypsy heroin pusher. It was a shame really because Pu provided great entertainment and was a distraction from the boring grind of prison existence. His bulging thighs squeezed out from a ridiculous miniskirt, making the mincing gait look ever so funny as he teetered across the yard to camp it up with his tranny pals.

Like all newcomers to heroin, Pu-Rambo was going through the heaving and retching his guts out routine in the *sala*, the main hall, where most blokes sat to write or watch television amidst the chaos of the place. The urge to puke was instant so nobody ever made it to the toilet as the jet of stinking bile and vomit rocketed up through the gullet to explode around the feet of guilty bystanders. False teeth usually shattered or ricocheted into orbit as they were launched out by the heroin-fuelled puke with so much force that it had the pukers up on tiptoes. Pu-Rambo's energy-sapping chunder ruined his eye make-up as his tears washed the mascara down his cheeks to mingle with the dripping slime running off his chin, the vile mixture splashing down between his big tits and ruining his silk blouse and two hours' work in the mirror. Within the space of a few weeks the image he'd attempted to cultivate of a twentieth-century lady of fashion quickly gave way to a near millennium sack of shit wearing baggy jeans and trainers. The gewgaw jewellery disappeared, as did the daily half-pint of war paint, as the heroin took charge of his personality and quickly had him on his knees in the shower cubicles sucking cocks all day or being rogered for a fix.

Pu-Rambo's best friend was a transsexual called Maria, a 6-ft tall, lantern-jawed bruiser who looked equally ridiculous in a micro-skirt and fishnet tights. If he bent over slightly, you could see his bollocks dangling in the gusset of his tights – hilarious!

Maria became so distressed at the change in Pu-Rambo that he attacked the gypsy pusher and practically bit off half his face. The screams were a treat as that big lantern jaw closed on a mouthful of lips and cheek and then, like a tiger-shark, ripped off the flesh in a shaking motion. Blood flew all around as he did it again. He then bit down on the skin of the forehead to force it under the eyebrow as his teeth clamped together, trapping the eyelid in the folds of flesh, then he let rip with his head and the screams frightened the pigeons on the roof. Other gypsies finally dragged him off just as he was pulling the gypsy's jeans down to bite his dick off. He managed to grab his bollocks and stretch the scrotum nearly to his knees before letting go.

Three other trannies came running to assist Maria, but the screws were on the case before they could swing a handbag. However, the shouting match was great to watch as trannies and boyfriends confronted the gang of gypsies in the most camped up, rip-roaring squabble I've ever seen. One of them wore a plaid ra-ra skirt, just like a tiny kilt. Each time he turned during his tantrum, the skirt flared to reveal flimsy blue shreddies, which were too small to hold everything, so bits were hanging out. You couldn't pay to see stuff like this. The spectacle continued for a few more minutes until the gurney arrived to take away the trashed gypsy, then the screws flashed the truncheons and everyone fucked off sharpish as Maria was yanked off down the block, just for one night. Pu-Rambo was moved off the wing and I was told some time later that he had managed to kick the habit.

The following day was very funny because Maria became Didi's new cellmate, hot on the heels of Pu-Rambo. This prompted another round of ribbing from Jake about who was going to bite the pillow that night. Fortunately I had refused Pu-Rambo a loan shortly before his transferral: maybe it was because I had never lent money to transsexuals before, or perhaps it was intuition. Maria and I reminisced about this sultry August day four years later when I met him again in Malaga prison.

The heat in the Carabanchel's gymnasium was insufferable, so I put the combat class on hold, giving me the opportunity to work one-on-one with Ali Safave, practising dangerous techniques to do with neck breaking using various applications of the neck-wrench and silent killing techniques. I spent a few days teaching him holds and throws from Kempo ju-jitsu and Spirit Combat ju-jitsu but mostly, because of the heat, we practised Kyusho-jitsu: nerve strikes and pressure-point fighting.

As usual we had an audience and the usual sprinkling of ringside experts who simply did not know when to shut up and fuck off. Ali had applied an armlock on me to keep me face down on the mat as he shoved his knee into my shoulder to keep me where he wanted me, because he was about to change the armlock to a one-handed wrist-control technique, which was what we were practising. I was making things difficult for Ali by fighting the technique. My elbow joint was taking the strain of a 240-lb experienced fighter when suddenly it exploded into pain as a Spanish spectator decided to help Ali by grabbing my forearm and pulling it back against the joint, shouting, 'Más!' meaning 'more'. The bloke was immediately knocked out by Ali's head-butt and swiftly dragged off the mat.

Then an argument started between Ali and the interloper's *compadres* about how he'd come on to the mat to correct Ali's technique because Ali seemed to be fucking around instead of ripping my arm out of its socket.

The discussion lasted all of five seconds then exploded into the most ferocious battering as Ali flew into an incredible rage. He punched two men to the ground and grabbed a third by the throat and testicles to lift him above his head, then stepped out from under him, letting him crash to the concrete floor, saying, 'Breakfall that one, you spick cunt.'

Everyone could see there were four men hurt, so it would have taken a brave bullfighter indeed to try their luck now. It ended there: or so we thought. This incident led to an attempt on Ali's life, because one of the injured men was the son of a face in Madrid. This prominent gangster put a price on Ali's head. It must have been substantial, because nobody in their right mind would attack Ali Safave, and somebody did end up having a go.

I first got wind of it from Ricardo again. He'd been offered the job, but sensibly he turned it down, knowing that the *Mezclado* would rip him to shreds should he get lucky. I addressed the problem immediately after Ricardo told me about the hit. The English table was the best place to discuss this with the gang and lunchtime was the earliest opportunity to get everybody together anyway, so when everyone had eaten most of their stinking fish, I started to tell them about the price on Ali's head.

Looking around the table I could see the silent hatred beginning to pulse into a palpable ring of steel around Ali, forming the most dangerous forcefield in this Spanish pisshole. Each face was expressionless, but the eyes were alert, revealing a pure, merciless aggression smouldering within. Each man on this table held a special hatred for the Spanish, and their faces reflected this as they gazed at those of the surrounding spicks. I told everyone about the approach made to Ricardo and his refusal: silence. I went on to explain how we all had to stick together until the threat was removed and that the family who put the price on Ali's head would be truly worried about their boy when they found out just who they were fucking around with in here.

Vito was brooding into his *bandeja* in his hard-boiled, 'Victor Mature' manner. 'Cripple the bastard now,' he whispered across the table. 'Then it'll be all over.'

Everyone sat pondering for a moment, then, 'Good idea,' said Jake, 'but we all need to do him so we all qualify for a price.'

Ali said loudly, 'Nobody in this prison will get prize money for my head.'

'That's right, Ali,' I said. 'And we're here to make sure they fucking don't.'

I felt better now that we all knew about the threat to Ali because his back was now well covered and the chances of a frontal assault would be as high as finding Christ's bones: not at all likely.

The duty screws came in to turf everyone out so we moved as one away from the table. Vito and Jake moved in behind Ali, while the rest of us slotted in around him. The few spicks that tried to squeeze in behind Ali were chucked out of it and slung between the tables, wondering what the fuck was up. We went up the stone steps to the bottom level of cells where everyone shuffled around waiting for the *galería* gates to open, then went up to the cells. The lower level was packed with shuffling inmates trying not to collide with each other as the herded throng swirled around clockwise in the poorly lit unpleasantness of this ghastly pit.

We, the *Mezclado*, reacted violently to any crowding of our space.

Even Dutch approached warily as he said, 'What the fuck's up with you lot?'

I quickly explained about the gangster whose son Ali had battered.

'Oh, fuckin' hell. They're the Krays of Madrid,' he said. 'They won't want to lose face in here – this is their fuckin' back yard.'

'They haven't lost face yet, but they fucking will if they keep this up.'

'How the fuck are you gonna stop it?' said Dutch, furrowing his brow like Sid James.

'Surely they realise the shit their boy will be in if anything happens to Ali,' I said.

Dutch took a big toke on his spliff (a Marlboro ciggie boosted with cannabis, rather than a blatant joint, in order to deceive the hawk-eyed screws) and said, 'They think everyone is so frightened of them that nobody would attempt such foolishness. They obviously don't know about you fuckin' lot, so some fucker ought to tell 'em.'

'Who, for instance?'

'Your fuckin' lawyer. Every lawyer in town knows that fuckin' lot.'

I thought about Dutch's suggestion, then decided to have a chat with Tupak to see if Ivan the Terrible could get the message across. Ivan was an ex-KGB assassin and was Tupak's man on the outside, so a notorious family firm in Madrid should have been easy for him to find. In the meantime, I asked Vito and Jake to tell their lawyers to pass on the good news about the young spick's dismal and very limited future.

I don't know how long it took for the message to get through to the crime family, but an assassin made a move on Sunday morning in the shower block. He didn't actually 'strike' as such, because his attempt was thwarted by Chinky, who was watching the shower-block entrance from the yard. He was sipping his coffee when he noticed a stranger, a gypsy type who'd come onto the wing the day before, strolling by with a towel and toiletry bag. Chinky fell in behind him and followed him in.

The gypsy's composure started to break down upon quickly checking the first three cubicles and finding them empty, save for the hot water cascading onto the floors and the steam it generated. Further into the shower block everyone was using cold water, including Ali, so there wasn't the usual thick cloud of steam obscuring everything, which would have made it easier for the assassin. As the stranger appeared out of the steam around the entrance, Chinky snatched the folded towel and a gleaming *pinchou* clattered to the floor in front of Dutch's cubicle. There was a flurry of movement as everyone grabbed their towels and stepped out of the cubicles. The gypsy was slim and athletically built, but his jaw sagged and his wild eyes closed as Chinky rattled his brain with a tremendous punch into the nape of his neck, dropping him like a log.

The spike was clean, polished and sharp as a needle, with no shit grooves in it. We quickly searched the would-be assailant but nothing more of significance was found. We got dressed in a hurry, anticipating the 7th Gypsy Cavalry to come galloping in; but nothing: he was a lone assassin.

Vito checked his ID card and found his *lugar* (home town) stated: Durango, SA., so he was Mexican.

Just then Rico came in and said, 'I was wondering what that cunt was up to. He was put in with me yesterday from *galería siete* and he's been acting strange since he got here.'

Rico was an Italian hit-man who had worked quietly in London for many years. His preferred life-story was too complicated to remember, but he said he was involved in the hit on 'God's banker' in London, a bloke by the name of Calvi. Apparently this bloke was the head of an Italian bank and also dealt with the Vatican Bank, hence: God's banker. The thing that surprised me most about Rico was his Craft handshake. I'd never guessed that Mafia members were in the Brotherhood of Freemasonry. Rico was a big pal of Enrico's and dined often with us, regularly bringing an excellent bottle of Etna, a full-bodied red from the slopes of the volcano in Sicily, thus indicating he also had friends in high places. This was not any old red wine, you see, but his favourite from Catania, his home town.

Rico was excellent company. You would have thought he was in the Diplomatic Corps (he probably was). His English was very Terry Thomas, with lots of 'old chap', and according to Gilbert the frog his French was *très* Sorbonne, but he still called everyone 'cunt'. Even so, he was certainly the most refined professional killer I've ever met, much like Foxy in *The Day of the Jackal*.

'What are you going to do with him now, gentlemen?' he said, looking at me in particular.

'We assumed he came to do Ali. That's why he's lying there,' I said.

'The chiv might have been for protection. Most of these cunts carry one, and I've told him to shower every day that he's staying in my cell.'

'Borrocks!' shouted Chinky. 'Dat cun' come in 'ere to stick dat spike in Ali.'

176

'It doesn't matter now,' I said. 'Let's get him out of here and sit him on a shitter next door pronto. We can question him later.'

An hour later the Mexican was taken off the wing and never seen again. We all agreed that it was an attempt on Ali, but we would give the young, connected spick the benefit of the doubt and not shred his scalp to send home to his family.

I only had the use of Enrico's mobile phone for the first two weeks of August because the new government of his country came into power early in the month and, for reasons that I can't go into here, Enrico was granted a release just a few days later – he'd be out in a week. Enrico quickly became euphoric and he no longer gave a toss about a thing. He stupidly told Oscar Bonilla about the mobile phone and that he could occasionally use it if he asked me nicely. I knew instantly that the mobile phone was now just so much ratshit; it would be grassed the moment Enrico walked out of here because Oscar wanted to be the big man amongst the South Americans and he would brag about the phone to his *paisanos*. I told Enrico that telling Oscar about the phone was most foolish and the *cacheros* would be here searching for it before the week was over. He couldn't have cared less; he was out, for fuck's sake.

'No, Christopher. Oscar is too crafty to risk losing *my* telephone,' he said, with a hurt expression on his face.

'It's not your fucking telephone when you've gone, is it? You shouldn't have told him,' I said angrily, knowing I couldn't possibly work with this man when I got out.

I must have imparted this thought to him because he wanted to go over the plans again for the Irish job.

His last day in the Carabanchel was hectic to say the least. He gave away all kinds of stuff to his *paisanos*, and about a dozen blokes came to me saying that they would call by my cell to pick up this and that. I told each of them that should they come anywhere near my cell they'd be picking themselves up off the fucking floor.

Enrico was walking around like Father Christmas, shaking hands and waving to every fucker. There was a continuous '*Si, si, si*' coming out of his mouth as blokes asked him for things. Three blokes who were sharing a cell rushed across the yard to tell me they'd collect the television at lunchtime. They were told exactly the same as everybody else: 'Fuck off!' There must have been 40 new owners of the electric fan and 60 blokes wanted the carpet. Fuck off! Fuck off! Fuck off! Fucking hell, I was getting fed up with this. At least a hundred foreigners learned two new words of English today.

At last Enrico was gone and I was alone in my cell revelling in the privacy and silence of it all. I had inherited a television, telephone, pots and pans, an electric kettle, table lamps, in fact everything that was Enrico's was now mine. I gave away a lot of kit because I didn't have a servant to cook for me and I couldn't be arsed to cook and clean up pots and fucking pans all over the show. I kept the bare necessities to knock up a bit of chuck for myself whenever I got pissed off with the *comedor* crap, but I wasn't prepared to be Fanny Craddock for two or three guests every fucking night. So now I would spend more time with the *Mezclado* on the English table. I rented out Enrico's telly because I had my own hidden under my bed.

Oscar Bonilla asked for the mobile phone the day after Enrico walked out of the prison. I asked him where he would be using it and he told me he'd use it in his cell that night. I asked him how it would be kept secret with two other men in his cell. He winked and tapped the side of his nose like Fagin, as though I could imagine him whispering under the bed-sheets.

'Get fucked, you daft cunt!' I told him, and then patiently explained that he should get himself locked into my cell for the recreation hour, where he could use it without anybody knowing. He said that was fine as long as he could bring Fernando, his Spanish pal, in with him because he had promised him he could speak to his wife and kids that night.

'Oh, fucking hell's fucking fire! You gormless spick wanker! How the fuck did you get to Madrid? You should have been caught before you got on the fucking plane.'

I told him to go away until tomorrow morning when he could have the phone all to himself because I didn't want it any more. I knew that as from tomorrow the telephone's life was going to be very short and somebody would be going down to solitary for a couple of weeks. That night I had a nice long chat with my Susan and another with my mother in England. I don't know how much credit was on that phone, but there couldn't have been much left. I was glad about that as the *cacheros* would be getting their hands on it and trying to use it up pretty soon.

The next morning at breakfast I passed the phone to Oscar and told him the battery was low and needed charging. He stuffed the box containing phone and charger under his shirt then beamed at the South American tables, indicating he now had the telephone. This was Saturday morning. By teatime the phone was being used by the *cacheros* because Fernando was so pissed off about having to wait an extra day to talk to his family that he grassed Oscar. *Cacheros* came on the wing that afternoon and tore apart each South American cell until they found the telephone; not in Oscar's room, but in his next-door neighbours', where it was sat in its charger, plugged into the wall socket for all to see. Three protesting South Americans were dragged down the block wondering what the fuck was going on because Oscar had bribed one of them to charge the phone for him in exchange for the next vacancy in the *zapatería*.

The day after the *cacheros* took the telephone, Oscar came to me in the *zapatería* to ask if he could share my cell. Oscar was married to a lady judge in South America. He was very well connected and was supposedly a major player in the Charlie game. I asked him if he knew about any work involving Kennedy or Enrico. He said he didn't, but he would be interested to share some of his cartel connections with me for future business ventures. I thanked him for the offer then politely refused his accommodation request, telling him I wished to live alone in my cell for as long as I could. I made a mental vow never to tell Oscar Bonilla the time of day.

Don Rafael was on duty that night, so when he came to my cell I asked him to make sure that nobody got put in with me.

He passed me his mobile phone and said, 'I've got to dash. I'll be back in half an hour. Don't worry about your cell, it's yours. I want to hear more about sailing tonight, so we'll have a chat about the sea when I get back.'

He locked me in and was gone. I called Susan and she told me about the carry-on with Kennedy, Don Pablo and the other guests. Apparently everything was fine and the huddles had now ceased so they were all very happily enjoying their holiday at my home.

Kennedy came on the line to tell me all was agreed and the job would start when I got out. Don Rafael returned to my cell so I said my lovey-doveys to Susan, closed the line and gave him his mobile phone back.

He sat in my chair and plonked his big feet on the bottom of my bed. 'How are things at home?' he asked, delving into his bag for the booze.

'Oh, the usual,' I said. 'Feeling lonely, but getting by.'

He pulled a bottle of rum and two large plastic cups from the bag. 'Ah, that reminds me,' he said. 'You prefer to be alone at sea. Why's that?'

He poured half a dozen fingers of rum into each cup then rummaged for the Coke bottle. I took the proffered cup so he could fill it to the brim with ice-cold Coca-Cola.

'It's not a case of preference; it depends on the vessel. I can't sail a big yacht alone around the Med with two or three tonnes of hashish on board. I need to sleep and eat, so I need a crew of two, especially if I'm going to sea for a couple of weeks.'

'So what about *gomas*?'

'They're different. Straight across and back in one night, shit off a shovel jobs they are. Unless you are going up to Alicante: then you wish you had somebody with you because after eight or nine hours of scanning the horizon looking for patrol boats and spotter planes, you're fucking knackered and you're only halfway there.'

'And you've done that on your own, with nobody to give you a break?' he said, with his eyes wide open.

'Oh yeah, fucking hell, the adrenalin and chocolate bars keep you going, but when you unload and get the boat out of the water, you fall asleep in the back of some fucker's car for the journey back to Malaga. Then you suffer from jetlag for a week.'

His eyes were still wide open as he took a long swig of his rum and Coke.

'Cheers,' I said, as I also took a long swig and looked at his wide eyes over the rim of the cup. 'But when you are with me,' I said, putting the cup down, 'it will be much better because I will be able to sleep while you take the helm.'

'What do I do if I see something like a patrol boat or an aircraft?'

'Shout me awake immediately and cut the engine down to idle speed so we stop making a wake. It's the wake that the helicopter or the spotter plane sees. They don't see the fucking boat. If a Heineken comes anywhere near us, don't cut the revs. We may have to fuck off sharpish.'

'What the fuck's a Heineken?'

I put my drink down and got off the bed to find one of my glossy magazines to show Rafael a Heineken lager advertisement.

'What the fuck are you looking for?'

'I'm looking for an advert for Heineken so I can show you the colours of the *Guardia Civil* patrol boats. That's why we call them Heinekens.'

'I'm not fucking colour-blind and every fucker knows those colours, so stop looking through those *revistas*.'

I threw the magazine on the table and clambered back onto my bed and grabbed my drink. 'Just so long as you can recognise a Heineken so we can get the fuck out of there before they get into shooting range,' I said, wondering whether I had said too much, because I didn't want to frighten him.

'Those patrol boats are fucking faster than a RIB,' he said, eyes popping out of his head now.

'Not when we throw the cargo over the side they fucking ain't. And we don't throw the cargo out till they are on our tail. If we time it right, they'll crash into one or more of the bales of hashish, knocking a big fucking hole in their hull. When we're empty, they'll never catch us.'

'Thank fuck for that,' he said, refilling our cups. 'What about when we unload in Alicante. Will I come back to Malaga with you?'

'No, my plan is for us to stay in Morocco, so we will refuel and double back to Nador at a great rate of knots. Depending on sea conditions we should crack 60 mph all the way back to Morocco.'

'Fucking hell! So we could be back in seven or eight hours?'

'Yep. But we will be absolutely shagged out by the time we get back,' I said, taking another long swig of my rum and not so much Coke. My head swam slightly when the fumes of the rum assaulted my nostrils, making me feel good in Satan's lavatory.

Don Rafael took a gulping mouthful of nearly neat rum and said,

'So how long have we got between trips? What happens to the RIB when we get back? I've got a shitload of fucking questions to ask.'

'That's all right, ask away. I've got a shitload of fucking time to answer your questions. A number of things determine when we take another cargo. First of all, when we get back, we recover the RIB from the water and put her in the workshop. Then we fuck off and live for a few days: have a rest, get pissed, get fed, get fucked and when we're ready and feeling good, we sort out the next job. If we haven't got a brand new RIB for the next trip, then we service the one we just used. Great care is taken with the servicing and I insist on clean fuel tanks because the tanks have been filled from jerrycans or *jarafas*, so there's always shit in the tanks after a job. Every filter is replaced with new ones and the water separators are stripped and cleaned regardless of how clean they look. The Moroccans always have a marine engineer to look over the engines, but you can't trust the fuckers. When they're finished, I always check over their work, then remove and check each spark plug to make sure they're new. When I'm happy with the RIB, I'll take her for a spin. Then she can be loaded and made ready to sail.'

'You take lots of precautions,' said Rafael, stretching to fill up my cup.

I noticed the bottle was well down and wouldn't last much longer. 'When you break down at sea and you fuck around trying to find the fault, you'll always find that the problem is a bit of shit blocking something up. Once when I broke down, it was the fucking spark plugs; the illustrious marine engineer had replaced the spark plugs but had forgotten to tighten them up: one fucked engine, one fucked job.'

'What did you do?' Big wide eyes now.

'Fortunately, I was only about a mile out from Cabo Negro, east of Ceuta, when it conked out. Obviously I couldn't see the damage, but I was later told it was the end of the loose spark plug melting onto the piston. I managed to limp back to the beach and get unloaded, so at least the cargo was saved.'

Rafael rummaged through his bag to find two bread rolls and a packet of Serrano ham. He made himself a ham roll then tossed the makings over for me to have one.

He was chomping on his ham roll and talking at the same time: 'When did you first go to sea?'

I had to think for a moment. Christ, what a question! '1964 was when I first handled a yacht. That was at the Royal Engineers Yacht Club at Kiel, Krautland, on the Baltic Sea.'

'Fuck! That sounds cold,' said Don Rafael, spluttering his lips as though he was freezing, sending a shower of breadcrumbs down his shirt front.

'No, it was a lovely late summer. I remember it well. Maybe if the weather had been bad, I would never have gone to sea, but it wasn't, it was beautiful. I was thrilled to bits with the whole thing. I remember thinking that I wish I had joined the Navy instead of the fucking Army.' I took a big bite of my Spanish buttie and a swig of rum and Coke, rolling it around my mouth savouring the dark meat and the tang of the rum. 'The yacht club was right next to the German submarine pens and was part of the massive naval base. I remember having loads of piss-ups and the occasional punch-up in the kraut boozer across the road from the main gates.' My memory started to fade in the fumes of Navy rum, but bollocks, that was in a previous life. We polished the bottle of rum off and swung the chandelier around the jungle and the desert for an hour or so, then Don Rafael left, with the promise that I'd remain alone in my cell until the Carabanchel closed in October.

August was truly a crap month, with inmates rotting and rioting in prison while Spain went on holiday. Prisoners could just about hack it when they thought somebody was working on their case, but moping in here, knowing nothing was happening while all that paperwork was sitting on some fucker's desk for a month caused bewilderment, anger and depression. Spanish prisoners mutilated themselves by slashing their forearms with razor blades. I told several bleeding spicks that a much better result could be achieved by slashing the carotid artery, or having a go at that big vein near your groin.

August was the time when the heroin pusher got lucky. Sudden attacks of vomiting were noticeably increasing during this month as the jet-propelled chunder roared out of the mouths of new junkies to splash on nearby sunbathers or drench the flip-flops of passing strollers, causing much annoyance and fighting. Luckily I spent much of my time in the gymnasium so I missed most of the chundering.

Chinky and Jake kept me up to speed with whatever was happening on the wing, so each time I sat at the English table I would get a report on who did what and if it affected the *Mezclado*. August affected everybody in one way or another.

Strangely, the wing population increased as the month wore on. The reason guessed at was the height-of-season tourist-mugging spree. Some of the creatures that came onto the wing should have been drowned at birth. Scumbag is a term of endearment for some of these fuckers. They seemed to be loitering and lurking furtively wherever I looked. They were in the corners, the sloppy shithouse and even the showers, where they stuck out like racing dogs' bollocks because they never washed. There seemed to be a heightened hostile atmosphere, which would soon materialise into a blood and snot answer to the intimidating environment being created by the Madrid underclass. Oddly, they had a superiority complex that gave them a confidence and cheekiness. This was completely farcical and inevitably very painful for many of them.

One of them must have thought I was a tourist: he tried to mug me in the coffee queue. I was chatting with Bernhard, a big kraut ex-Paratrooper, when I felt a sharp object poking into my ribs from the side. It was a *pinchou*.

A harsh voice started to stage whisper, but before the sounds had translated to words in my brain, the voice was stifled by the larynx-crushing point of my elbow as it smashed into the thyroid cartilage and trachea of the mindless guttersnipe who was about to have a bad day out. I heard the bones cracking as I folded his hand over against the wrist joint so I could remove the spike from his numb fingers. I immediately plunged it into his right buttock, where it would be discovered later by the examining doctor over in the *enfermería*. But right now he was struggling to breathe through his damaged windpipe. He couldn't quite force the cry of pain through his swelling airway, so a pathetic squeal passed his trembling lips as the *pinchou* entered the flesh of his arse.

My fists set about changing his dark, good looks as I battered his face with hard, crunching punches that would cause serious facial disfigurement lasting several weeks. Each time he looked in the mirror he'd be reminded never to stick a spike into the ribs of the flint-hearted Anglo-Saxon, and to stick to mugging old lady tourists: it was safer.

A passing Moroccan stooped to look at the bleeding face, then grunted with recognition as he grabbed the ankles and pulled him across the dirty floor away from the *economato* queue. He let go of the ankles as he reached a group of his countrymen, who first looked at the face, then spat into it. Apparently the battered muckworm had been busy with his *pinchou* and I had just saved his bacon because the Moroccans were about to dispatch him just as he'd tried to mug me. They'd held back for a moment to see the cabaret.

Don Francisco, the English-speaking thug in prison officers' garb, stood over the bleeding gypsy with his feet apart, holding his long truncheon behind his back under the cheeks of his arse. He was rolling back and forth on the balls of his feet, reminiscent of a New York cop. He thought the Arabs had battered the gypsy, but the Spanish grasses soon had him looking in my direction. His fellow prison officer, Don Isidrio, organised the getting of the gurney, while Don Francisco slowly, menacingly approached the *economato* queue, heading straight for me. Bernhard the kraut suddenly stepped in front of him, gobbing off in rapid Spanish, apparently explaining the attempted robbery with violence by the witless, unlicked cub.

Don Francisco brought the truncheon to bear on Bernhard's upper arm, moving him aside with a quick jerk of his head, indicating for him to get out of the way. Bernhard momentarily resisted, then thought better of it, realising he was blocking the path of a uniformed lunatic who would crack his skull unmercifully if he didn't cooperate. I looked into the dull eyes of the dipsomaniac. The stink of whisky hung in the air in front of his face: a common occurrence amongst the keepers of the Carabanchel.

'You Eengleesh cunt! You theenk you can fuck with my *paisanos* and walk away?'

'I fuck with nobody, especially your *paisanos*. But if one of your *paisano ratas* tries to stick his *pinchou* in me, then I'll show you how I fuck your *paisanos.'*

'Where is the *pinchou*?' he snarled, panting whisky fumes across my face.

'I think one of the Arabs shoved it up his greasy arse,' I lied.

'Which wog cunt did that?' he shouted, turning to glare at the nearby Moroccans.

'I'm fucked if I know. But I'm chuffed to fuck that someone gave it back to him,' I beamed.

'Just because you are Don Rafael's *maricon* [queer] doesn't mean you are safe from me, you Eengleesh cunt!'

The dull eyes had now come to life and showed the watery glitter of insanity as the nerves in them tried to unravel inside the numb skull of the uniformed nutter.

'Are you saying that Don Rafael is a homosexual? He will be pleased to hear that his colleagues think he's a fucking queer,' I chuckled sarcastically.

'You will keep your fucking trap closed, Meester fucking Eengleeshman. You cause trouble here and you fucking die, you cunt!'

He was spitting his words now. Angry as fuck he was, so I held my tongue, because to further the confrontation now was risky. His knuckles were white as he gripped his truncheon, so I said, 'OK, *jefe*, I'll say nothing to Don Rafael. *Adios*,' and I turned away quickly and took my place in the coffee queue, noticing that the *Mezclado* were strategically placed all around me. The gurney arrived for the guttersnipe and away he went, never to be seen on this wing again.

Don Francisco stupidly got himself amongst the Moroccans in an attempt to locate whoever had stabbed the spike into the arse of the guttersnipe. The chances of Lord Lucan stepping out of the crowd had better odds.

An old Moroccan wearing a jellaba and a fez suddenly broke into song as he thrashed a battered guitar that was completely out of tune in what was obviously intended as a piss-take of Don Francisco. A jolly crowd of Arabs immediately formed around Mohammed Chet Atkins and started clapping and drumming on the tabletops, creating a most alarming cacophony of typical shite Moroccan music. North Africans, large and small, danced with imaginary sultry tribal maidens. Rif mountain-men momentarily lost in dreams of home, eyes closed in remembrance of family celebrations, danced with arms outstretched, swivelling around on one foot while trying to look like corrugated iron. Not quite the image of a whirling dervish; more like a shit-kicker's shanty. The only things missing were sand and camels.

The audience of Europeans thought the whole thing was quite ridiculous, but the Arabs enjoyed themselves tremendously, seemingly unabashed at what would cause most Europeans to inwardly cringe if called upon to perform likewise without a belly full of ale. The sand-shanty troupe continued their shuffling jigs accompanied by the desert choir until teatime and the whole thing was truly abominable on the ears, but I had to laugh at the antics of Arabs acting the goat. Some of them were blowing into empty plastic bottles while others had taken the dominoes and put them in plastic buckets to rattle. In fact there was a whole host of improvised instruments. No one made any attempt at a rhythm; any momentary beat was purely accidental and was quickly fucked up and brought back to Moroccan standards. Melody was also accidental and derived at by chanting, shouting or a shrill yodelling sound, yet they seemed to know what it was all about and there was plenty of backslapping for some obscure solo performance that the trained ear somehow missed.

It was funny to see Mohammed Chet Atkins turning the tuning keys on the guitar strings as he cocked his head in an attitude of listening to the strings twanging into tune, then smugly nodding to the ensemble, letting them know he was ready to go. Then, with his fez skew-whiff, reminiscent of a brown, bearded Tommy Cooper, his right hand flew into action in a blur of tuneless strumming, while the fingers of his left hand wandered up and down the fret-board like a nervous crab, producing sounds that no other guitarist in the world could copy. Some of them had wrapped a comb in a piece of newspaper and were blowing sounds through it like a kazoo.

I watched two men performing a dance of intricate gawky movements which definitely bore no relation to the noise of the band, but they were strangely coordinated and the noise didn't put them off as they delighted everyone with something handed down from their tribal ancestors. I wondered what it was: possibly a sand dance or a desert ballet, probably based on the avoidance of stepping in camel shit or on a scorpion. These people were making me laugh, but not everybody was happy with the Arab cabaret.

A group of spiteful gypsies gathered across the yard from the Arabs and tried to compete with a couple of guitars and syncopated clapping, but they were no match for the rowdy chaos clattering out of the pipes and drums of the Camel Corps Band. Everything ended on a bum note as the screws came out, whistling us in for the evening meal.

The shimmering air distorted my vision of the rooftops of Madrid on the final evening of August. I was standing on the table in my cell with my elbows resting on the bars of the window. I was daydreaming about where the aircraft could possibly be flying off to when Don Rafael let himself in.

'Here, take the phone. I'll be about half an hour, so I'll see you later.'

Then he was gone. I called Susan and told her there might be a hiccup with the telephone because Rafael was on holiday as from tomorrow and Don Pablo was due back shortly but I didn't know when. She told me he had promised to make my life dead easy when he got back, and I would be able to use his office phone whenever he couldn't give me his mobile, so there was no need to worry about telephones. Susan told me that the Colombian girl who was Don Pablo's bit on the side had given her a contact number in Madrid and another one in Cali, Colombia. She told Susan that she wanted to keep in contact with us forever, saying that these contact numbers were a secret and that not even Don Pablo knew them. Susan was puzzled as to why she would do such a thing. I told her to put the numbers somewhere safe and forget all about her until I got home. I wondered if the women were trickier than the men? Fucking right they were: what a silly question.

I asked her if Kennedy was at the *finca* and she told me he'd gone to sea that morning but his missus was still in their apartment, seemingly pissed off because he didn't tell her he was working.

Apparently he would be away for a week. That snippet of information told me that Kennedy was working the Nador to Alicante job, so there would be plenty of cash around next week.

I felt the slight wind pressure as Don Rafael pulled open the cell door, so I told my sweetheart how much I loved her, then cleared the line.

'All's well? I hope,' said Rafael, grinning all across his face.

'What's so funny?' I said, passing him his mobile phone.

'I'm on holiday as from tomorrow.'

'Yeah, yeah, don't fucking rub it in. I'm not in the mood.'

'Ah, but I am,' he chuckled.

I quickly tidied my bed then stretched out on it as Rafael pulled the chair across to make himself comfortable with his feet up on their usual spot.

'I'll be away for two weeks so keep your head down while I'm gone and don't upset any *funcionarios*. Some of them don't like you, so beware.'

The concerned look on his face disappeared as he pulled out the bottle of Navy rum and two large plastic cups.

'You're gonna fuckin' miss this,' he chuckled.

'What did I say about fucking rubbing it in?' I chided.

He laughed and said, 'Your pal Don Pablo will be back in a day or two, so I'm sure you can expect something nice from him.'

I did expect something nice, especially after he'd had such a nice time at my house. And, of course, I did get something nice: new underwear and T-shirts, new socks and trainers, a box of toiletries and several jars of vitamin and mineral pills. But for now I had a bottle of Navy rum to polish off.

'I wouldn't be surprised if Don Pablo went to Jerusalem for his holidays,' said Rafael, not knowing, of course, where he'd really been. 'He's tighter than a duck's arse and he looks fucking Jewish.'

'No. He looks more like a mafioso to me: slicked down and swarthy,' I argued, 'never done a day's work in his fucking life.'

'That's why I think he's a fucking Jew. Have you noticed his jewellery? The rings and tiepins he fuckin' wears? The smarmy bastard.'

Don Rafael's eyes were glowing green with envy as I replied, 'Yes, the jewellery is old Masonic jewellery, probably handed down through his family.'

I remembered admiring a gold signet ring inlaid with jade upon which was carved the square and compass symbol of the Brotherhood of Freemasons. I had noticed other fine old pieces, all with the Brotherhood's markings. But one piece in particular stuck in my mind, and that was the beautiful gold tiepin with the all-seeing eye inlaid in lapis lazuli between the legs of the compass: the mark of the Grand Master.

Don Rafael poured the rum and added Coca-Cola, then handed me the brimming cup.

'I don't know anything about Freemasons,' he said. 'They had a club in Nottingham, but I thought it was just like a working men's club.'

'Nobody knows much about Freemasons because they're a secret society. Mind you, in the UK there are loads of coppers and screws boozing in Masonic lodges, so it can't be that fucking secretive, can it, and if the Krays and Kenny Noye are members then they should change the fucking name to the Kennel Club.'

I smiled at my little joke, then Rafael said, 'Well, they can't be up to much fucking good if Don Pablo is one of them.'

'Maybe he isn't one of them,' I said, swigging my rum. 'Maybe he thinks it's cool to wear the jewellery. He obviously knows what it is and likes to be an impostor.'

'I don't think so. He rubs shoulders with the aristocracy and jet-set of Madrid, so his circle of friends wouldn't like to think he's an impostor,' said Rafael.

The thought occurred to me that Don Pablo and Enrico were big pals and Enrico's circle of friends included the Diplomatic Corps and high-placed officials on the Madrid government scene. But I suspected Don Pablo was not a Freemason, and that nor was Enrico. They were more likely Knights of St Colomba. But who gave a fuck? We had that rum to get down us, and August was just about to fade away.

FIFTEEN
LUCKY

A new black face arrived on the wing from *galería siete*. He came across the yard and sidled up to me, adjusting his step to mine.

'How're ya doin', Chancer?' he asked in his Rasta accent.

'Who the fuck wants to know?' I replied.

'Lucky,' he said, 'Lucky Johnstone, from Tenerife.'

'Well, you ain't from Tenerife and if you're in here, you ain't fucking lucky. What do you want?' I said, as the camera whirred on its axis to follow us around the yard and the *Mezclado* kept watch from various lookout points.

'I'm a pal of Billy Rigby in Gib. You was supposed to take a tonne of pollen out of Larache and take it to Tenerife but you got fucked into here instead.'

'How the fuck do you know that?' I said, glaring into his shiny black face. His eyes were brown and showed no sign of substance abuse. He was lean and looked fit, but there was a shiftiness about him that made me feel slightly uncomfortable.

'Bad news travels fast. Lenny, your shipmate, had to find another skipper *rapido* and he ended up with that big fat cunt, Peter Zantmayer, the Swiss fella.'

'So what has all this got to do with you?'

'I was waiting for that cargo in Tenerife. Part of it was mine.'

'So what happened with the job?'

'It was four days late and the shit had to be stashed in Larache,

191

which cost extra, but the problem was with that grabbing cunt Zantmayer. The bastard had us over a barrel and wanted too much money. He wanted more than double what you was gettin' an' he wanted a hotel in Tenerife to rest for a week before he returned to Spain. The shithead wouldn't take the fuckin' boat back to Morocco to get ready for the nex' trip.'

'But Lenny got the job done?'

'Yeah, but fuckin' hell man, it . . .'

I cut him short right there. 'Stop fucking dripping about a job that's been done. You're fucking lucky Lenny found another skipper willing to do it. Anyway, what do you want?'

We walked in silence for a moment, then Lucky Johnstone said, 'I wanna be with your lot on the English table, an' I'm 'earin' there's room in your cell.'

Whenever an inmate changed wings, the screws would let them onto the yard first to see if they knew anybody they could share with. If this didn't work, they allocated him the first single-occupancy cell to hand. As far as I was concerned, this is what would be happening with Lucky.

'You can join the English table if the others don't object, but I'm fucked if I'm letting you share my cell. Don't even fucking think about it because you ain't.'

'What if the screws put me in with you?'

'Don't worry, they fucking won't, even if you ask.'

'That's a big shame,' he said sadly. 'I was 'opin' we could make some decent plans for the future. There's loadsa scope on Tenerife. It's growin' an' growin', man.' A genuine expression of concern spread across his face, exposing the whites of his eyes. 'Tryin' to find a fuckin' skipper dese days is a fuckin' joke, especially to do de Atlantic. Nobody's got da fuckin' bottle,' he said, despairingly.

I wondered how much tactical knowledge Lucky had of the coastline and landing points on Tenerife. I decided to pick his brains later, when he was settled in. 'We can discuss all kinds of fucking plans, but you're not living in my cell just to make plans. We can do that out here in the yard.'

We did several laps of the yard, then Chinky beckoned me into the shade for coffee.

'I'll go and sort a cell out,' said Lucky, avoiding the inevitable meeting with the *Mezclado*, heading off in the direction of the screws' office.

'Who's the coon?' asked Jake, as I sat on the concrete plinth to drink my coffee.

'Oh, he's an acquaintance of an acquaintance,' I replied, smiling at my cute reply. 'Apparently he was a customer of mine who I hadn't yet met.'

'A coon customer, eh?' laughed Chinky.

Everyone chuckled as the penny dropped.

'He wants to join us,' I said, looking at each face in turn.

'I don't know if I could rely on him,' sneered Jake, letting slip his lack of enthusiasm for black friends.

'You didn't have a problem with Kennedy, or did you?' asked Ali Safave.

'Nope, but he was different. He was here when we formed the *Mezclado* and he was reliable.'

'Maybe,' said Ali, 'but we won't know how reliable Lucky is if we don't let him in. I know him from *galería siete* and he's a good man.'

That clinched it. If Ali Safave reckoned he was a good bloke then that was good enough for me.

'OK, that'll do. He's in, at least for now,' I said. 'Unless someone has an objection apart from the colour of his skin.'

Jake harrumphed loudly as we all laughed at the ridiculousness of everything. We jangled like fishermen's wives for an hour, then Lucky Johnstone wandered into view. Lucky's dawdle seemed to be jet propelled in comparison to a group of African blacks who he overtook, though. These blokes moved around the yard like the zombies in Michael Jackson's *Thriller*. Everything about them had an air of creeping slackness, as though they were sleepwalking. Occasionally they would wake up to kick a football around the yard, but generally they would inch along trance-like. I no longer wonder why Africa is so fucked up.

Lucky ambled up to me saying, 'I've been put in with Rico. Is he here?'

'No, mate,' I said. 'He's over there, playing chess. He's the Italian bloke with all the muscles. Don't go over there yet. He enjoys his chess and he wouldn't thank you for disturbing him.'

'Especially with the good news you are sharing his fucking cell,' added Jake.

Everyone chuckled disparagingly except Ali Safave, who said, 'If he kicks up a fuss, you can share my cell.'

'I'll go and get the coffee,' said Chinky. 'How do you like yours?' he said to Lucky's face.

'*Cortado*,' said Lucky, showing lots of white teeth.

'C'mon, Jake, gimme a hand.'

Lucky sat on the concrete plinth between Ali and Vito and was quietly gobbing off about how he knew me and the general goings-on in Tenerife, when Rico strolled across from the big metal table full of chess boards and pieces.

'I have just been informed that you are moving into my cell. Is that correct?' said Rico, looking hard into Lucky's face.

'Yeah, man. I hope dat's OK wid you.'

'You will shower daily and you will launder your clothes regularly. You will not smoke, spit, shit or wank, nor make any remarks about which programme is on my telly. You obviously know Chancer here, so I will permit you to live in my cell. Behave like a cunt and I'll push you right through the fucking bars to drop into the yard below.'

'OK, man, no fuckin' sweat.'

Rico turned to face me, winking with the eye Lucky couldn't see. 'He'll only be with me for a month. I've been told I'm going to Lugo prison in Galicia the first week in October.'

Rico was lucky. He was one of the only ones who knew for certain where he'd be going when the Carabanchel closed in October. A flutter of apprehension ran through me as I realised I would be leaving the hell I knew for a hell I didn't know. Anywhere was better than the Carabanchel, but when you've learned to cope and survive in the most disgusting Stygian creek, the notion of a sideways move is unsettling.

Confusion is part of the layer cake of prison mentality and can make the most gifted intellectual capable of imbecilic thought. For a split second there, I actually experienced misgivings about leaving this abysmal dungeon in order to move to a new and better place.

LUCKY

There was no worse prison than this in the whole of Spain, possibly the whole of Europe. Fuck me! They were destroying the place in an attempt to erase the stigma and slur on Spain's new European face: a bit like Max Factor making up Frankenstein's monster. It was going to take a long time to mask all those scars and pustules: pus would always ooze out of this Augean stable, no matter how much concrete they hid it under. Anyway, I would be out of here soon so I'd ask Don Pablo if he knew where I would be sent to. Maybe he knew already.

SIXTEEN
GIFTS

It was in the *zapatería* during a coffee break that I saw Don Pablo for the first time after his holiday at my house in Coín. He entered quietly and made his way through the empty workbenches towards me. There was a flurry of movement as the South Americans scurried back to their benches, such was their affection for the job of making slippers: just another aspect of their fawning, bootlicking nature.

I was sitting supping my coffee as he held out the right hand of fellowship. I gave his knuckle a squeeze and he belatedly squeezed back, more an afterthought, as though he had forgotten about his Masonic jewellery.

'Come to the office, Creestoffur, I have things for you.'

His English had improved noticeably. We strolled across the workshop yard, chatting amicably like a couple of old pals. Obviously the pending closure of the Carabanchel had diluted the snobbishness that his rank had given him. We wended our way through dark corridors, chatting about Susan and my lovely German shepherds, Max and Sammy, and Roxy, my Rottweiler, while puzzled or smirking prison officers allowed us to pass through the gates.

Don Pablo was dressed like a country squire. His well-cut trousers matched his Harris tweed hacking jacket, and his open-necked shirt with a silk cravat reminded me of Foxy in *The Day of the Jackal*. On reflection, he did look a lot like a dark, oily James Fox, but more short-arsed.

We entered his plush office and he waved me to the telephone on his beautiful desk.

'*Llame* Susan,' he said, as he pulled open the ornate doors to the drinks cabinet. He brought out two cut-glass port glasses and filled them from an ancient ship's decanter. 'Susan say you like best port,' he said, proudly confident in his improved English.

'Oh lovely,' I said, holding out my hand to receive the glass.

'*Llama* Susan *ahora*, speak Susan now,' he said with his thumb to his ear and his little finger to his mouth.

'OK,' I said, lifting the receiver and dialling the number.

Don Pablo disappeared as I spoke to Susan. He left the drinks and locked me in his office, first indicating by holding up his hands that I had ten minutes.

I listened to Susan's soft voice buoying my spirits and assuring me that all would be well. On and on we talked. It was wonderful. I was truly emboldened by the best pep talk I have ever received. My lovely wife is not only self-reliant, but her boldness of spirit makes me wonder if she is a reincarnation of Joan of Arc. If not, then without doubt she is an Amazon.

Don Pablo returned and we enjoyed several glasses of port and chatted about Kennedy and the Big Job. Then he escorted me back to *galería cinco* with my new sports bag full of goodies. His presence prevented any would-be rummagers discovering its contents. Fuck that! He didn't lug this all the way from Coín just to be turned over by some manky fucking screw. He said cheerio and patted my shoulder, just like an old chum. He seemed not to care a fuck who was looking as he waved me into the *galería*, where I quickly found my friends in the yard.

Chinky met me and told me he was en route to the *economato* then pointed to the shaded corner of the yard, where the *Mezclado* were huddled playing *pachis*, a dice race.

'What's in the bag?' said Jake.

'I don't know yet. The missus sent it.'

'How the fuck did she get it in here? I can't even get a fucking parcel sent in.'

Jake wasn't envious, he was just being nosy.

'A pal of Enrico's brought it through *ingreso* for me.'

'A screw, you mean?'

'Yeah, Susan sent it to Enrico and he gave it to the screw last night,' I lied.

'It is nobody's concern how he gets things in, is it,' said Ali Safave angrily.

'Oh, fucking pipe down, I was only curious,' said Jake, getting up to give Chinky a hand with the coffee.

Lunchtime came and I had another foul experience with prison food. It was tripe and onions and the stink made me heave, so no way could I put this clart in my mouth. This was without doubt sapfu (surpasses all previous fuck-ups) from the kitchen. It nearly caused a riot, as everyone threw it away and remained hungry till the evening meal. Fortunately there were three large tins of salmon and a jar of pickled onions in the sports bag so we had a beano with salmon butties, all thanks to Nike, the goddess of sports bags, and my lovely Susan, who filled it with nice things.

As soon as my cell door was locked, I emptied the rest of the bag's contents onto the bed. I was delighted with the newness of everything and the fact that my new trainers were Nikes and fitted perfectly. Susan was an astounding woman: the sports bag was full of lovely surprises and I will love her forever. Susan has always been full of surprises. Two years ago she came with me and Stuart, an associate of mine, to collect some money from an East End face living in an urbanisation on the Costa del Sol. We didn't expect a problem but Stuart was a coward so had asked me to accompany him. He was then going to treat us to lunch.

The face had clocked us parking the car and had left his poolside sunbed to go indoors, closing the *rejas* (folding metal gate) so we couldn't get to him. Susan was standing close to the *rejas* as Stuart was asking nearby sunbathers which apartment the face lived in. Suddenly there was a shout as a pistol appeared through the *rejas*. A shot was fired at either Stuart or me, but unfortunately the gun was inches away from Susan's head, and the bang deafened her in her left ear for months. Very coolly she punched through the bars into his nose, knocking him onto his arse, but he still held the pistol. Pandemonium broke out as sunbathers grabbed their children and dashed indoors to call the police. We quickly returned to the car and were driving down the *carretera* (highway) to Fuengirola as police cars with sirens wailing and a helicopter flying overhead were racing to the scene. Susan's brave punch possibly saved a life or two that day and she has never said a word about it from that day to this. The face was arrested and banged up in Malaga prison, which was a good thing for him, because if I'd been able to get to him, I'd have ripped his fucking head off.

Anyway, I stowed all the nice things back in the sports bag and zipped it tight so no cockroaches could get in, then I relaxed with a big bar of Bourneville dark chocolate: my favourite. I bet King Farouk with all his millions has never felt the joy that that bar of chocolate gave me.

The evening meal that day was atrocious: flaky fish with oily salad served with a couple of slices of Spam. There was a hot soup, but the smell of putrefaction made me gag. The pudding was an apple, but I had to peel it to scoop out the bruises. What a shambolic fucking shitpile this Spanish-run hovel really was. The lousy bastards knew they only had another month before the prisoners left, so they didn't care a fuck about the welfare of the inmates. Some people wonder why I do not think well or highly of the Spanish; all they see is the jolly Costa del Sol, sangria and the stamping feet of flamenco dancers. Oh, and the fucking 'Birdie Song'. I will live with the horrendous scar of the Carabanchel for the rest of my life. To me this prison, though closed down, is the real, corrupt Spain, superintended by a Spanish government whose abysmal stewardship allowed molestation, depravation and malevolence to thrive at the hands of xenophobic officials. It was a place where every Spaniard I met was ingrained from birth with the *denuncia* syndrome (grass, nark, stool-pigeon, informer, *chivato*), unable to keep any secret, driven to report the slightest misdemeanour in their pursuit of a place in the toad-eating championships; a place where primeval desires like watching the slaughter of bulls on national TV and feeling another man's cock up your arse was as natural an urge as breathing. This appalling environment was nurtured by the pitiless, ill-disposed prison officers, most of whom were corrupt, cruel and maladjusted. Which reminded me to ask Don Pablo if he knew where I'd be sent from here.

SEVENTEEN

NEWS ABOUT A MOVE

The following day Don Pablo came to the *zap* and took me to his office so I could use his telephone again to speak with Susan. On the way I asked him about the pending move. He told me that I was going to La Moraleja prison on the outskirts of Dueñas, near Palencia, further to the north of Spain. The prison was brand new and there would not be any Spanish prisoners going there from here. It was Spain's international prison, built solely for foreigners.

'Do not worry, Creestoffur. I have said to Don Marianno that you will be soon there.'

He went on to explain that Don Marianno was his opposite number in La Moraleja and he knew to look after me. He would later give me his calling card with a message on the reverse stating that I was to be cosseted. This card opened many doors for me in La Moraleja, such was the power of corruption and the reputation of Don Pablo.

I told Susan about La Moraleja. The news saddened her because she'd hoped I would be moved to Malaga or perhaps Jaen, where it would have been easy for her to visit. During the three and a half years I ended up spending in Spain's jails, I never once allowed my wife to visit me. Her distress did not need to be doubled by a visit to Satan's lavatory. I explained that my trial would be at the Audiencia Nacional (high court) in Madrid, so being transferred to Malaga was out of the question. Maybe after the trial there'd be a possibility of getting a transfer to Malaga, but until then it was La Moraleja.

It was around this time that Don Rafael came back from holiday. He confirmed I was going to La Moraleja and told me he had a couple of pals up there. He quietly let himself into my cell and quickly set up the rum and Cokes.

'I bet you missed all this shit didn't ya?' he said, grinning all over his face. 'You'll have to make the most of this 'coz you won't be able to booze and deal until my friends get to know you up at La Moraleja.'

'Yeah, I realise that. It's a shame you're not coming.'

'Fuck that! My seniority doesn't count up there. Besides, all the management posts are taken and I'm fucked if I want to run another *galería*. No, I'm out. I've already explained all that.'

'Ah well, it was just wishful thinking,' I said, taking a luxurious swig of Navy rum, savouring the taste and feeling the glow creeping through my guts. I then topped it up with Coke. 'When do you think I will leave here?' I asked.

'You will be with the last batch to leave, right at the bitter end, which should be on 15 October, so you haven't got much time. Just think; you are part of history, being the last Englishman to leave the Carabanchel prison,' he chuckled, as I pondered on the thousands who had gone before me. Was Julian Grimau García kept in this cell? Whereabouts was his bullet-riddled body buried inside these walls of shame? He was the man who'd refused the blindfold when he was executed by firing squad in the Carabanchel prison yard. He was much luckier than Arregi's brother, who was tortured to death. Was it his ghost I'd hear moaning in the night? I remembered entering this dreadful place for the first time, when first I walked under the inglorious masonry and roof, where the ghosts of past prisoners were buried in the stone and cement of this Spanish monstrosity. My imagination was running wild then with all kinds of terrifying thoughts, all part of the Spanish plan to unhinge anybody who was unlucky enough to be sent here, to the dark, infamous Carabanchel.

'I'm fucked if I want to be remembered as the last Brit out of here,' I snapped, as he guffawed loudly.

NEWS ABOUT A MOVE

'The Carabanchel's last Chance!' he crowed, laughing his fucking head off.

'Was you in the fucking pub before you came to work today? You're fucking pissed!'

'No I'm fuckin' not, I'm just enjoying myself. Here, I've got some ham and pickled onions, an' there's a loaf in my bag,' he chuckled as he rummaged around in his sports bag. He put the makings of a sandwich on the table. 'Help yourself,' he said, then, wearing a concerned expression on his face, said, 'You will need to close down the booze racket in a minute and you'll have to be careful with your bank because people will be on the move to other prisons next week.'

'Yeah, I've been thinking about that. We'll pack the booze in this weekend, but I was hoping you could tell me who will not be going to La Moraleja so I know who not to lend money to.'

'Oh, that's fuckin' easy,' he smiled. 'All you foreigners are going to La Moraleja and you are all supposed to be going on *modulo* 8. But be careful 'coz I just heard they are opening two new *modulos*, so you may lose some of your friends and customers. If I was you, I would close the bank now and pull in what's owed.'

'Yeah, I'll do that on Thursday when everyone's been paid,' I said as I lifted my lovely ham-and-pickled-onion buttie. 'I bet you haven't got any mustard in that bag.'

'I fuckin' knew you was going to ask that,' he said, bending over to reach into the bag. '*Oualla!*' he cried as he produced a jar of Senf: kraut mustard.

'Fucking champion,' I said, as I poured a dollop onto my buttie.

I was about to take my first mouth-watering bite when suddenly the cell door swung open and Don Luis, a novice screw on Rafael's shift, stepped in. He babbled something in rapid Spanish to Don Rafael, who then got up and said, 'I won't be long, some cunt has slashed his wrists. Don't drink all the fuckin' rum.'

And they were gone.

EIGHTEEN
MARICONES

I devoured the buttie and washed it down with Coca-Cola straight from the bottle. I was just wondering who the nut was who'd slashed his wrists when Don Rafael returned.

'Fuckin' idiots plague my fuckin' life,' he muttered as he closed the cell door. 'That fuckin' *maricon* Madonna . . .'

'What's up with him?'

'He let that cunt Guillermo get up him in the shower block the other day.'

'So what? All the other gypos fuck him.'

'Guillermo came in off the street last week and his blood test came back this morning. He's HIV pos.'

'So Madonna thinks he's got a dose?'

'And not just that; every fucker knows about it, so Madonna's arse will dry up.'

I have seen Madonna sucking cocks in shower cubicle no. 3. Shower cubicles no. 1 and no. 2 were occupied by Maria and Pu-Rambo respectively. Shower cubicle no. 4, which ended the first section of the shower block, was taken by Nuala, a slim, black transsexual with big, red pouting lips and a masterpiece of home grown tits, the likes of which could only be found here and in Hollywood. This fellow could make a fortune in the Houses of Parliament, but here he was, sucking unwashed cocks and flogging his hole for peanuts.

I had to walk past these four shower cubicles to reach the main shower area, where there were possibly 15 to 20 more cubicles. In the early morning those first four were never occupied, so we used to turn on the hot-water taps in them to waste Spanish hot water. We used cold water for our showers to cool ourselves down.

Many times after a training session in the yard I would enter the shower block and walk past these four cubicles, where I would see slurping cock-suckers and back-scuttling gypsies shamelessly emptying their sacs into each other. Such horrible images will live with me forever. I am constantly reminded of such scenes whenever I see men dressed as women in comedy shows on TV.

'Who shares his cell?' I asked as Don Rafael shoved his buttie into his mouth.

'I've just put him in with Robin Hood,' he said through his mouthful of buttie.

'I thought his wrists were slashed.'

'Oh yeah, the usual scratch on the surface with lots of noisy drama.'

'Robin won't be fucking happy with Madonna in his cell.'

'I don't care a fuck about that thieving cunt. He'll be in the office in the morning complaining all over the place.'

Robin Hood's real name was Francisco, or the shortened, more popular name, Paco. He was about 50 years old and was a well-known jewel thief. He was reputed to have stolen jewellery worth 200 million *pesetas* over a three-month period and now he was host to a disease-laden brown-hatter whose end would be caused by contaminated seed. I couldn't imagine the distress caused to Robin Hood by having Madonna in his cell; on the other hand, he might have been getting a suck at that very minute.

Madonna was a man doing his best to become the ugliest woman in Spain, but he had a lewdness about him which exuded *double entendres* as though he was saying, 'I'm a woman, but I'll let you bite the pillow if you like.' His hairy legs had been shaven so often that he now had a five o'clock shadow beneath his knees. He wore his skirts longer than the other queers and his tits didn't seem to hang right. He was always on the lookout for a regular boyfriend, but because he'd had so many, he was a bit of a soiled dove. Now that Guillermo had contaminated his freckle, the adventure of being a burlesque tart would die the death, unless he took Guillermo to be his husband; then they could both die the death together. The leprosy aspect was apparent the next day; everyone avoided Madonna for fear of being contaminated. All the modern-day Aids education doesn't quite touch the nerve of acceptance in fellow human beings. The deep-rooted animal instinct of shunning the sick still persists in the survival world of prison.

Everybody was waiting for the inevitable rumpus, for there were too many points of convergence in this place to evade your enemy for long. Guillermo's payback happened in the yard as he made his way across it with a cup of coffee in one hand and a *revista* in the other. Madonna moved in behind him and stabbed him in the back. The *pinchou* must have struck the scapula because it did not penetrate; it seemed only to go in half an inch. The cry of pain was heard all around the yard as Guillermo dropped the coffee and bolted to the shower block, followed closely by a screaming Madonna and a flock of Spanish sheep-shaggers looking for entertainment.

I was entering the shower block when it happened, so I stepped aside to allow the fleeing Guillermo into the cul-de-sac where Madonna's ilk lay in ambush in their shower cubicles. The transsexual brute Maria downed Guillermo with a leg trip, flattening him, with his arms outstretched on the wet floor. Nuala, the black tranny, rushed out of trap 4 holding a heavy mop-bucket right over him, which he then dropped onto his head. It was one of those metal mop-buckets with castors and a mechanical mop squeezer, so it was a formidable blow, capable of breaking a skull. The impact smashed Guillermo's face into the floor, which stunned him and put a lump the size of a golf ball on his head. Nuala stomped on the mop-bucket, trying to make more lumps, but Madonna shoved it away and started to hack at his ear with his spike. He quickly became fed up with the ear and attacked the buttocks in a frenzy of stabbing and slashing. Maria and Nuala stepped back sharply when the blood started to fly about. Fuck that for a game of soldiers. The grasses were all squeezing into the shower block to witness the demise of Guillermo in order to gain brown-nose points with the screws.

I postponed my shower and turned to exit the block before the Keystone Kops arrived. A path cleared for me the instant I went against the flow and I made my way out. Just as I stepped out of the doorway, a tranny by the name of Sylvia collided with me in his belated rush of support for his gender-bender *compadres*. He knocked me off balance into Romulo, a scowling, scar-faced gangster from downtown Madrid. I didn't see the punch that split my lip, but his garlic breath was like a cloud of vapour in my face as he tried to lock his arm around my neck, pulling me in for a big bite. I forced my head down under his chin to avoid his tainted brown teeth and to take a meaningful bite of Adam's apple, while simultaneously driving my knee up into his crotch. My knee rocketed into his bollocks three times as I tore away at his throat. I was really missing my broken teeth just now, but the ones remaining were well embedded. I clamped off his windpipe with the aid of my left arm behind his neck, forcing him into my mouth. I was pulverising his guts with my right fist when suddenly he was ripped out of my grasp and slammed into the concrete by Ali and Jake.

'Get out quick. The screws are here,' rasped Ali, as I grabbed my shower bag and instinctively moved into the crowd milling around the door.

Don Francisco, the English-speaking thug, was first on the scene, with Don Juan, the little Hitler, right behind him. Sylvia, whose real name was Sylvestre, was about to explain the decking of Romulo to Don Francisco, when Chinky grabbed his elbow to steer him away. Sylvia was reluctant at first, but became more compliant when Chinky grabbed one of his tits and pulled him painfully out into the yard to enlighten him regarding grassing.

Madonna, Maria and Nuala were taken to the screws' office as the gurney arrived for Guillermo. Romulo had recovered and was nursing his throat and bollocks in the recreation room. I had mixed feelings about him because I didn't finish him off with a good hiding. If you don't give these people a hard enough beasting, they tend to come after you for revenge. I wasn't wrong. For days after Guillermo's demise, Romulo could be seen peering intently at me, always from the midst of his group of friends. The *Mezclado* kept him under surveillance for a little while, then we all became fed up with it all, so one day I strolled across to his group and gave him the eye.

'*Servicios!*' I said, nodding in the direction of the spattered porcelain shed. I turned away and started walking towards the shithouse, knowing the *Mezclado* were strategically positioned in case anything irksome happened behind my back.

I didn't walk into the stinking bog. I stood by the door and waited. A tall, skinny bloke came over from Romulo's crowd and told me in bad English that the incident should be forgotten; it seemed Romulo didn't want to know. I took that remark with a pinch of salt, but agreed with the messenger. I would be careful over the next couple of weeks, then I'd be gone from this place.

NINETEEN
DEBT COLLECTING

Peculio day (payday) was busy for me at the end of September. I managed to collect all debts, bar three. I expected this because blokes were being sent to different prisons this week, so, human nature being what it is, some of them hoped to get away without paying me.

Alfredo was keeping out of my way, so I suspected he was up to something. I checked with the duty screw to see if he knew who was being transferred this week and guess what? The three musketeers who owed me money were listed for transfer to Valdemoro prison on Monday, and they were: Alfredo, Javier and Paco Rabane. I immediately went in search of all three to get my money back.

I found Alfredo in the shithouse, chasing the dragon. He was a junkie, who earned his dough trading Charlie and smack but regularly used my bank to finance deals on Tuesdays and Wednesdays when cash was scarce. I hated coming in here. The stink made me gag and the filth was everywhere, but I had to find the three musketeers before they blew their dough on smack.

Alfredo was in trap 3, sitting on the filthy pan with a drinking straw in his mouth, sucking up the fumes of the scorched heroin as he held his cigarette lighter beneath the silver foil upon which was the brown sugar. I didn't disturb him; this was his moment of euphoria, his time to chew the clouds. Nothing else mattered to him right now, so I would gain nothing by fucking it up for him. I waited until he finished then I calmly asked for my money. He gave me the usual Spanish spluff about his *madre* and his dying *abuela* (grandma) needing money, so while he was feeling on top of the world, I relieved him of his watch and told him to deliver his television to my cell before the recreation hour tonight. He started to bleat about watching his favourite film star that night, so I informed him about all the stars he would be seeing if he didn't bring it. He was glazing over with smack now so I fucked off out of that stinking pit and started to walk around the yard doing deep-breathing and total-exhalation exercises in order to dispel the excremental fumes I endured in having to speak to that lowlife spick in his lair. I hated that terrible place. I felt contaminated by it. Ugh!

That night Alfredo came to my cell, pleading to keep his TV and promising to pay me on Tuesday after he had fixed a drugs deal, obviously unaware that I knew he was being transferred to Valdemoro on Monday. I pulled him into my cell and drove my knee up into his bollocks. He doubled up, clutching his crotch. I quickly turned him sideways on and blitzed his leg with a volley of knee strikes, then I spun him around to even up the damage by doing his other leg. He writhed on the floor, rubbing anaesthetised thighs and crushed gonads. I grabbed his throat and yanked him to his feet and shouted, 'Television, *ahora!*' Then I pulled him out onto the landing and pushed him in the direction of his cell, which was across the bridge on the opposite landing to mine.

The bridge was a narrow walkway joining the two long landings on either side of the wing. It was cluttered with grimy dustbins, which exuded a special smell all of their own, much like the inside of a dustman's glove. They were yet another health hazard, as well as being a dangerous obstruction so high above ground level. I wondered where Alfredo had got to, as I hadn't seen him cross the bridge. I leant on the handrail looking all around at the toing and froing of the wing: blokes nipping in and out of cells, shouting obscenities at each other, using sign language and gathering in huddles outside of various cells – the hubbub of prison wings the world over. The members of the *Mezclado* were all out; leaning on the handrail observing everything, waiting to see the TV being delivered, knowing that one of them would inherit it tonight.

DEBT COLLECTING

Chinky was down on the *segundo* (second level, or 'twos' in English prison parlance), waving to attract my attention. Ali spotted him and shouted across to me, pointing him out. When I clocked him, he pointed down towards the screws' office then gave me the grassing hand signal, opening and closing his fingers and thumb, indicating that Alfredo was gobbing off with the screws. Chinky, Jake and Vito made their way up to my level and positioned themselves near the bridge on the opposite side of the wing. Ali, Abdulla and Lucky joined me, leaning on the handrail. We all knew who was on duty tonight: Don Francisco, the nutter.

At last the duty screw arrived with the grassing Alfredo in tow.

'Hey, you English cunt! Extortion will get you another two years.'

That was the moment when he noticed he was completely surrounded by the *Mezclado*. There was no escape; he was too far away from the office and reinforcements. He realised he was very near the gap between the safety net and the gable end of the wing; this could be the beginning of a really bad day out.

'I'll let it go this time,' he said, bravely, 'but if it happens again you will get a problem.'

His eyes were wide with the sudden fear and uncertainty thrust upon him by the surprise ambush. This was his moment of enlightenment; the moment most feared by all prison officers: alone, in the midst of the people who hated him most. His blue serge armour was just like so much blotting paper right now, ready to soak up the piss of fear, the shit of alarm and the blood of impact with the floor below.

'OK, *jefe*,' I said. 'I will leave him alone just so long as he pays me what he owes me before Monday.'

I looked deep into the eyes of the lunatic prison officer, willing a message into his tangled brain that he was a very lucky man to be able to walk away from the monstrous mistake he had just made. Such was the misguided confidence of these stupid men that they thought they could do anything so long as they were in uniform. Had any prison officer in a British prison (like Parkhurst), put himself in the same situation, he would most certainly be dead. He would have been launched right through that fucking gap.

While everyone was intent on what was happening outside my

cell, Chinky had slunk away and raided Alfredo's cell. He put Alfredo's TV into a plastic refuse sack and took it to the opposite end of the wing. Don Francisco's bubble burst with the resounding crash of exploding television as it arrived on the bottom floor, just outside the screws' office. Chinky had chucked it over the top handrail to plummet through the other gap at the far end of the wing to land (hopefully, he thought, on the head of a screw) just by the screws' office door. Don Francisco seized the moment to fuck off from whence he came as the wing erupted with laughter and gleeful faces leered over the handrails at the glittering debris below.

The duty screw didn't have a clue what it was until he joined his *compadres* down below, but the penny had dropped for Alfredo. In his heart he knew it was his TV as he dashed past all the laughing spectators leaning over the handrails. There was a hushed silence as Don Francisco picked up a piece of television with Alfredo's name written across it in shocking-pink marker pen. He slowly looked upwards at the leering crowds of prisoners gawping down at him.

'*Hijo de putas!*' screamed Alfredo, as the *galería* erupted with shrieks of laughter and cat-calls. It seemed that everyone knew about Alfredo's plan to piss off without paying the *giri*. He couldn't resist telling his pals about it, so being Spanish, they had to tell everybody else, hence the uproar. The howling laughter pissed off the screws so they quickly banged us all up for the night.

The following day Alfredo was sandwiched between Ali and Vito in the *economato* queue and was informed that failure to pay the debt would result in his being transferred to Valdemoro in a wheelchair. It is surprising where money comes from when you really need it: Alfredo coughed up the next day.

Paco Rabane's idea was typically Spanish; he approached me to ask for a further loan to pay for a heroin deal on Sunday, so when he had sold the smack on Monday, he would pay me in full on Tuesday. This creep was called Paco Rabane because he stank like a whore's boudoir. He used a jasmine-scented brilliantine to slick back his hair in the fashion of a poncey flamenco dancer, or maybe he thought himself a ballerina. He used lashings of cheap aftershave and perfume on his face and clothes, but it did nothing for his halitosis. His mouth was like a horse's arse.

DEBT COLLECTING

I agreed to give him a further loan and I told him that I'd pass it to him on Saturday morning in the shower block. We all knew he was having a *vis-à-vis* visit with his wife on Friday, so I knew he would have cash and smack after the visit.

Vis-à-vis is the conjugal-rights visit when the prisoner is allowed to shag his missus in one of the fuck cells situated in the visiting block. The fuck cells provide the prison with all manner of drugs: heroin, cocaine, hashish and all the various pills that dreamers seek. Great quantities of this stuff is brought in, hidden you know where. Whole families pile into the fuck rooms for a visit. Wives, mothers, sisters and children discharge the contents of various holes then hug and kiss and traipse out, leaving the wife behind for a shag.

I've seen blokes come back on the wing with a kilo of hashish, brought in inside family holes. Four nine-bars make a kilo and a nine-bar is six or seven inches long by about two and a half inches wide and is an inch thick, so there are some big old fannies out there. Still, if a baby's head can get through, a couple of nine-bars is a piece of piss.

Many times I watched the outer wrapping being passed around so everyone could have a sniff of whoever's fanny had brought it in. They would rip it up so they each had a piece for a pudding bashing later on. Sometimes the shit came in wrapped in porno magazines so the boys had the bouquet effect along with the visual titillation. This became a very popular side product and was traded briskly amongst the tribal wankers.

I had breakfast on the English table on Saturday morning and we all clocked Paco Rabane's first regular customers paying for their fixes. Chinky remarked that he must have been up half of the night making *papelitos*, the tiny packets of heroin that make a fix. Trade was brisk. He served 17 blokes at his breakfast table and his main sales would take place in the shithouse in about a hour's time when the *economato* opened.

The *economato* queue got quite long and often out of hand on Saturday mornings because there was no work and everyone was on the wing. Consequently, the screws concentrated on the queue because scuffles were inevitable, with Moroccans barging in at the front and bully-boy gypsies refusing to queue because it wasn't macho. So a great deal of pushing and shoving happened at the front of the queue, where steaming hot coffee was often the first wash of the day for some.

The trannies were always at the front of the queue because they had lists of shopping for their boyfriends and favourite gangsters. They carried plastic bags and large trays, big enough to hold 20 or more coffees, so there was always a delay until they were served. They were under constant hassle to hurry up, so there was always diva-quality yelling at the ignorant twats who barged in front of them. When the *Mezclado* were near the front of the queue, nobody barged in. I remember how the boss of the gypsies got his comeuppance one Saturday morning. Queuing for anything was beneath him; he would walk straight to the front of any queue, whether it be the *economato, comedor,* telephone, mail, doctor or methadone queue, and nobody challenged him because of who he was. He was always surrounded by his heavies and nobody said a word, until he stepped in front of me, so I told him to fuck off and get behind me.

The *toreador* posturing was instantaneous as the hard, black eyes looked me over. The gypsy's four heavies were taken out the moment they stepped towards me. The unrelenting knuckles of the *Mezclado* paved the way for a quadruple choke-out as each of them fell victim to *hadake jime* (chokehold) in less than one minute. I then invited the boss of the gypsies to attack me, but his bottle had gone and he really didn't want anything from the *economato.* That happened a few months ago and the boss was taken off the wing, so a new boss was installed. He never jumped the queue when we were in it.

As usual the screws were occupied by the noisy *economato* queue as Paco Rabane dealt with his regulars in the bog. We kept him under surveillance at all times so when we reckoned he had enough cash on him to pay his debt, we moved in. He was never alone because he always paid a couple of lookouts to keep nicks on the screws and he had plenty of hangers-on hoping to share a fix with him.

The lookouts were dealt with first; they were easy. Ali simply told them to go for a coffee, so off they went, feeling lucky because they weren't in the shithouse with Paco Rabane. I took a deep breath of fresh air before going into the foul, gut-churning atmosphere of fresh-laid shit mixed with heroin fumes.

Paco Rabane was completely startled in that moment of recognition, especially when my left hand grabbed his windpipe as my right hand crushed his gonads and whisked him into the nearest empty shitter. I forced him up against the wall as Chinky started to turn out his pockets. He couldn't cry for help because I had blocked his airways with my grip on his gullet. His oesophagus was probably closed as well because my hand was clamped around his larynx and Adam's apple and was driving the rest of his neck against the wall, so he was busily dying as Chinky finished his search.

'Got everything?' I rasped, as Chinky pulled off the shoes and socks to empty out the *papelitos* that were stored therein.

'Jus' about. Lerrim go,' said Chinky, scooping up the remaining *papelitos*.

I released his bollocks and slammed him into a sitting position on the feculent pot, then I released his throat. His breaths came in great gasps as he started to recover, but the heroin he had inhaled that morning wasn't helping him now. He began fighting for his breath and was starting to panic. I guessed his epiglottis had closed so I punched hard into his jaw, knocking him cold. I yanked him out of the shitter and laid him in the recovery position in a pool of acrid-smelling piss. I grabbed his tongue and nearly tore it out of his head as I pulled it in an effort to free his epiglottis. He was wheezing and hiccuping, then he started to breathe deeply and evenly for a moment. He then relaxed into normal breathing. The silence was broken by my instructions.

'Quick! Get his pants down; sit him on the shitter. The fucking screws'll be here in a minute.'

Vito and Jake swiftly lifted him into a sitting position on the shitpan with his trousers around his ankles. 'Right, Chinky, put that silver foil on his knee and open a *papelito* onto it.'

I was looking around for his cigarette lighter.

'Here irriz,' said Chinky, trying to put it in the sleeping hand, realising what I was up to.

'Let it fall to the floor; it doesn't matter. The screws'll find it anyway,' I said, making sure it looked like he'd OD'd.

I scanned the shithouse to see how many grasses I had to deal with and Ali said, 'Don't worry, we cleared them all out when you started on him.'

I knew then that the screws wouldn't be long in coming.

'OK. Let's get out of here before I fucking choke to death,' I said, striding for the exit.

On entering the yard, everything looked normal, but everyone knew something had gone down in the shithouse. Before I had finished my first lap of the yard, the screws were heading for the shithouse. My ruse must have worked because we didn't hear another word about it. Paco Rabane was taken to the *enfermería* with a suspected overdose of heroin and was sent to Valdemoro prison on Monday morning, possibly in a wheelchair.

Now I had only one more debt to collect, so there I was, standing silently in the doorway of Javier's cell. He was startled when he clocked me in the shadow of the cell door. The television was on loud and I spotted two more on the floor under his bed. Javier was pulling in his rental sets before leaving on Monday. He quickly pulled the counterpane across his bed, letting it drape so it covered the televisions with the overhang.

I pointed to the set that was switched on. '*Esta tele es mi gusto,*' I said, smiling and friendly. '*La tomo ahora,*' I said, more sternly.

Panic was in his eyes as they darted about, looking for something. I followed his gaze but could only see filth and debris in his cell. He leaned forward to reach a porno magazine and took out a *diez mil* note (10,000 *pesetas*) from the centrefold.

'*Toma,*' he sneered. I snatched it from his grasp and pocketed it.

'*Seis mil más,*' I snapped, telling him I wanted a further 6,000 *pesetas*.

'*Te pago el martes,*' he lied, smugly.

Chinky appeared behind me. 'I would like dat one,' he said, pointing to the television that was switched on.

'He just told me he will pay me six *mil* on Tuesday,' I said, 'so help yourself. He deserves a slapping; he'll be in Valdemoro on Monday.'

Chinky unplugged the television and was disconnecting the antenna when Javier started to protest. I slammed him onto his bed, cracking his head against the cell wall, which was covered with centrefolds of homosexual men in various sickening poses. Chinky was gathering up the television when Javier, panic-stricken, rummaged under his pillow and quickly produced another *diez mil* note. He pleaded with me to leave him the television because hiring out these sets was his only income and could he please have the 4,000 *pesetas* change. I nodded Chinky out of the cell empty-handed, then took the money, telling him I'd give him his change on Tuesday. Fuck you, Javier.

TWENTY
TAKING THE BURN

Now that I had closed the bank and near enough finished the booze trade, I concentrated more on my personal training, so I designed a stretching routine to keep myself supple during the transition period between prisons. I was told I would be finished in the gymnasium on or around 12 October and my job in the *zapatería* would end on the Friday before 15 October. This gave me a few days to organise my gear and pull in the televisions I had out on hire. I redistributed the tellies amongst the *Mezclado*, so they each had one to take to La Moraleja. Unfortunately for me, my television was stolen by a prison officer on the morning of my departure. But for now I was busy training.

I was in my cell practising and compiling my new training routine when a big black fly flew in through the bars of my window. It was noisily buzzing around until it landed on the wall, level with my head. I was standing in the fighting stance called *zenkutsu dachi*, the forward-leaning stance (*gong jian bu* or *deng shan bu* for Chinese styles), when I remembered another fly-on-the-wall situation that had happened four years ago.

I was in San Clemente, a southern Californian seaside town drenched in sunshine, a most wonderful place to be. It was also in October, 22 October to be precise, and it was the opening of Gary Forbach's Kajukenbo Institute, which fell on the anniversary of 20 years of his teaching martial arts in California. The *dojo* was full of eager students waiting to see the first lady of kung fu: Malia Dacascos Bernal, the mother of Mark Dacascos, the film star. On the billposter was an array of well-known martial artists: Master Ted Sotello; Master Eric Lee; Sifu George Kikes; Sifu Julio Hernandez; Sifu John Bishop; Si Gung Gary Forbach, 7th degree red and black belt, and right at the bottom of the bill was yours truly, billed as the London *Sensei*. Boy, was I proud of that!

The reason the fly made me think of this was that Malia had us all in an elongated *zenkutsu dachi*, which she called the Glass Horse stance. This was because the stance was so low, you could balance a glass of water on your knee. She had us all in this stance, and it dawned on me that this was an endurance test to see who would be the last to collapse. I was the only Englishman there, so national pride was at stake. There was no way I was going to fall over in front of a crowd of Yanks. A black fly buzzed around my head and then landed on the wall in front of me, so I studied it there, willing it not to move, so that I could ignore the pain of tensed leg muscles for 20 minutes. I won.

Now I was studying this big black fly on the wall of my cell as I elongated *zenkutsu dachi* into Malia's Glass Horse stance. I braved it out for 20 minutes then changed legs for a further 20 so one leg didn't get jealous of the other. A hard attitude to training is crucial in prison and a high pain threshold is essential. The self-discipline required to perform these daily rituals stems from a self-belief that you can endure the necessary pain to improve and strengthen your body and mind. Confidence comes with fitness and the ability to dynamically defend yourself in surprising and perilous situations where the odds are stacked against you. This is especially true if you can deal with ambushes by multi-attackers and backstabbers and skuzzballs sneaking up behind you to slide a chiv into your kidneys. In the Carabanchel these mostly came from the denizens of the heroin world, where desperation drove the underclass to even lower levels of depravity and subhuman behaviour.

I gave myself a quest rather than a penance. My quest was to survive mentally and physically, rather than adopt the sackcloth-and-ashes attitude encouraged by overseers. Most prisoners hate their cells; mine was a sanctuary, my well of good sense. This mentality enabled me to see as far through a brick wall as anybody. Time was in abundance; it was one thing we all had. My sympathy went out to those men who could not meditate or focus on ways to accept their lot. I became aware of many things during the lonely hours of my imprisonment; my thoughts dwelt on life and death, though I did develop the ability to focus on the positive path of life rather than think negatively about death.

Philosophy is a creep; it seems to worm its way across all kinds of no man's lands to fuel thought in the thickest of skulls. Soothsayers abound in life: people telling us from childhood that our destination is heaven or hell and our life is a journey towards one or the other depending on how we use it. This philosophy of life is instilled from birth by prophets in white collars, but here in my cell I found time to discover that the Sea of Galilee was not the only source of my spiritual refreshment.

Because of the eclectic nature of my collection of books, and because I had plenty of time to read and reflect on various aspects of the love of life, I came to the conclusion that it was a great pity that the 'mystical' Eastern influence seemed only to have infiltrated the West in terms of curry. Somehow, I felt that the curry crusade was as far as it was going to go; it was resting while the Islamic crusade overtook it, though I very much doubted that sheep's eyes would be as popular as curry.

Anyway, I was thinking along those lines when I received a visit during recreation from one of my codefendants: Pavarotti. He was given that name because of his girth and facial resemblance to the famous tenor, absolutely not for his prowess at opera singing or anything else to do with the man. However, he was probably fair at singing 'The Green Green Grass of Home' in Spanish. I wondered if the Spanish national anthem had the word 'grass' in it.

Pavarotti's visit was an attempt at bribing me to take the blame for the hashish being in my minibus, thereby exonerating everyone else from the case. Obviously my codefendants had had a meeting (excluding yours truly) and come up with the brilliant idea that I should take the burn for them. The fucking useless tossers were a liability. They'd brought it all on top with their careless use of telephones and casual chatter. Anyway, I heard him out and perked up a little when he offered 11,000,000 *pesetas* (£45,000 approx). I knew I had no chance of getting off the charge, but I thought I had a good chance of getting bail, so I told him I would sleep on it and tell him tomorrow what I would do. The next day, Paco came to see me to tell me that he would take the burn because he needed the 11,000,000 *pesetas*. I didn't argue or even discuss it at length. I merely said, 'OK, you take the burn.' Just a couple of days later, Pavarotti and another codefendant got out on bail. That meant that we should all have got out on bail, but this is Spain, a member of the EU, where money talks and fuck all else matters.

Pavarotti had 12 previous convictions for drug trafficking and another for armed robbery. His mate's rap sheet was just as bad. Nevertheless, they qualified for *fianza* and were released before the Carabanchel closed for destruction. His lawyer, who was also my lawyer, told me we would all get bail now that those two had been released. Spanish law states that everyone on the case should be treated equally, so, because I had a clean sheet, I should be the next to get bail. But first the lawyer needed 5,000,000 *pesetas* to smooth it with the judge. I was skint, so I told him to ask Pavarotti to pay my bail. I heard no more from the lawyer until after I was removed to La Moraleja prison and then it was only via a clerk from the office who came to tell me my trial date.

Pavarotti was married to a Moroccan girl whose family were big landowners in Morocco, growing hectares of hashish, hence his numerous convictions for drug trafficking. Prior to his release he'd told me how, over the years, he had lost tonnes of hashish in the Mediterranean Sea. His major problem was finding courageous skippers to do the job. Every time the spick skippers clocked a dot on the horizon, the shit went overboard *rapido*. He was really pleased with himself months earlier when he discovered that Kennedy and I were skippers, and had thought I was duty bound to skipper for him, seeing as how he was paying the lawyer. Much later, when I was due for release, he contacted Susan to arrange a meeting in Malaga. Susan told me that he was surprised to hear I was still locked up. She said he would make contact again whenever I got out, as he'd find out my release date from my lawyers. It is a wonder the telephone didn't melt in my hand, I was so angry. I told

Susan, 'Should he call again, please tell him to go away in short, jerky movements: in other words, fuck off!'

The point I must make here is that Paco volunteered to take the burn for 11,000,000 *pesetas*, so we all relaxed, thinking that when the trial happened we'll all walk. The trial took place at the Audiencia Nacional in Madrid and, true to Spanish form, Paco reneged on the day and tried to wriggle out of it by telling his own lies about not knowing any of us, thereby fucking up any chance we had of getting off. How I despise these fucking people. I used to be a professional soldier; I am so pleased that I never had to serve with the Spanish military. I reckon the first sign of trouble and they'd be away like fucking long dogs, leaving you to it.

At the end of the trial Pavarotti walked out of court because he was on bail and had appealed. I later learned that he received a longer sentence than mine, but I found it strange that he could contact my wife as a free man when I was still locked up. Ah well, that was Spain, the land where money did all the talking. And while we're on the subject of money . . . the bank was closed, but the smack was still pouring in, so cash in the prison was in short supply.

TWENTY-ONE
BEGGARS AND THIEVES

Vito was the first to complain about being pestered for a loan, then each in turn started dripping about begging junkies. Heroin was on the wing but cash was scarce so frustration set the scene for desperate measures. Heroin addicts are not like cocaine or hashish users; they will do anything to get a fix, whereas Charlie and puff smokers can get by without it and tend not to kill for it.

Everyone on the wing knew that the bank was closed, but that seemed not to matter to the gypsies and junkies; they had a God-given right to demand money with which to buy heroin, or grab a fix no matter how. The first to feel the pinch were the junkies themselves, then the dealers, who refused to hand out fixes without first getting the cash. The pressure then came my way because the desperados would kill for a fix. At first it was aggressive begging; then the dealers accompanied the junkies, reinforcing the demand for money. Then came the robbery with violence when the penny dropped regarding the bank being closed to everyone.

The *Mezclado* closed ranks during the dying days of the Carabanchel because the screws had practically ceased patrolling the wing as their interests now lay in their new posts in the various Spanish prisons they had been allocated to. Don Francisco was appointed to Madrid V, better known as Soto de Real, a nearly new prison where most of the Carabanchel's Spanish inmates were destined to spend the remainder of their sentences. He was now concentrating his efforts into coercing the spicks who were going with him into becoming his eyes and ears in his new post. Rigorous coercive methods were not needed by Don Francisco; he merely ignored his grasses' misdemeanours, and besides, they would happily push their noses up his hole anyway.

One morning before breakfast I had shot the bolt on my cell door and made my way down to the shuffling throng. I was crossing the bridge on the *segundo* to call on Chinky when I glanced up towards my cell and thought I saw the door close. It was almost as if I had imagined it because it was just something that caught my eye in a fleeting moment. My instincts made me turn around on the bridge, race back up to the top level and rush headlong along the narrow gallery, colliding with pissed-off inmates who were in my path. I could see the bolt had been drawn back and the cell door was open just a fraction of an inch. My anger knew no bounds when I realised someone was in there. I hauled open the heavy iron door and stormed in.

There was a big fat gypsy frantically shredding my mattress with a metal *pinchou*. Another was clasping my television set to his chest, gathering up the flex and antenna, ready to leave. I sensed a movement behind me and a quick glance showed it to be Ali Safave watching my back and keeping nicks for what was about to happen.

The oily, olive-gobbling twat with the TV quickly put it down on the table, shrugged resignedly and tried to get past me as though his presence in my cell didn't warrant an explanation. The heavy-set scuzzball continued slashing my foam mattress, oblivious to all around him in his desperate attempt to find the rolls of banknotes he had been told were hidden therein. I noticed my pillow had already been slashed to ribbons and my kitbag had been slashed from end to end and the contents were all across the floor. They could only have been in here for about two minutes and look what they'd done already!

The scuzzball had his back to me, with one knee on my bed and his other foot on the floor, steadying himself as he tore away at my mattress, seemingly unaware of my presence, his quest for drug money leaving him bereft of any sense of danger. I grabbed the television thief by the ear, with my thumb squelched firmly into his eye socket and yanked him screaming to the doorway where I broke his face with the most savage head-butt I have ever delivered. His girlish scream bubbled to silence as his nose disintegrated and the blood drowned the noise in his throat. The unconscious heap was then pulled clear of the door by Ali Safave, who swiftly broke the fingers of each hand before heaving him over the handrail to fall into the safety net, where he lay motionless as his blood poured out of his nostrils to drip onto the shufflers far below.

The fat scuzzball was busily hacking away at my mattress when my fist deadened his leg. He screamed in agony as I raised his dead leg with an ankle twist to pull him off the bed, landing him heavily on his back on the floor. I screwed his foot into an excruciating ankle twist as I kicked his arsehole and stomped his bollocks in my attempt to pack the whole lot into his pelvic girdle. I stepped across him to stomp my foot into his throat, then, with all my weight on that foot, I choked off the echoing screams that were reverberating around the high rafterbacks of the *galería*. These were unforgettable screams; unnerving screams, the cry of the wounded underclass, the sound of the injured monkey who would plunge that evil, glittering spike into a nun's heart just to get his fix.

I clasped his ankle tightly as I pulled and stretched it as high as I could before slamming his foot down next to his ear, thereby doubling him over in an attempt at pinging his hamstring and giving his gluteus-maximus muscles a stretch like they'd never had before. I then gave him an axe kick just beneath his sternum, which sent him immediately to his dreamland of earth-packed floors and boiling hedgehogs. His front teeth were stained and rotten, so I knocked them out with the chair leg, then set about his eyebrows with my fists. I split each of his eyebrows by punching them several times very hard indeed, ensuring two really good sabre scars that a cavalry officer would die for. I shoved his *pinchou* up his arse, then Ali gave me a hand to toss him over the handrail to join his thieving brother in the safety net. I had a good feeling in my heart that the two-year-old little boy who died at the filthy hands of this snivelling gypsy turd was giggling from behind the enchanting clouds of heaven with his mother, who was raped and murdered with him.

CARABANCHEL

From that day on I always waited for the duty screw to come up to lock my cell before I left it, as did all my pals. The normal thing to do on leaving the cell was to slide home the bolt on the closed door; then the duty screw would come along turning his key in each door in turn, locking the bolt in the closed position.

We all thought the example of Pinky and Perky in the safety net would prevent further problems, but the mysterious yearning for chasing dragons drives men on to all kinds of slippery slopes, inviting the sword of Damocles to dangle over their heads.

Heroin has its own toxicological traits, which induce men to take risks that no other drug can hope to compete with; hence heroin being the devil incarnate of the drug world. Here in the Carabanchel the drive to sustain the habit is relentless in its skulduggery, so a state of constant awareness is necessary to fend off the incessant attempts at relieving you of your worldly goods in order to pay for the essential fix.

The *Mezclado* constantly bristled with awareness and any approach to any one of us caused an immediate response that any world leader would give his left bollock to have on-hand for his personal protection. Not forgetting, of course, that these men would be a monstrous pain in the arse for any world leader's protection team. These men were tried and tested professional killers and were the absolute racing dog's bollocks when it came to sorting blokes out. But we still had to be alert in the gutters of the heroin world, especially in the desperate sewers of the Carabanchel.

The days of Chinky going alone to the *economato* for a tray of coffee ceased during those dark, closing hours of the dying beast. Danger lurked not only in the shadows and stairwells, but also in the bustling coffee queue, where a sharpened animal bone could be slid into your kidneys for the price of a few cups of coffee.

It was at this time that news of our departure dates filtered through in dribs and drabs. Though we all thought we were going to La Moraleja together, we were shocked and dismayed when Chinky was informed that he was to be detained in Madrid, but they didn't yet know which prison he was going to. Jake was also told that he was to be sent back to Brussels to face the music there. They

230

didn't know exactly when, but he could expect to be taken to La Moraleja within a week.

During those unforgettable days we all stuck together and battered the many thieving faces of the would-be assassins and robbers, one of whom was the memorable Diko, a Portuguese smackhead who was locked up for killing a Spanish priest. His story was that the priest was a *maricon*, who had provided him with a room in the vestry of the church. Diko took umbrage when the priest jumped into bed with him on the first night to practise his holy orders in corned-beef inspecting. Diko throttled him, then stove in his skull with a silver-plated chalice. He was caught with a sack full of church silver and a box full of offertory coins. His story about the queer priest didn't hold much holy water with the Spanish Old Bill. So here he was, furtively seeking a victim to rob in order to pay for a fix.

He made a big mistake by selecting Abdulla as his victim. He snuck up behind him as he entered the shower block, but Vito was just two seconds to his rear, which was very unfortunate for Diko. As Diko stalked Abdulla, Ali Safave and I were already in the shower block getting ready to take a shower. Diko pulled out a polished bone *pinchou*, fashioned from a leg of lamb, then sprang forward to ambush Abdulla, but Vito was already airborne, having anticipated Diko's intentions. Vito punched Diko on the back of his neck with a blow that could have felled an ox. He slammed into the raised concrete gully that was in front of the shower stalls to take away excess water. His teeth tinkled across the metal cover as they bounced out of his mouth due to the impact of colliding with the edge of the gridiron. Vito removed the bone *pinchou* from Diko's hand and held it for Abdulla to see.

'Shove it up his hole,' said Abdulla, 'then we'll get rid of him.'

The stunned Diko tried to move slowly under the restraining hand of Vito, then started to moan and whimper, but jerked into sudden, painful reality as Vito lay into his buttocks with the shiny bone. One final thrust and it was embedded in his arsehole as Abdulla stomped his head onto the gridiron, knocking him unconscious and cutting off the most splendid Alfred Hitchcock scream. That scream must have touched Abdulla's heart because

Diko's attempt on his life warranted a death sentence in the ranks of the mujahidin. And because Abdulla was a warlord in that adamantine tribe, Diko's death would have been no more than a passing cloud. Lucky Diko was swiftly hauled out of the shower block and sat on the filthy shitpan in trap no. 1, next door, where he would eventually be found and taken to the *enfermería* for treatment.

TWENTY-TWO

FAREWELL CHINKY AND LUCKY

With Diko safely out of the way, we enjoyed our shower with the usual laughing and joking about the size of Lucky Johnstone's cock. As we relaxed and dried ourselves, talk soon got around to our new destination: La Moraleja.

We all sat there on the wooden benches, drying our various bits and chatting like any team of players, but instead of discussing our next match, we were talking about our next prison. I noticed that Chinky had become quite morose and he remained quiet throughout the banter about the prospect of change and new prison officers. The talk was of rookie officers with no experience of handling hardened criminals, which was partially true, as we would soon discover. Chinky's pensiveness seemed to deepen as everyone else cheered up and towelled themselves dry.

'Cheer up, Chinky. They'll send you to La Moraleja prison with us. You'll see,' said Jake. 'They won't let you contaminate their posh new prison in Madrid.'

Jake didn't know it yet, but he was only a couple of days away from being taken back home to Brussels. He thought he was coming with us up north.

Chinky rapidly went downhill mentally over the next few days. He had convinced himself that he was to be extradited to Australia to serve the outstanding 20-stretch from a previous conviction. He'd been given 20 years for a heroin bust, but was sentenced *in absentia*.

CARABANCHEL

Chinky was grassed by the Australian wankers he worked with, in a deal that gave them shorter sentences. He narrowly escaped capture by the Malaysian police, who responded to information passed to them by the Australian court. Had they caught him, he would most certainly have been put to death.

Prisoners would often fluctuate between the highs and lows of depression, from volcanic overwroughtness to subdued simpering, but perpetual stress in various degrees of intensity pecked away at your integrity. A lot of stress was self-imposed, simply because of the inability to control one's thoughts. Despair was never far from the mind in the Carabanchel; the cell walls could sometimes overwhelm the inmates' thoughts with a dramatic sense of claustrophobia that stifled all hope of freedom. This was a mental phenomenon inexplicable to the layman who never set foot inside the Carabanchel prison. Tricks of the mind allowed dead men to talk to you through the weeping concrete, men like Paco Granados and Joaquin Delgado: innocent men who were tortured and put to death here not so long ago. Did they pray in my cell? And politicos like Julian Grimau García, who was first pushed out of a first-floor window, breaking both arms and fracturing his skull, who later walked alone to the Carabanchel wall, refused a blindfold then died a violent death under a volley of shots fired by the Spanish, who smiled as they performed their duty. *Schadenfreude* should have been a Spanish word: it was mainly practised here in Spain.

I became more and more concerned about Chinky's mental health as he became totally acrimonious to the Spanish and discourteous to the *Mezclado*. I knew something was terribly wrong when he gave me the frozen face as we all laughed at a particularly good joke. His sudden brusqueness was hard for me to take in a gentlemanly way, especially in front of the others. But I did. I bit my tongue rather than compound his disturbed reasoning. Vito tried to soften the blow by trying to explain away Chinky's rapidly changing behaviour. But secretly we all knew this was the precursor to the ultimate rejection: suicide.

The powers of darkness had forced their devil into the fragile mind of their victim, turning him into a lost soul in the dark, unholy corridors of prison eternal, which was to be Chinky's destiny. Over the next few days we concentrated on relieving the pressure in Chinky's mind. We each in turn tried to console him, to bring him out of his terrible depression; then fate stepped in.

We got up one morning and he was gone. We were at breakfast when Jake asked, 'Where's Chinky?'

A freezing trickle of alarm seeped down my spine as a horrible sensation of foreboding gripped the English table, commanding silence. Normally, Jake would know Chinky's whereabouts because they shared a cell, but because men had been transferred already, there were plenty of empty cells, so Chinky had moved across the *galería* to be alone. Not a smart move, but you cannot prevent a man from living alone when he has the opportunity. Everyone stopped chewing and coffee cups were placed back down on the table as the bird of ill omen cast its shadow across our hearts.

Ali Safave resignedly lifted his leg out from under the table and scanned the *comedor* for the duty screw. He clocked him standing behind the steaming coffee urn, then slowly made his way against the flow of bodies to speak with him and ask about Chinky. We sat in silence as Ali returned to give us the news. The screw told him that 15 men had been transferred to Soto de Real at six o'clock that morning and that they had to shackle Chinky and subdue him because he'd refused to go.

I wondered if he had wanted to say goodbye to each of us before he was removed from the wing. Maybe that was why he struggled with the screws. My heart sank with the sadness of it all – another mental cross to bear, another lying-awake session in my cell, thinking about my Chinese friend.

We ate our breakfast in silence, each with our own thoughts centred on Chinky. That night, in the stillness of my cell, I prayed to Jesus and to every saint I had ever heard of, especially Saint Jude, to calm Chinky's thoughts and oust the demons. Later, in La Moraleja, I was informed that poor old Chinky had topped himself shortly after leaving the Carabanchel. To this day and forever, I will always think that he was another victim of the fiendish Carabanchel, and each time I visit a house of God, I pray that He plucked Chinky's soul out of that graveyard of fallen angels.

Jake was affected most by Chinky's removal; he offset his misery by telling the most funny Chinese jokes he could dig out of his copious repertoire.

'Why did they bury the Chinaman on the side of the hill?' he asked across the table. Everyone looked blankly at him. "Coz he was fuckin' dead!' he roared, in his attempt at cheering himself up and cracking a few smiles around the table.

Chinky was quickly forgotten as we continued our churning journey through the heart of darkness. Our next blow was when Lucky Johnstone took a beating as he chatted to someone he knew in the *sala*. He had just brought in a tray of coffee and biscuits accompanied by Vito and Jake when he spotted someone he wanted to talk to strolling across the yard to the *sala*.

Ali Safave sensed something was wrong when he clocked two known grasses hurrying towards the screws' office. He nudged me and nodded in their direction with a concerned look on his face. A sudden stab of apprehension had me off my arse and running towards the *sala* like shit off a shovel.

'C'mon. You can bet your fucking life it's Lucky,' I roared as I ran.

By the time I reached the *sala*, blokes had started to scurry away from the entrance, while at the same time curiosity was enticing others in to gawp at the black fellow being kicked around the litter-strewn floor.

Lucky's unconscious face was smearing blood across the floor as he was being kicked and stomped by a gang of snarling gypsies. Many onlookers were bowled over and umpteen tables and chairs went flying as the *Mezclado* steamrollered through the entrance and into the kicking gypsies.

I heard bones crack as I side-kicked a stomping junkie in the small of his back. I was in full flight as my right foot nearly snapped him in two, which was my intention. I followed his hulking frame to the floor and stomped the back of his head so that his nose flattened itself against the unforgiving floor. He managed to roll over onto his back, which suited me because I wanted him to have an unforgettable day out.

The sound of pounding flesh and screams of pain were all part of the chaos of combat as I pounded his eyebrows into everlasting scar tissue. I finished him with a knee-drop onto his clavicle, noisily breaking the collar bone with a crack that was heard above the sounds of battle.

The hospital case I had just created was Gustavo, a heroin dealer and notorious bully. He was a *preventivo*, awaiting trial for raping members of his own family: a truly obnoxious specimen of this particular species, who should really have been put down at birth. Certain close relatives now wish he had been sacrificed at birth, to Olive, the gypsy goddess of oil, which they all love so much.

The screws entered the *sala*, all whistles and truncheons, so we quickly lifted Lucky to his feet and carried him fireman-style around the rear of the spectators and into the shower block, where we undressed him and bathed his wounds.

Abdulla spotted the end of a bone *pinchou* sticking out of Lucky's black arse. He couldn't pull it out because the bone was smooth and slippery with blood. Jake took on the task with his great strong fingers, but failed to move the buried bone. Grunting loudly he eyed each of us in turn with an expression that said, 'Tell anybody about this and you're fucking dead!' With that he lunged his face towards Lucky's buttocks and shoved his big nose right up into the crack of his arse in order to clamp his teeth around the end of the slippery bone. The bone squeaked as Jake heaved at it, his powerful neck muscles bulging with the effort. A slurping sound, much like a wet fart, escaped from Lucky's arse as the bone was yanked out. The bated breath gushed out of us all in a triumphant cheer, which immediately collapsed into helpless laughter at the realisation that Jake had truly brown-nosed Lucky.

The laughter ceased instantly when Abdulla took the bone and wiped it clean, revealing the shit grooves at the sharp end of it. We had to assume that ratshit was in the grooves when it was stabbed into Lucky. The anger in Vito boiled over noisily as he uncharacteristically cursed all the gypsies on the planet. This incident would affect all of us during the few days left in the dying Spanish beast.

We quickly realised that Lucky needed professional help. He wasn't coming to full consciousness. Umpteen kicks to the head had severely concussed him and several of his beautiful white teeth had been kicked out. On checking the inside of his mouth, I could see he needed stitches to at least two deep lacerations as well as his external wounds.

Ali Safave strode off to the screws' office to get help, pronto. Vito and Jake kept everyone out as Abdulla and I cleaned and nursed Lucky as best we could. The screws came to check him first, and a few minutes later the gurney arrived to take Lucky away. I didn't see him again until weeks later when he arrived at La Moraleja.

Lucky had unwisely followed his friend into the *sala* to ask him if he was destined for La Moraleja, but he had been quickly surrounded by Gustavo and his *compadres* because they thought he had money. The gypsy perception of the *Mezclado* was that we were all wealthy *giris* (foreigners), and one of us out on our own was fair game for the hyenas. There weren't any questions: just a savage mugging.

I knew trouble was brewing all around me. The dying beast wasn't going to die quietly; it wanted to drag as many souls as possible down into the depths of Hades, where it belonged. Vito was deeply incensed by Lucky's unnecessary battering, so now he was hell-bent on retribution and the extermination of the verminous gypsies. The flamenco tribe had created a terrible enemy. Any one of them who came within striking distance was instantly decked by this man who represented the pure spirit of Sicilian hostility; a true mafioso, whose very shadow was enough to terrify the many unfortunates who had fallen under his mallet fists. My friend Vito had changed his outlook on life: another evil spell cast by the Carabanchel.

TWENTY-THREE
VENGANZA

It wasn't mere conjecture that vengeance was in the air; it was in the faces of my closest friends, plain for me to see. They were hungry for retribution for the ignominious treatment at the hands of unworthy prison officers and the impudence and strut of the lowly gypsies who threatened and pestered the shit out of everyone. Vito especially was fired by the vendetta spirit as the dying gasps of the Carabanchel impelled him to return the compliment to as many oily gypsies as he could lay his relentless fists on.

I became more concerned when I noticed the glint of resentment in Ali Safave's eyes whenever certain prison officers appeared. My concern was not for the screws, but for Ali, should he become consumed by the Carabanchel cacodemon. For should he kill a prison officer, his life would be forfeit and I would lose a dear friend. I touched his forearm one morning as the daggers flew from his eyes into the heart of Don Francisco, the English-speaking thug.

'Things will be different in La Moraleja,' I said. 'That piece of Spanish shit is not worth the effort. Look at him, he's dead already. He'll be rotting in prison long after we get out.'

The hard eyes softened somewhat as he muttered, 'Vengeance is like jealousy; it is a sickness. I must learn to console myself or I will kill that particular infidel.'

'That's right, mate. Look at him: he's dying on his feet. He is so full of piss and pus, happiness is something he will never know. One of the screws told me they all shag his missus when he's on nights.'

As I looked at Don Francisco, I silently wished he would live a long life behind the heavy doors of whichever Spanish shithole he was sent to to earn his piss-poor prison officer's pension. I fervently hoped that I would never set eyes on him again because I knew if ever I should meet him in the street I would thrash him to within an inch of his life.

Jake never left Vito's side as the vendetta spirit gripped his soul too. This formidable pair took it upon themselves to escort Abdulla to the *economato* several times each day. Never has the getting of coffee and biscuits broken so many teeth and noses in the history of queuing. An ambulance-chasing lawyer would make a fortune following behind Jake and Vito. The *economato* queue would erupt in an explosion of boots and fists each time we had coffee. The smouldering anger against the bigoted gypsy tribe, with their delusions of grandeur exhibited by their haughtiness, caused magnificent bruising and loss of blood during those final hours. A frenzy of retribution swept through *galería cinco* like a pox in a brothel.

The screws hardly ventured out of their office because the palpable atmosphere of fear and hate could be felt throughout the *galería*. The dying beast had become an anarchist's delight, though I must reveal that many anarchists bit the dust under the fists and boots of the *Mezclado*.

Vito was in his element; his release of frustration was near complete as he battered his opponents all over the yard. He and Jake became their own mobile 'no-go area'. When the *Mezclado* went for coffee, the gypsies and the meek and mild tended to move aside and beckon Abdulla to go in front of them.

One might think the *Mezclado* had now become the bully, but that wasn't the case. There were many scores to settle from the days before the seed of the *Mezclado* was planted. Gypsy spivs who had taken gargantuan liberties with solitary chaps were now paying for their talk-tall threats and posturing piss-taking. Men like Vito had long memories, so now there was a sense of urgency to balance the books. Even the trannies who had made cheeky passes at him in the past stayed well out of his way.

Whenever the prison officers were required to sort out a scrap, they responded mob-handed and showed no mercy to foreign or gypsy inmates, but they did exercise restraint when handling their *paisanos*.

On the night following Chinky's removal Don Rafael was on duty, so he joined me in my cell after final lock-up. He quietly let himself in, closing the cell door noiselessly behind him. I was sat on my bed reading the *Combat* magazine that Susan sent me every month. She knew it would bring me great joy each time I got it, especially as she always hid a *Telefonica* phone card between the first couple of pages, where the editor, Paul Clifton, had his comments. She put it there because I'd told her that the Spanish prison officers flip through the magazines in reverse, starting at the back page and working their way to the front. Susan would glue Paul Clifton's comments page to the facing page, hiding the phone card between the two. I never lost a phone card to the screws, but I never got to read the editor's comments because I had to rip that page out.

'You need to tell your lot to quieten down,' said Don Rafael. 'The gypos are going to kill one of you before you leave here.'

'They're always going to kill someone,' I said, reluctantly closing my *Combat* magazine.

'Anyway, it's caused a fuckin' stink; tomorrow you will all get a spin. *Cacheros* are gonna rip the fuckin' wing apart to make sure there's no fuckin' *pinchous* around.'

'What fucking use is that?' I said. 'Everyone knows the weapons are hidden in the shithouse and rat-holes around the yard.'

He pulled up the chair and sat with his feet plonked on my bed. Reaching into his bag he produced a couple of cans of San Miguel and passed one to me.

'Enjoy this, 'coz you'll be gone shortly and you'll have to do without until you get sorted in La Moraleja. Don't worry, there's a bottle of rum in the bag with some Coca-Cola.'

'Oh, that's nice,' I said. 'At least I've got something decent to drink to Chinky's health.'

'Oh yeah, Jackie fuckin' Chan. He went fuckin' crazy 'coz he couldn't see you before he was taken away. They really had to lay into him and shackle him up tight. He'll have had a rough time in transit 'coz he busted a *Guardia Civil* nose as he was being shoved into the prison bus.'

For a horrible moment I remembered the beating I'd received at the hands of the gutless Spanish police, for I was also shackled when they beat me. My heart went out to Chinky as I visualised the clubbing he would have received on the fetid floor of the filthy prison bus.

'I'll call one of my pals in Soto de Real later, so I'll tell you tomorrow how Jackie Chan is getting on.'

'Yeah, OK. Thanks. He is on my mind so I appreciate that,' I said, taking a swig of beer whilst trying to shake off the enmity I felt to all things Spanish, especially as Don Rafael was Spanish and I couldn't let him think I held any ill will.

'Oh, talking about my pals, I had a chat with Pepe. He's up in La Moraleja. Your reputation has beaten you to it. I called him yesterday and told him about you. He said he is looking forward to meeting you, seeing as how he is a big-time aikido man. He's always on TV up there whenever there's anything to do with martial arts. He said he's heard about you already.'

'Will he be bringing stuff in for me?' I asked.

'No, but he will help with getting you installed in the *polideportivo* (gymnasium), he is influential in that department. Don Marianno is the payroll director and he and Pepe are big pals, so don't worry about the job in the gym.'

I remembered that Don Marianno was Don Pablo's counterpart in La Moraleja and Pablo had also told me I'd be getting the job in the *polideportivo*, so I was doubly sure of it now. This was to prove correct as I did become the *jefe del polideportivo* shortly after my arrival at La Moraleja. But that is part of another story.

'Don Philipe, Don Isidrio and Don Roberto are the officers in control of the *polideportivo*. Don Philipe is an old pal of mine and he will look after you. You must not approach him, or anyone else. He will let you know what's going down in his own good time. He's got to get to know you before he'll work with you.'

Inwardly, I was all agog with what was being mapped out for my future. During my six months of incarceration in the Carabanchel –

242

a place of constant danger and foreboding – I had gone with the flow of events to find myself not only surviving, but earning sufficient amounts of money to help keep my wife in Coín and to live reasonably well in this pisshole. I had the use of a telephone potentially every day, and I had my own cell. I was under the patronage of senior prison officials who shielded me from lunatic screws: and it was all because of my martial-arts skills, my Bushido philosophy and my serendipity. Oh, and because I was a skipper.

Don Rafael delved into his bag to produce a bottle of Navy rum and a large bottle of Coca-Cola. Two large plastic cups appeared, which he promptly filled to the brim with the delightful mixture. I do not relish any memories of the Carabanchel, but it was somehow gratifying to be indulged by the *jefe del modulo* with his booze, his treats and especially his mobile phone.

'Here, call your missus,' he said, handing me his phone. 'I'll just go and check the office before we sink that bottle of rum.'

'Yeah, OK. I need to speak to her tonight. She knows I'll be in transit soon.'

Looking at me thoughtfully, he said, 'You better tell her that tomorrow night will be the last call on that phone, 'coz you'll be out of here the day after tomorrow.'

A pang of apprehension fluttered through me as I wondered how many days would go by before I could speak to Susan again. I need not have worried because, thanks to Bellerophon, the god of telephones, I was reconnected quite soon after my arrival at La Moraleja prison.

Susan told me that Kennedy was spending too much time at sea. His wife was constantly moaning; not even the BMW muscle car he had bought her could shut her up. I knew what Kennedy was up to. He was working the long-haul ribwork to Alicante or Sagunto as much as he could before the onset of winter. Not that there is a winter there, as such, but the Mediterranean Sea becomes unpredictable weatherwise between November and March. It's not so important for the short journey from the coast west of Marbella across to the Tetouan area; but to take a couple of tonnes out of Mar Chica, near Nador, in a RIB that is loaded higher than the sponsons on a journey as far as Sagunto, north-east of Valencia, is a bit of a challenge to any Old Salt. I have experienced weather and sea-condition changes happening in less time than it takes some blokes to drink a pint of bitter.

So my pal Kennedy was really at it. Susan said that each time he came home from the sea, he was like a zombie. His wife was making great demands for some kind of social life, especially as she was sat on so much cash, but he stoically carried on with the work.

I explained to my wife about tomorrow night possibly being the last telephone call for a couple of days or so, but she fobbed it off as being just a little annoyance. I love that woman.

Don Rafael came back as I said my goodbye, so I handed him the phone.

'You can have a bit longer tomorrow night,' he said. 'Now where's that fuckin' bottle o' rum?' He sat in his usual place with his feet up. 'We've just had a message that the Belgian police are here to take your mate back to a prison in Brussels.'

'Christ! When is he leaving?'

'Oh, he'll be out of here by six o'clock in the morning.'

'Take me along to his cell now so I can say goodbye to him.'

He looked longingly at the rum bottle.

'Fuck that!' I said. 'We can sup that after I've seen Jake.'

'OK, *venga*, let's fuckin' get it over with.'

He quietly opened my cell door and walked along the gallery as I gently closed it. When we got to Jake's cell, he unlocked the door with his key and quietly slid back the bolt.

'You've got ten minutes,' he said, then he pulled the door open to let me in. 'I'll lock you in. See you in ten minutes.'

Jake's eyes opened wide as I entered his cell.

'What the fuck are you doing here?'

He sat up on his bed and turned down the volume on his telly.

'I've come to say goodbye. You're off tomorrow morning.'

'How the fuck do you know that?'

'The *jefe* just told me that the Old Bill from Brussels are here to take you home early in the morning.'

'Why has he told you? He should fuckin' tell me.'

'He's just found out, so he let me come and tell you. Don't worry, it's official. Someone will be along to tell you in the morning and give you two minutes to pack and get out. At least the *jefe* was decent enough to let me come and see you.'

I could see that Jake was excited and couldn't believe his ears. He grabbed me in a bear hug and we danced a little jig in the middle of his cell.

'Fuckin' hell! Fuckin' hell! Fuck, fuck, fuck!' he roared. Then he flopped onto his bed as tears rolled down his big, hard face.

'I can't fuckin' believe it,' he sobbed. 'I'm leavin' this scumbag fuckin' country. You wouldn't shit me, would you?'

'No, you big lucky cunt. You'll be eating fish and chips tomorrow in a civilised land, you big lummox.'

'I've got your details so I'll keep in touch,' he said, fishing around for something in his pocket. 'Here,' he said, 'you can have this. I'm not setting foot in this fuckin' shithole of a country ever again, not for any fuckin' thing.'

He handed me a key.

'What the fuck's this?' I asked, palming the key.

'It's in Barcelona airport car park. It's a fuckin' new car I bought when I first got here. Like a cunt, I left it there and got the fuckin' train. That's how I got caught: on the fuckin' train. Anyway, you can have it.'

'No, you fucking keep it. Get one of your mates to fly in and pick it up. I'll be inside for a while so it's no use to me.' I handed him the key. 'But I'll have the fucking telly,' I said, pointing my thumb at it.

'Take every fuckin' thing. I'm takin' nothing from here that will remind me of this fuckin' place.'

'No, I'll just take the telly,' I said, as I heard the door bolt being slid back. Then the door was pulled open by Don Rafael.

'This is all fuckin' true, *jefe*? Will I be out of here in the mornin'?'

Don Rafael stood there grinning. 'Yep! You are on your way to that pisshole of a country called Belgium.'

Jake roared with laughter and held his guts as he spluttered, 'What the fuckin' hell's this place then?'

'C'mon,' said Don Rafael, beckoning me out. 'I've got to lock him up before the officer from *ingreso* gets here to give him the glad tidings.'

'Just a minute, I'm taking the telly.'

I unplugged the set and coiled the lead as Jake got off the bed to give me a hug and a farewell handshake.

'I'll never forget you, Chancer.'

'No, Jake, and I'll not forget you.'

I picked up the telly as Don Rafael held open the cell door for me.

'Good luck, Jake, and Godspeed you back home.'

I walked out of his life. The cell door closed and the massive steel bolt slid silently home. A strange sensation of silence seemed to engulf me, as though I had cotton wool stuffed into my ears. That deep feeling of loss and grief at the departure of a fellow prisoner came over me again.

Back in my cell Don Rafael tried to be jolly. He knew Jake's departure had affected me. He'd been in this job long enough to know all there is to know about sadness.

'How many fuckin' TVs have you got?'

'Oh, this is for one of the boys. It's no use to Jake any more.'

'Yeah, he'll be out on the streets of Brussels tomorrow night . . . on the piss.'

'How the fuck do you know that?' I asked, as I took a big swig of rum and Coke.

'It always happens with the Belgians, especially as it's only theft. They think the Carabanchel is so cruel, their sentence is over once they get them home. You should see the faces on the cops when they come in here to collect them: you'd think they had never seen a fuckin' rat or cockroach.'

'Winston Churchill once said that you can judge a country by its police force,' I said seriously.

'What the fuck is that supposed to mean?' growled Don Rafael.

'It is possible that the Belgian authorities take a dim view about rats and cockroaches sharing their prisoners' food and accommodation.'

'Bollocks! Rats are everywhere.'

'Did you see any in Nottingham?'

'No, but I did in Algeria.'

The eye of wisdom often closes when philosophers drink rum, so I changed the subject. We wittered into the night talking shite about all and sundry, which was much better than prowling around the cell like a caged animal.

The morning saw the departure of Jake, the Belgian bouncer. We didn't see him go; he went at 6 a.m. Vito was down in the dumps, but he cheered up slightly when I told him I had taken Jake's telly. We sat at the English table eating our breakfast of bread and coffee.

Ali Safave said, 'Today is our last full day together. Tomorrow we go to La Moraleja, so I suggest we all stay together today because the gypsies have noticed how few we are.'

Vito slowly got to his feet and glared intently in the direction of the gypsy tables. He hissed loudly like a snake as he slowly drew his forefinger across his throat. The *comedor* fell into silence as everyone looked at the fearsome Vito wearing his spurs of wrath.

The challenge was there for all to see and the insult to the gypsy tribe was unmistakable as Vito vehemently spat, with an exaggerated stoop in their direction. The looks of hatred glowered across the *comedor*, but none were more hateful than Vito's. The dark eyes smouldered in the chiselled granite face of this extraordinary Sicilian as he sent his message of ill will across the dining hall. Just for a moment he seemed alienated and alone, then the *Mezclado* rose to their feet as one and turned to face the gypsies. Just a few seconds of simmering, naked, eye-balling aggression was enough.

'OK. Sit down. Message sent.' Fuck me! I nearly laughed as I realised I was barking like a sergeant-major, but it worked; we sat down as one.

There must have been a face or two amongst the gypsies with whom Vito still had scores to settle because the anger didn't leave his expression when we all sat down, and there seemed to be a couple of scuzzballs looking very uncomfortable at their tables.

TWENTY-FOUR
THE DYING BEAST

Dutch nipped across from his table, all smiles on a smug expression. 'Chancer, you are going to *modulo* 8 when you get to La Moraleja.'

'How the fuck do you know that?' I asked, surprised.

'I know one of the screws in *ingreso* and they have the lists of names and *modulos*. We are leaving here tomorrow by bus, then tomorrow night we will be bedded down in *ingreso* until the following day when we go onto *modulo* 8.'

'What about the rest of us?' asked Abdulla.

'I don't know about you personally,' said Dutch, 'but Ali Safave is going on *modulo* 8 with Chancer. Hopefully we'll all be on the same wing, but they are opening *modulo* 9 because 8 is full, so you may find yourself on 9 with the krauts and the frogs.'

'Don't worry, Abi,' I said. 'Let's see how everything pans out and if you are not on with me, we'll soon fix it so that you are.'

'You seem to have a plan, my brother. Do you know something that we don't?' asked Ali Safave.

I nodded at Dutch and said, 'I'll tell you when this nosy clog fucks off.'

I laughed as Dutch's facial expression changed to something resembling Barney Rubble out of *The Flintstones*.

'I come over here to give you some info and you call me a nosy fuckin' clog! What kind of fuckin' friend are you, you 'orrible cunt!'

249

'A good one, so relax, I'm only joking, and we'll have less of the 'orrible,' I said.

'Good. I've been wondering what you lot will be getting up to when we move.'

Dutch swung his legs over the bench to make himself comfortable and sat with his elbows on the table and his chin in his hands, waiting.

'Right,' I said, 'the bank will open just as soon as we get the hang of the place. The main tribes of the prison will be South Americans and Arabs, so there won't be much in the way of smack. It will be Charlie and hashish, so we'll avoid the smackheads. There will be a delay with the booze, but I reckon a few weeks after I start work in the gym we can start trading.'

Vito had cheered up a wee bit now. 'What about our training?' he asked.

I thought for a moment, then decided that it would be a good idea to keep everyone together with a bit of training in the yard, so I said, 'I will start training sessions in the yard until I get the job in the gym. Then we'll have our regular combat classes again.'

Dutch wore a smirk on his face and I thought I detected a bit of the green eye of envy when he said sarcastically, 'How the fuck do you know you'll get a job in the gym? And if you do, how do you know they'll allow combat classes? Who have you got in your pocket? He must be fuckin' big.'

The table fell into silence for a moment, then Ali Safave growled, 'Why would you ask such a question? You never go to the gym and you never do any combat training. Why should you ask who is in anyone's pocket? Even the *Mezclado* would not ask about such things. Now go back to your own table.'

We all frowned at Dutch as the penny dropped for him. He knew he had stepped over the mark with his prying. Resignedly he lifted his legs over the bench and with a big sigh said 'sorry', then strolled back from whence he came.

We were in a huddle on the English table chatting about La Moraleja when the duty screw strutted over to our table. He slapped his truncheon into the palm of his hand noisily, then, in a low, threatening tone of voice so beloved of posturing bullies, croaked, '*Afuera, giris.*'

THE DYING BEAST

A shockwave of silence enveloped the lone prison officer as he watched us scan the dining hall as though he were not there; the moment of revelation hit him like an express train as it dawned on him that we were looking for his *compadres*. In that instant – the worst moment of his life – all of his years of experience were reduced to just so much ratshit as he realised he was alone amongst some of the most dangerous men on the planet. One look into the eyes of Ali Safave made it abundantly clear that life was about to end, abruptly. I watched the screw's eyes flutter as a gruff, bass voice roared, 'Fee-faw-fum,' somewhere in the back of his mind. The armour-plated uniform was now a blue serge duvet, full of white feathers as the contents of his shoes began to quake. Had this person been anyone other than a Spanish prison officer, I would have felt some pity for him, but because he was Don Carlos, a notorious bully and pervert, I gloated inwardly as his world liquefied in his gonads.

The galvanised silence seemed to expand as the intensity of the moment grew. The screw was now paying for his crass stupidity with the nightmare of the prison authority's *bête noire*: the brutal killing of one of their own. The horror-struck screw glanced into Vito's eagle eyes, and that glance initiated the jetstream of adrenalin which had him back-pedalling like Fred Astaire exiting stage left.

We strolled out into the yard, in case the idiot came back with reinforcements, and joined the throng of strolling prisoners aimlessly shuffling through time. Vito bristled with aggression as we strolled past groups of hostile gypsies who were gathered at various points of the yard. They were ignored as La Moraleja fuelled our chatter.

We spent the rest of the day talking about the move up north and I discovered that the weather would affect us; it actually snows in Palencia during the winter, so I would need a fleece or a combat jacket. I had such clothing at home, so that final night in the Carabanchel I would ask Susan to send me a jacket.

That afternoon, everyone was busy getting ready for the bedlam that would happen tomorrow, so I was stowing my kit when my cell door opened and a strange screw beckoned me to follow him. I had never seen this man before so I asked him where he was taking me. He told me 'Don Pablo'. He escorted me through the alleys and corridors, down through the bowels of the beast, then up some steps that I had never seen before until we arrived at Don Pablo's office. He ushered me in and then stood guard at the door. Don Pablo welcomed me with a glass of port and a platter of Serrano ham and cheese slices. He handed me the telephone and beamed, '*Llama* Susan.'

I called my wife as he tinkered about in the office next door. I told Susan that I would call her again later with Don Rafael's mobile phone. Anyway, we had a nice chat, then Pablo came quietly back into the room, so we said our lovey-dovey bit and rang off.

Don Pablo did his best to make me understand that I must not jeopardise my future by befriending heroin dealers or otherwise blotting my copybook. He gave me his calling card with a personal message in his own handwriting on the reverse. This calling card did me a hell of a lot of good; it opened many doors in my new prison and gave me *mucha fama* (kudos) with some of the prison officers, especially the older, experienced screws who knew him.

We said our farewells with promises of a celebratory reunion and a pledge to sail around the world with precious cargoes. After a hug and a handshake I was escorted back to my cell by way of the secret passageway. The mystery screw looked deeply into my face as he closed my cell door; he would appear in my life in another prison, but that is not for this book.

By the time Don Rafael arrived in my cell, I was all packed and ready to move. All I had to do now was sleep, shit, shave and fuck off out of this pisshole. But first, there would be a little farewell party with rum and Coke, Serrano ham, cheese and pickled onions and Ali Safave.

I asked Don Rafael to allow my friends into the cell for a drink, but he didn't think it was a good idea. After he'd had a drop of rum, though, I managed to persuade him to bring Ali from his cell to join our fuck-off party. Don Rafael felt a bit awkward with having such a vibrant warrior as a drinking partner and I'm sure Ali felt much the same about him, but Navy rum works its special magic on all makes of human being, so we had a memorable closing-down party. Before Ali arrived in my cell, I had made my call to Susan, so I was feeling really buoyant after hearing the supportive words she had said to me. That woman is my life.

THE DYING BEAST

We laughed and joked our way through two bottles of rum, then it was time to hit the sack. We made our drunken vows and a pact to meet up when I got out. Then, with a final bout of back-slapping, hugging and handshaking, he locked me in and took Ali back to his cell.

There was a sadness in the eyes of Don Rafael that will live with me for a long time, but it didn't bother me then because I was well pissed as I lay on my bed and listened to the sounds of the night in the dying hours of the Spanish beast. In a few hours' time, they would open the sluices of this cesspit to allow the dead beast to discharge the contents of its infected arsehole: the bum's rush I'd been praying for.

The wailing siren had me out of my bed before it reached its highest note. I performed my ablutions and made ready to leave. I then relaxed on my bed, reading a magazine. *Recuento* happened with lots of noise, then we were allowed down for an early breakfast.

The *Mezclado* ate its last meal together on the morning of 15 October 1998. We ate in silence. Then, when I had finished, I placed my hand palm upwards in the centre of the English table and said, 'Right, I'll see you all in La Moraleja.'

Each man – a real man, a true warrior – slammed his hand on top of mine, making a stack of hands to mark the disbandment of the elite *Mezclado*. We left the table as one, then dispersed as we entered the gallery to hand in our bedding and grab our baggage for loading onto the transit trolley. The transit trollies would be rolled out to the waiting buses and loaded into the baggage bays. The televisions were being loaded onto a separate trolly and a screw was checking each set against the serial numbers and prison records on his list. My set didn't match the records, so the screw confiscated it and put it with two other sets on a different trolly. He told me it would arrive in two days' time after a further check against their paperwork. My name was written in indelible ink all over the telly, but I knew it was goodbye telly. The screw didn't need to have 'thief' tattooed on his forehead; it was written all over his greasy face.

We were slowly and noisily processed out of *ingreso* into the outer

253

yard, where *Guardia Civil* officers awaited us. They roughly frisked us and bullied us into an alley at the end of the yard where we were issued with a plastic bottle of water and a bag of stale bread rolls. The press of the throng pushed us through the opening at the end of the alley where frenzied *Guardia Civil* officers handcuffed me to the nearest inmate, who happened to be the mad American. My left wrist was shackled to his right, and then we were pushed and kicked across the yard and prodded with truncheons into the stinking, filthy single-deck bus. We were then poked with pistols and truncheons into a square-metre metal pen with a cold metal bench seat in it. Snot, phlegm and piss were everywhere as we gingerly sat down, making sure there wasn't any under our arses. These buses had been used recently to remove the Spanish from here.

The steel door was slammed and locked as the next pair of prisoners was poked into their own metal coffin behind us. The bus was quickly filled with protesting non-Spanish prisoners. The screams of a claustrophobic kraut were silenced with what sounded like a truncheon singing around his head. The Yank soon settled into a snore as I sat peeping through a slit in the perforated metal sheet that served as a window. I watched as the buses filled up and departed. Apparently the senior officer was to travel on my bus, so we were the last to leave the yard.

At last, the bus pulled out of the yard and the Carabanchel gates closed behind me. I had slipped out of Satan's fingers; it was like stepping out of a minefield unscathed after lugging a mine-detector for six months.

The journey to La Moraleja was to take over six hours of cramped, shackled rattling, with stale bread and warm water to be eaten or drunk with the encumbrance of Spanish shackles and the acrid stink of Spanish piss: an unforgettable journey at the end of the twentieth century in a member country of the European Community – my fucking English arse! I wish I was prime minister; I would make Gibraltar into a massive naval base, full of nuclear submarine facilities, and shun Spain completely. Anyway, I had more important things to think about as the bus rumbled away from the dead Spanish beast.

THE DYING BEAST

My thoughts were on survival. If I'd survived Europe's most evil dungeon, I reckoned my Bushido mentality would make La Moraleja seem like a Florida theme park. Roll on Disneyland; here I come, you bastards.